DEDICATED TO ALL THE NON-FAMOUS AND UNKNOWN INDIVIDUALS

WHO ADVOCATE FOR NON-VIOLENCE AND PEACE,

ESPECIALLY TO ALL THE DESERTERS WHO REFUSE TO FIGHT AND KILL,

YOU ARE OUR TRUE HEROES!

JAY B JOYFUL

PEACE

REAL POWER COMES FROM LOVE, NOT HATE.

A BOOK ABOUT PACIFISM,
NON-VIOLENCE AND
CIVIL DISOBEDIENCE

Joyful-Life.org

Bibliografische Information der Deutschen Nationalbibliothek:
Die Deutsche Nationalbibliothek verzeichnet diese
Publikation in der Deutschen Nationalbibliografie;
detaillierte bibliografische Daten sind im Internet
über http://dnb.dnb.de abrufbar.

Second Revised Edition
© 2025 Dr. Jörg Berchem, alias Jay B Joyful

Verlag: BoD · Books on Demand GmbH, In de Tarpen 42,
22848 Norderstedt, bod@bod.de
Druck: Libri Plureos GmbH, Friedensallee 273, 22763 Hamburg
ISBN: 978-3-7693-5288-7

Content

Preface

Dear Reader,

Peace be with you and with all people and living beings around you!

Nothing shocks me more than to see that at the end of the first quarter of the twenty-first century, humanity is not only continuing to pursue old ways of acting and reacting to violence and war, but seems to be increasingly welcoming them again and developing ever more perfidious and inhumane ways of manipulation, aggression, injury and killing through technical possibilities. Humanity does not seem to have learnt from its long and horrific history.

That said, I must admit that this fact cannot diminish my unshakeable belief in the goodness of man and his capacity for compassion. It will not change my believe that Love is the seed from which creation was born and that Love is also the motor of evolution.

No sane person in this world desires war or violence - not once they are confronted with reality, overcome trauma and can speak honestly about their feelings. Nobody hates another person, as soon as they really know them, and accepting their own injuries and vulnerability, their humanity.

"The population does not want wars and must therefore be lied into wars," says Julian Assange, the greatest hero and martyr of this century, whose case shows that humanity and the powerful remain stuck in the thinking of the Middle Ages, when people persistently tried to suppress uncomfortable truths by imprisoning, torturing and executing truth seekers and messengers.

This must end! The only way to put an end to this is for each individual to engage with the everlasting truths of Peace and a science of Peace. We do not need a science of war. We should not accept and war ministers (often misleadingly called "defence ministers"), but create Peace ministries and have Peace ministers. No one should serve in an army, but everyone should be involved in an alliance of Peace, self-responsible and non-violent, for a peaceful and just world. Instead of spending billions on weapons and the military, every individual should insist that their taxes are used for Peace, healing and justice. The military-industrial complex should be abolished, destroyed and banned. I dream of a world where this is so, and where people switch off their televisions and movie programmes, stop reading newspapers and so-called social media, so that they escape the brainwashing that holds them captive, and instead they go out, walk towards each other, embrace as one human family and together realise their dreams of a peaceful, honest and just world in a solid and inspiring cultural diversity. I firmly believe that these dreams can become reality, if we only want to and do it.

This book is intended to be a modest contribution to this. It should inspire faith and trust in Peace. It is meant to be a profound exploration into the philosophy of pacifism, a timeless call to understand, cultivate, and champion the transformative power of Peace.

As we stand at the crossroads of history, where the echoes of past and present conflicts reverberate and the shadows of new challenges loom, the need for a paradigm shift in our approach to conflict resolution has never been more urgent. This book endeavours to be a guiding light on this path, inviting readers to embark on a journey that transcends the conventional narratives of violence and war.

The pages that follow weave together the threads of historical reflection, philosophical contemplation, and real-world examples to unravel the essence of pacifism – a belief system that advocates for non-violence, justice, and the resolution of disputes through dialogue and understanding. The narratives within are not just the stories of distant peacemakers; they are the stories of individuals who, well-equipped with the conviction that Peace is not merely the absence of war but the presence of a healed and intact condition, have forged paths of reconciliation and cooperation.

In these pages, you will encounter the diverse tapestry of pacifist thought, from the teachings of ancient philosophers to the wisdom of modern visionaries. Through the lens of compassion, empathy, and a commitment to human dignity, the book seeks to inspire a collective awakening to the potential within each of us to be architects of Peace.

This collection of essays, quotes, speeches etc. acknowledges the complexities of our world and the challenges inherent in the pursuit of Peace. It recognizes that the journey toward a more harmonious existence requires not only the dismantling of structures that perpetuate violence but also the nurturing of a profound shift in our individual and collective consciousness.

You will see that, in a departure from standard orthography, I begin the words "Peace", "Love" and "Life" with capital letters. I have made a habit of doing this to express my respect and esteem for Peace, Love and Life.

As you delve into the chapters that follow, may you find not just a manual for Peace but an invitation to introspection, dialogue, and action. Together, let us explore the transformative power of pacifism and embrace the timeless truth that, in the words of Martin Luther King Jr., "Darkness cannot drive out darkness; only light can do that. Hate cannot drive out hate; only Love can do that."

In a world yearning for healing and unity, this book extends a hand, urging us to embark on a shared journey toward a future where Peace is not only a distant dream but a lived reality.

December 2024, January 2025

Dr. Jörg Berchem, alias Jay B Joyful

I. Prologue

1. About the Author
Jörg Berchem: Peace as a Philosophy of Life

by Lusungu Nkwera

> Do not struggle
> to be yourself.
> Just be yourself.
> Do not fight for Love.
> Be Love.
> Do not fight for Peace.
> Be Peace.
>
> Jörg Berchem

Dr. Jörg Berchem, a prominent philosopher and scholar of human ecology, holistic natural medicine and development studies, has developed a unique and insightful understanding of Peace. His perspective on Peace is deeply rooted in philosophical and psychological inquiry, interdisciplinary research, spirituality and a commitment to addressing the complexities of conflict and global challenges in a multi-disciplinary way.

Berchem's work is closely tied to conflict resolution and international relations. He explores the role of international organizations, diplomacy, and Peacebuilding efforts in preventing and resolving conflicts. His insights emphasize the importance of respectful cooperation among nations and the establishment of mechanisms for peaceful dispute resolution.

Jörg Berchem's understanding of Peace draws upon a rich philosophical foundation. He engages with the works of renowned philosophers such as Immanuel Kant, Hannah Arendt, and Eugen Drewermann, integrating their insights into his own scholarship. Kant's idea of perpetual Peace and the concept of "cosmopolitan right" play a central role in his thinking, emphasizing the importance of human rights, international cooperation and the rule of law.

Berchem's perspective acknowledges that Peace is a multifaceted and complex concept. He understands Peace not as the mere absence of violence but as a dynamic state characterized by justice, equity, and the absence of structural violence and inequality. This nuanced approach underscores the need to address underlying causes of conflict, such as socio-economic disparities and political injustice.

One of Dr. Jörg Berchem's notable contributions is his commitment to a multidisciplinary approach. He recognizes that understanding and achieving Peace require insights from various fields, including philosophy, psychology, political science, sociology, and law, but also from ecology and spiritual wisdom. By bridging these disciplines, he offers a comprehensive view of Peace that considers political, social, biological and ethical dimensions.

Ethics plays a central role in Dr. Berchem's understanding of Peace. He emphasizes the ethical imperatives that underlie Peace, such as respect for human rights, the duty to protect vulnerable populations, and the need to address global challenges like exploitation and poverty. His perspective underscores the moral responsibility of individuals and nations in the pursuit of Peace.

Dr. Berchem views the Peace process as analogous to a healing process. The goal is a state of wholeness and holiness, which should be understood as a purpose of life, creation, and nature. Compassion, forgiveness, and Love are essential prerequisites that, therapeutically like medicine, help facilitate and establish Peace. This applies to both inner Peace and external Peace, with inner Peace being considered the initial step.

His views on peaceful coexistence are based on a deeply Christian spirituality that understands all beings and the "co-world" (instead of the "environment") as a system characterized by fraternal connection and Love as a fundamental creative principle. His image of God is androgynous and thus reflects perfection in diversity. In his philosophy, Love is a reality, just like light and warmth. Hatred is merely the absence of Love, in the same way that darkness is the absence of light and cold is the absence of warmth. Cold and darkness don't represent any form of energy, but only the lack of it. There are no "cold rays" or "dark rays," only light rays and heat radiation. Therefore, we must confront hatred with Love, essentially compensating for the deficiency.

War is therefore also considered to be the absence of Peace, a state in which creation is meant and for which man, as a thinking and consciously deciding being, has a special responsibility. Trauma and manipulation cause people to lose faith and the feeling of connection and Love. In his opinion, war and hatred are only possible through lies, whereby the biggest lie is to regard other people as inferior, inhuman and unworthy of life.

Disarm and abolish the army now! Turn officers into caregivers for the elderly and soldiers into healthcare workers! Deport the War Ministers to countries they destroyed, so that they can be sentenced there. We need a Ministry of Peace!

Jörg Berchem refused his military service and has spoken out against violence and the military all his life. He rejects the institution of the military in its entirety, as he sees it as an exclusively destructive force. Training to become a soldier, he says, is nothing other than the legal torture of brainwashing and the deprivation of conscience and self-responsibility. Images of the enemy are installed and people are dehumanised in order to make the ordered killing possible.

Soldiers are worse criminals than contract killers. Contract killers have the freedom to refuse a contract, for example, to kill a child. Soldiers have so debased and sold themselves that they cannot even refuse this. Civilian employees of an army are guilty of complicity in murder. (inspired by Eugen Drewermann)

During the so-called "corona crisis", Dr Berchem organised peaceful protests against the restriction of human rights and the division of society. He argued in favour of the right to free self-determination over medical treatment and warned against classifying fellow human beings and isolating healthy people.

In conclusion, Jörg Berchem's understanding of Peace is characterized by a philosophical foundation, a recognition of the complexity of Peace, a multidisciplinary approach, a focus on conflict resolution, and a commitment to ethical imperatives. His work serves as a testament to the importance of rigorous academic inquiry in the pursuit of Peace, and offers valuable insights into the multifaceted nature of Peace in an increasingly interconnected and interdependent world. Dr. Jörg Berchem's scholarship contributes to the ongoing dialogue on how to build a more peaceful and just global order.

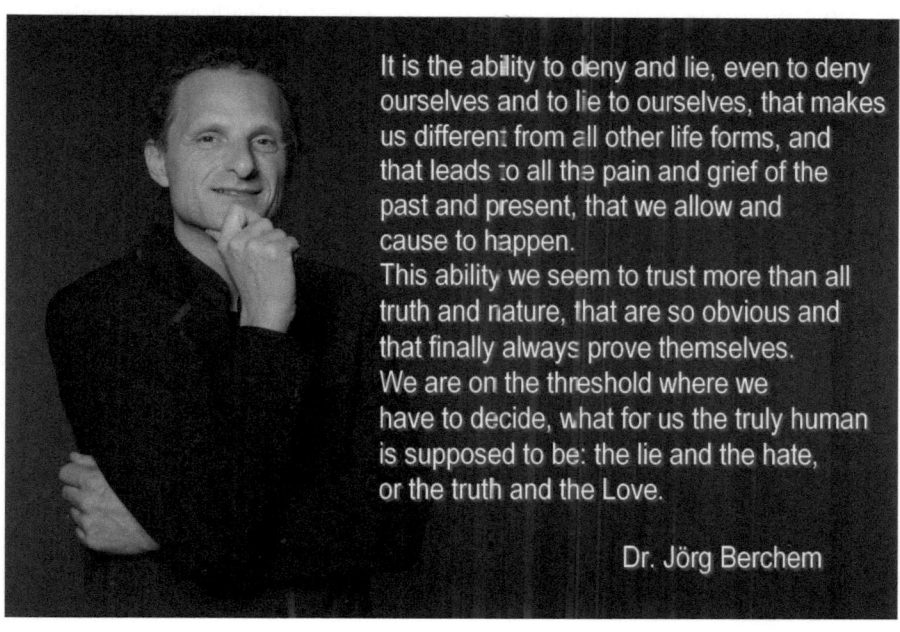

It is the ability to deny and lie, even to deny ourselves and to lie to ourselves, that makes us different from all other life forms, and that leads to all the pain and grief of the past and present, that we allow and cause to happen.
This ability we seem to trust more than all truth and nature, that are so obvious and that finally always prove themselves.
We are on the threshold where we have to decide, what for us the truly human is supposed to be: the lie and the hate, or the truth and the Love.

Dr. Jörg Berchem

2. The Joyful-Life Self-Declaration of Peace

As a citizen of the world community, I stand against racism, discrimination and intolerance of any kind.

Throughout my Life I will try to promote equality, justice and dignity among all people in my home, my community and everywhere in the world.

I believe that all human beings are born free, equal in dignity and rights and have the potential to contribute constructively to the development and well-being of societies and all Life on earth.

As I recognize the dignity and right to live of each individual, I condemn all violence, domestic, social, political, national or elsewhere in speech and action.

I am ready to live without the supposed protection of military armament.

I want to advocate for Peace without weapons to be developed and realized politically and socially.

I declare that this recognition of dignity and respect for being also applies respectively to the entire fellow world: e.g. to animals, plants and nature.

In humility, I want to respect, protect and preserve the foundations of Life, and I want to share them justly and equitably.

To fulfil this ambition, I want to align my Life with the mantra:

GOOD THOUGHTS

GOOD WORDS

GOOD DEEDS

The Joyful-Life Self-Declaration of Peace by Dr. Jörg Berchem, Joyful-Life.org

II. Faces of Peace: People, Visions and Quotes

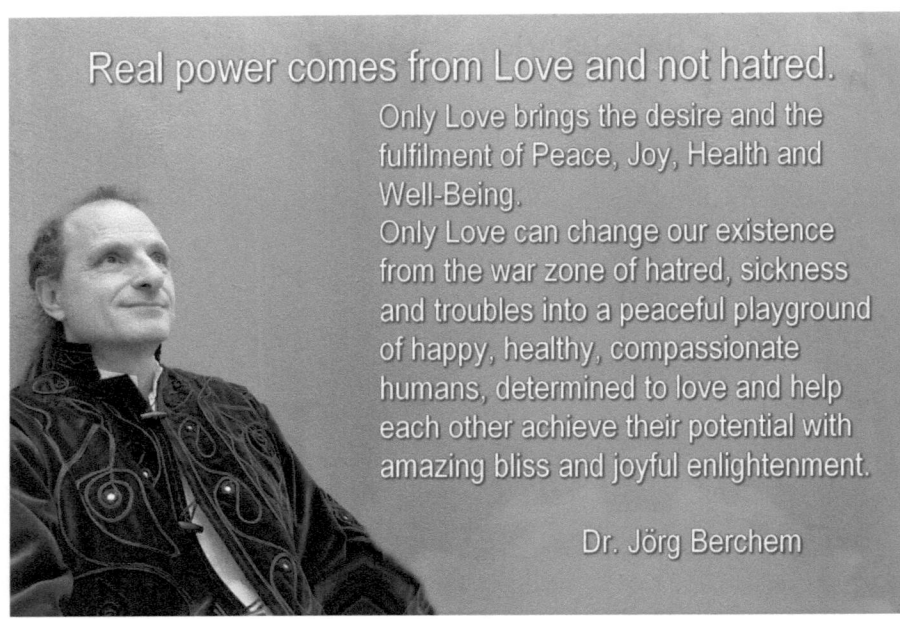

Real power comes from Love and not hatred.

Only Love brings the desire and the fulfilment of Peace, Joy, Health and Well-Being.
Only Love can change our existence from the war zone of hatred, sickness and troubles into a peaceful playground of happy, healthy, compassionate humans, determined to love and help each other achieve their potential with amazing bliss and joyful enlightenment.

Dr. Jörg Berchem

3   Introduction

The World Needs Positive Messages and Visions

Regarding the war rhetoric of the mass media and the proclamation of old and new concepts of the enemy, I felt the strong wish to send more stimuli of Peace and peaceful visions into the world, thoughts about compassion and words of Peace.

It was Nelson Mandela who indicated, that hate has to be learnt. Thus, everybody knows somewhere inside the desire for Peace and the feeling of disgust about war and hate. The mass media and politicians train the people to ignore these feelings and teach strong feelings of hate and violence. The desire and feeling for Peace and unity becomes buried under self-doubt, fear and manipulation.

By the means of power games and an economy which is based on exploitation and war, the people are trained with new concepts of enemy and are baited against each other. The willingness of politics to accept war as real means and instrument is alarming. The growing acceptance of war by so many people is even more alarming, and proves nothing, but the success of the manipulation of the masses. The bitter truth is: It still works in the twenty-first century. For their dirty business, the exports of weapons and war, often covered as humanitarian aid or "democratisation", need the distraction of the masses and the cooperation of parts of the population.

But do educated and free people really want to produce weapons, which are sent to exploited countries, where they kill many innocent people, traumatise, humiliate or kill children or their parents? Does a soldier, who is educated, liberated and freed from the brainwash of the military, go to war to fight against people he does not really know? Does he really for little money and questionable trainings fight, once he sees through the manipulation and realises that he is only used for the benefit of a few?

Prominent and popular people of the past and present know that Peace can never be achieved by violence. In simple and clear words they express that Peace is a possible reality, that it can be lived, and that only Love and non-violence can do something against the hate, violence and war.

Gandhi, Jesus, Nelson Mandela, Albert Einstein, Martin Luther King etc. – Were these brave men and women only insane dreamers? Or did they change the world and inspire us?

Should we continue to listen to the warmongers in politics, economy and mass media, or should we rather listen to the charismatic and wise men and women, whom we admire?

In 2014, I began to design postcard size posters of wise quotes on Peace. These postcards could be sent by e-mail. The idea was to send out positive, loving and peaceful thoughts and messages to touch the hearts of the people. Anybody can just choose which one likes and distribute them with all means. Don't forget to send to those who are called your enemy. If you can afford it, you may sponsor a billboard, e.g. in front of a military base or book an advertisements. – These postcards are the basis for this chapter.

The Vision

Only if people lose their fear, but discover their compassion, starting again to believe in Peace, they will refuse to follow the spiral of violence. When first a few and then more and more refuse to accept the manipulative concepts of enemy, refuse to finance war, refuse to demonstrate against each other, refuse to hate, refuse to become soldiers ... then Peace is possible.

Let us prove that the human race has really overcome the Middle Ages, also in mind and action.

- We can develop actions as signs of Peace.
- We can demonstrate for Peace and demand Peace.
- We can live Peace and get in touch with those people we are told that they are our enemies, whom the politics wants us to fear.
- We can celebrate concerts and festivals of Peace.
- We can create a place of encounter and exchange
- We can eliminate injustice and poverty.
- We can show solidarity with the persecuted and the suppressed.
- We can visit mosques, synagogues, churches, homes of asylum seekers, and we can get to know each other.
- We can publish articles, songs and films about our feelings, our wishes, our visions.

- We can share words of Peace on the internet.
- We can network and communicate directly and through the internet.
- We can express our wish for Peace and demonstrate our willingness to live Peace.
- We can print posters, batches, flags with messages of Peace and advertise Peace on billboards.
- We can write to our politicians and remind them of their responsibility.

Instead of demonstrating and talking against so much, we can stand up for Peace and develop hope and visions.

> *Let* us bring light into darkness, because darkness can only be overcome by light, hate can only be overcome by Love, violence can only be overcome by non-violence, and war can only be overcome by Peace.

Notes

We live in a time when politics often denounces people because they find some wrongdoing, some small blemish on their résumé. It's a time when fans abandon their idols as soon as a small spicy detail of their private life becomes known. A time when politicians are ousted from their positions if a mistake is discovered in their past. People lose their jobs because they are associated with an opinion that is not universally accepted.

In this book, people also speak who, like all humans, have not been or are not infallible but have achieved great things or positively inspired many people.

This book is not meant to idealize individuals. It aims to enrich with words of wisdom about Peace and harmonious coexistence. We encounter people whose dedication to Peace, courage and sacrifice, Love, and passion should inspire us. No more. No less.

4   A. J. Muste: Peace is the Way

The phrase "There is no way to Peace, Peace is the way" is often attributed to A.J. Muste, a Dutch-born American clergyman, pacifist, and activist. He was a prominent figure in the Peace and civil rights movements in the United States during the 20th century. While the exact origin of this quote may not be definitively traced to Muste, it is closely associated with his philosophy and advocacy for non-violent resistance and Peace.

Abraham Johannes Muste, often known as A.J. Muste, was a prominent figure in the American Peace movement during the 20th century. He held strong and influential beliefs regarding Peace and non-violence. A.J. Muste's ideas about Peace can be summarized in the following key points:

1. Commitment to Non-violence: A.J. Muste was a fervent advocate of non-violent resistance. He believed that non-violence was not only a moral stance but also an effective method for achieving social and political change. He was deeply influenced by the ideas of Mahatma Gandhi and his use of non-violent civil disobedience.

2. Peace Activism: Muste was actively involved in various Peace movements and social justice causes. He played a significant role in anti-war protests, particularly during the Vietnam War era. His activism was characterized by his unwavering dedication to achieving Peace through non-violent means.

3. Personal Transformation: A.J. Muste believed in the idea of personal transformation as the foundation for social change. He argued that individuals needed to embody the principles of Peace and non-violence in their own lives before they could effectively contribute to broader societal transformation.

4. Critique of Militarism: Muste was a vocal critic of militarism and war. He saw war as a destructive force that not only resulted in the loss of life but also perpetuated a cycle of violence and suffering. He actively worked to oppose the arms race and military conflicts.

5. Intersectionality: Muste understood that Peace was intimately connected to other social justice issues. He saw the need to address issues such as poverty, racial inequality, and economic injustice as part of the broader struggle for Peace. He believed in the interconnectedness of all these struggles.

6. Faith-Based Activism: A.J. Muste was deeply influenced by his Christian faith, and this played a significant role in his activism. He saw non-violence as an extension of his religious beliefs and a way to put Christian principles of Love and justice into action.

7. Advocacy for Civil Rights: Muste was also involved in the civil rights movement and saw the struggle for racial equality as an integral part of the broader Peace movement. He believed that civil rights were a fundamental component of achieving a just and peaceful society.

A.J. Muste's ideas about Peace were characterized by a deep commitment to non-violence, a belief in personal and societal transformation, and a dedication to addressing the root causes of conflict and injustice. His legacy continues to inspire those who work for Peace and justice around the world.

5   Albert Camus: The Absurd Condition

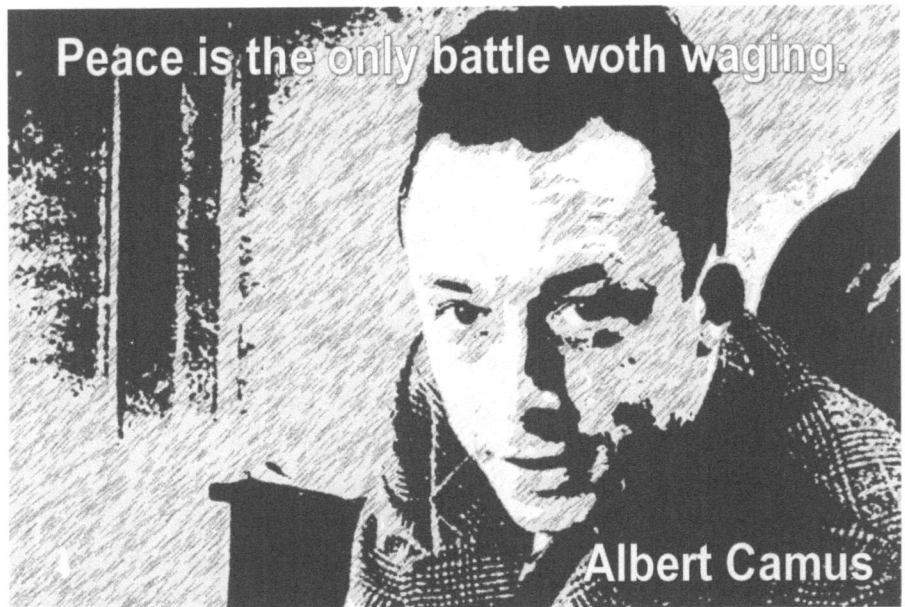

Peace is the only battle woth waging.

Albert Camus

Albert Camus, the renowned French-Algerian philosopher, writer, and Nobel laureate, possessed a profound understanding of Peace that was deeply rooted in his philosophical reflections, literary works, and experiences in a world marked by existential absurdity and the aftermath of World War II. Camus's perspective on Peace was characterized by his exploration of the human condition, the rejection of violence and oppression, and a commitment to the value of life. To appreciate Albert Camus's perspective on Peace, it is essential to explore the key elements of his philosophy, his literary contributions, and the enduring impact of his work on the pursuit of Peace and human dignity.

Central to Camus's understanding of Peace is his exploration of the "absurd condition" of human existence. He grappled with the inherent contradiction between humanity's search for meaning and the apparent meaninglessness of life. In the face of this existential absurdity, he emphasized the importance of finding a way to live with dignity and authenticity.

Camus was a fervent advocate for the rejection of violence as a means to achieve political or ideological ends. He experienced first-hand the horrors of World War II and the violence of the Algerian War, which deeply influenced his philosophy. He believed that violence, whether in the form of war, terrorism, or oppression, only perpetuated suffering and created a cycle of retaliation.

Camus's philosophy centred on the intrinsic value of human life. He believed that every individual had the right to live with dignity and without unnecessary suffering. This belief underpinned his commitment to Peace, social justice, and the preservation of life in the face of existential challenges.

Camus's perspective on Peace also encompassed the idea of revolt against injustice. He believed that individuals had a moral duty to stand up against oppressive systems and to challenge the dehumanizing forces that led to violence and conflict. His essay "The Rebel" explores the complexities of rebellion and the pursuit of justice.

As a writer, Camus recognized the potential of art and literature to convey his philosophical ideas and promote Peace. His novels, essays, and plays often grapple with themes of human existence, moral dilemmas, and the search for meaning. Through his literary works, he invited readers to contemplate the human condition and the choices that lead to Peace or conflict.

Albert Camus's impact on the understanding of Peace and the human condition is profound. His commitment to the rejection of violence, his advocacy for the value of life, and his exploration of the absurdity of existence continue to inspire individuals, writers, and philosophers worldwide. His work challenges us to reflect on our responsibility to seek Peace, justice, and dignity in a world marked by complex and sometimes inexplicable challenges.

In conclusion, Albert Camus's understanding of Peace was characterized by a deep exploration of the human condition, the rejection of violence, and a commitment to the value of life and human dignity. His work serves as a reminder of the moral imperative to stand against injustice and violence, even in the face of existential challenges. Camus's legacy stands as a testament to the enduring potential of literature and philosophy to inspire Peace and reflection in a world marked by complexities and contradictions.

6   Albert Einstein: The Abolition of War

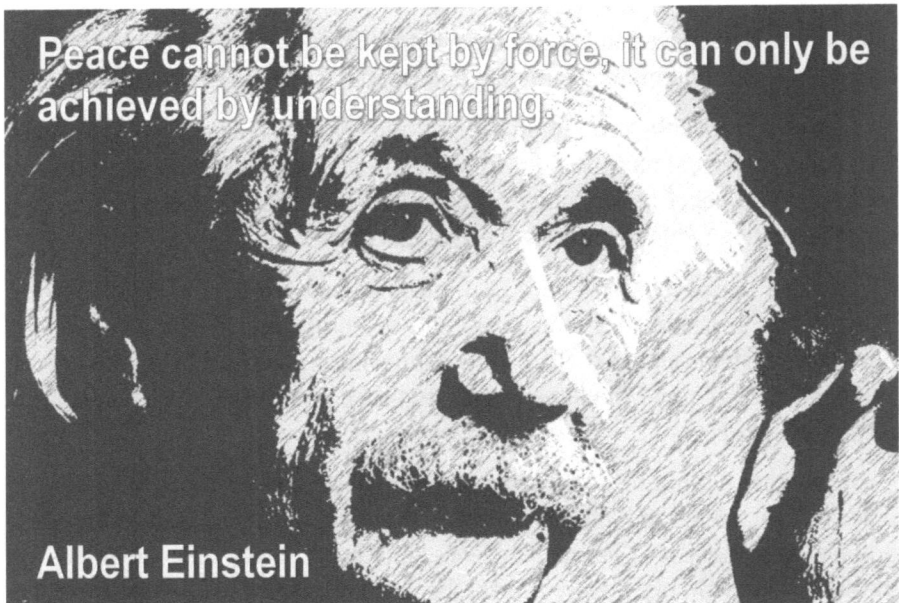

Peace cannot be kept by force, it can only be achieved by understanding.

Albert Einstein

Albert Einstein, renowned for his groundbreaking contributions to physics and for his intellectual prowess, held a unique perspective on the understanding of Peace. His insights into Peace were deeply philosophical and transcended the realm of science. Einstein's views on Peace were strongly influenced by the turbulent times in which he lived, particularly the two world wars and the development of nuclear weapons. To appreciate Einstein's understanding of Peace, one must explore the fundamental elements of his philosophy, his life experiences, and his enduring impact on the pursuit of global harmony.

At the heart of Einstein's perspective on Peace was the belief that true Peace could only be achieved through the abolition of war. He famously remarked, "You cannot simultaneously prevent and prepare for war." This notion was a clear reflection of his deep concern over the destructive power of warfare, particularly in the context of the burgeoning nuclear arms race during the mid-20th century.

Einstein's understanding of Peace was inextricably tied to his scientific work. He was well aware of the destructive potential of the atomic bomb, which he had indirectly contributed to with his work on the theory of relativity and the famous equation $E=mc^2$. Recognizing the cataclysmic impact of nuclear weapons on the world, he became an outspoken advocate for disarmament and the peaceful use of atomic energy. He saw that science and technology, when used irresponsibly, could lead to global catastrophe, and he believed it was his moral duty to prevent such a scenario.

Einstein's approach to Peace was grounded in his philosophical conviction that the common good of humanity transcended national interests and boundaries. He believed that nations needed to work together to maintain Peace and promote a just and equitable world. He was an advocate for a world government, which he saw as the ultimate safeguard against the outbreak of future wars. His 1946 essay, "The Real Problem is in the Hearts of Men," underscored the idea that Peace was not just a political or diplomatic matter but a question of human ethics and values.

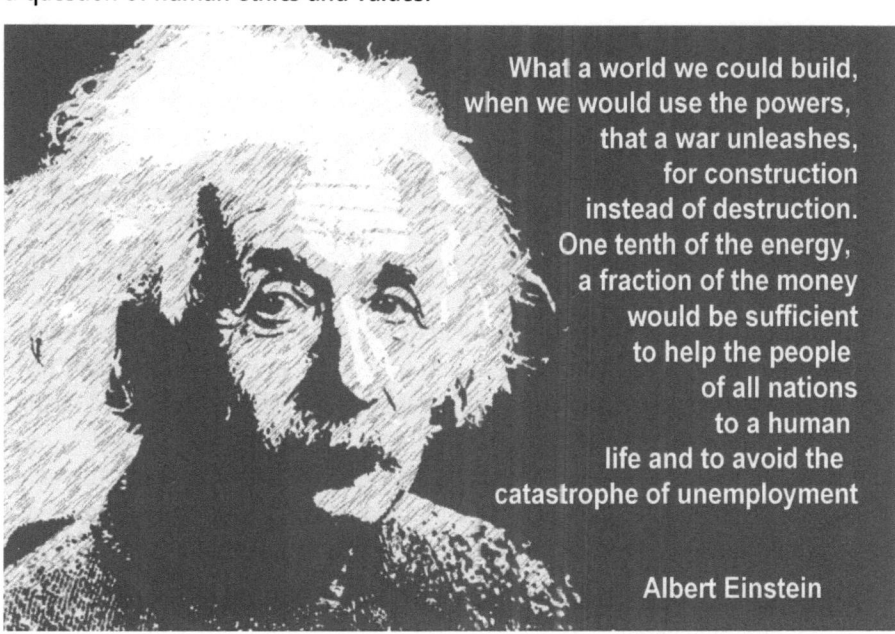

What a world we could build,
when we would use the powers,
that a war unleashes,
for construction
instead of destruction.
One tenth of the energy,
a fraction of the money
would be sufficient
to help the people
of all nations
to a human
life and to avoid the
catastrophe of unemployment

Albert Einstein

Einstein's life experiences profoundly influenced his understanding of Peace. As a Jewish scientist who had fled Nazi Germany, he had seen the atrocities of World War II and the Holocaust first-hand. This background intensified his commitment to working for a more peaceful world. He lent his voice to various Peace organizations and was a co-founder of the Bulletin of the Atomic Scientists, a publication that emphasizes the urgent need to address nuclear dangers.

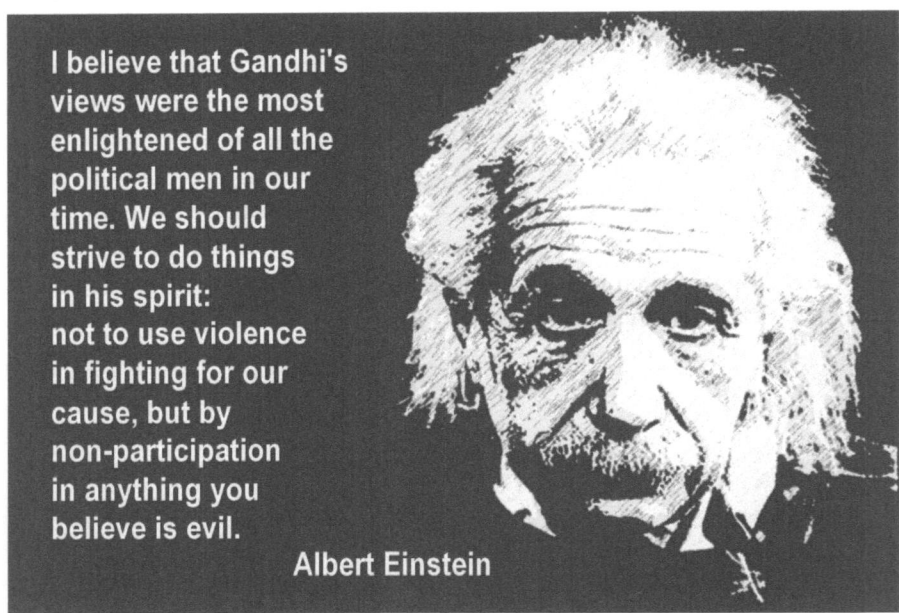

I believe that Gandhi's views were the most enlightened of all the political men in our time. We should strive to do things in his spirit: not to use violence in fighting for our cause, but by non-participation in anything you believe is evil.

Albert Einstein

Einstein's impact on the understanding of Peace extended beyond his lifetime. His advocacy for nuclear disarmament and his call for a world government have left an enduring legacy. The Pugwash Conferences on Science and World Affairs, which he inspired, continue to bring together scientists, scholars, and policymakers to address global security challenges. His warning about the perils of nuclear weapons and the need for international cooperation to ensure Peace remains relevant in contemporary discussions about global security.

In conclusion, Albert Einstein's understanding of Peace was deeply rooted in his moral and philosophical convictions. He recognized the dire consequences of unchecked warfare and the destructive potential of scientific advances, particularly nuclear technology. Einstein's advocacy for global cooperation and his commitment to the betterment of humanity continue to inspire those who work tirelessly to create a more peaceful world, free from the horrors of war and the threat of nuclear destruction.

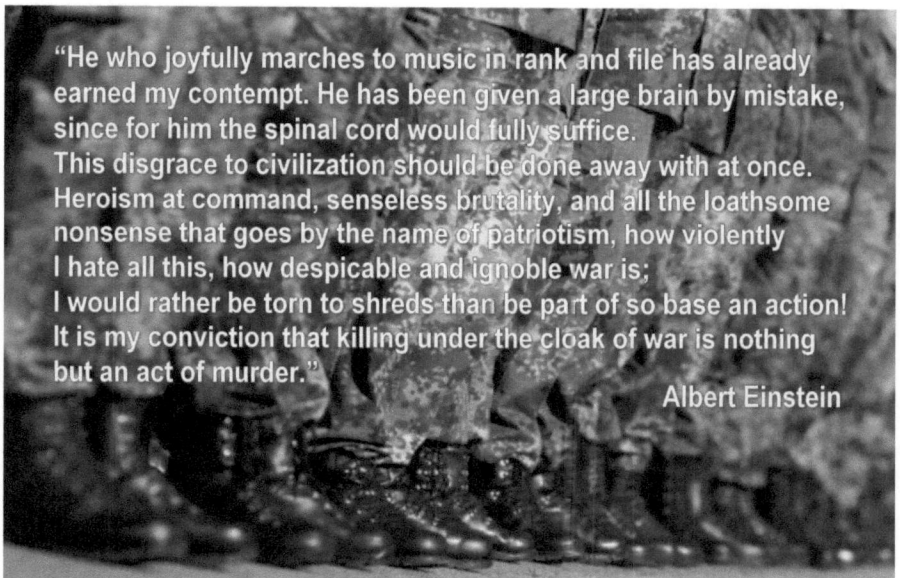

"He who joyfully marches to music in rank and file has already earned my contempt. He has been given a large brain by mistake, since for him the spinal cord would fully suffice.
This disgrace to civilization should be done away with at once. Heroism at command, senseless brutality, and all the loathsome nonsense that goes by the name of patriotism, how violently I hate all this, how despicable and ignoble war is;
I would rather be torn to shreds than be part of so base an action! It is my conviction that killing under the cloak of war is nothing but an act of murder."

Albert Einstein

7 Albert Schweitzer: Reverence for Life is the Highest Court of Appeal

True philosophy must start from the most immediate and comprehensive fact of consciousness: 'I am life that wants to live, in the midst of life that wants to live.'

Albert Schweitzer

Albert Schweitzer, a polymath and humanitarian, is best known for his philosophy of "reverence for life." This concept, deeply rooted in his personal experiences and philosophical reflections, became the cornerstone of his pacifist beliefs. Schweitzer's work in medicine, theology, and philosophy demonstrated the profound implications of his commitment to Peace and non-violence.

Albert Schweitzer's reverence for life philosophy is grounded in a profound respect for all forms of life. This philosophy impels individuals to recognize the intrinsic value and worth of every living being. It is a holistic approach that extends beyond humans and encompasses animals, plants, and the environment as well. Schweitzer famously stated, "I am life that wants to live in the midst of life that wants to live." This profound recognition of the interconnectedness of life is the foundation of his pacifist ideology.

Schweitzer's reverence for life philosophy is inextricably linked to his pacifist beliefs. He recognized that any form of violence, whether it was war, oppression, or cruelty to animals, was an affront to the sanctity of life. For Schweitzer, the principles of non-violence and pacifism were not just ethical ideals but practical imperatives for a more just and harmonious world.

1. Opposition to War: Schweitzer vehemently opposed war and the use of military force to resolve conflicts. He believed that the horrors of war resulted from a lack of understanding and a failure to appreciate the sanctity of life. He advocated for the peaceful resolution of disputes through diplomacy, negotiation, and dialogue.

2. Humanitarianism: Schweitzer's pacifism was intertwined with his humanitarian work. He dedicated his life to providing medical care in Africa, often in challenging conditions. His medical missions were grounded in the idea that alleviating suffering and promoting life is a more meaningful and constructive response than violence or indifference.

3. Advocacy for peaceful Coexistence: Schweitzer was a vocal advocate for international cooperation and the establishment of a global legal framework to prevent conflicts. He believed that nations should work together to address common challenges and that a commitment to Peace was vital for the survival of humanity.

Albert Schweitzer's philosophy of reverence for life and his pacifist stance remain highly relevant in today's world. In an era marked by ongoing conflicts, environmental degradation, and social injustices, Schweitzer's teachings offer a guiding light for those seeking a more peaceful and sustainable future.

4. Environmental Ethics: Schweitzer's philosophy anticipated the modern environmental movement. It underscores the need for ecological responsibility and sustainable living, reminding us of our duty to protect the environment for the sake of all living beings.

5. Non-violence Movements: Schweitzer's commitment to non-violence and his insistence on the importance of dialogue and understanding have inspired countless Peace activists and movements worldwide. His teachings continue to shape the discourse on conflict resolution.

6. Humanitarianism and Global Solidarity: Schweitzer's legacy lives on in humanitarian organizations and individuals who strive to make a positive impact in the world. His emphasis on compassion, service, and

global solidarity remains a guiding principle for those dedicated to alleviating human suffering.

In conclusion, Albert Schweitzer's reverence for life philosophy and his unwavering commitment to pacifism serve as a testament to the power of ethical principles in shaping a more peaceful world. His teachings challenge us to reflect on our relationships with all living beings and to recognize the profound interconnectedness of life. Schweitzer's enduring legacy reminds us that the pursuit of Peace and non-violence is not just an ideal but a practical and moral imperative for humanity's survival and flourishing.

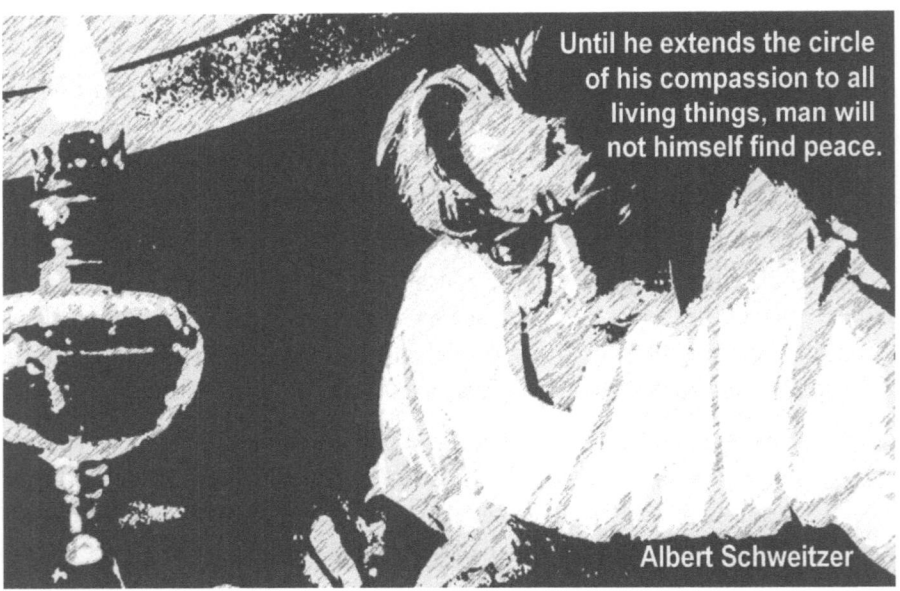

Until he extends the circle of his compassion to all living things, man will not himself find peace.

Albert Schweitzer

8   Alfred Adler: *Gemeinschaftsgefühl*

War is not the continuation of politics with different means, it is the greatest mass-crime perpetrated on the community of man.

Alfred Adler

Alfred Adler, the Austrian psychiatrist and founder of Individual Psychology, offered a unique perspective on the understanding of Peace. While primarily known for his work in psychology, Adler's views on Peace were informed by his broader ideas on human behaviour, community, and social dynamics. To appreciate Adler's understanding of Peace, it is essential to explore the fundamental elements of his philosophy, his life experiences, and his contributions to the field of psychology.

Central to Adler's perspective on Peace was his belief that human beings have an innate desire for social harmony and belonging. He emphasized the importance of social interest or "*Gemeinschaftsgefühl*," which he saw as the fundamental motivating force in human behaviour. Adler posited that individuals are driven by a deep-seated desire to contribute positively to their communities and to foster cooperation and social cohesion. In this sense, Peace was not just the absence of conflict, but the presence of mutual respect, cooperation, and a sense of belonging.

Adler's approach to Peace was closely linked to his holistic view of individuals and their psychological development. He saw mental and emotional health as intrinsically connected to an individual's ability to adapt and function within a community. According to Adler, individuals who felt socially connected and had a sense of purpose were more likely to experience inner Peace and contentment. This perspective suggested that societal structures and relationships played a significant role in an individual's mental and emotional well-being.

Furthermore, Adler's understanding of Peace encompassed the notion of social equality and justice. He believed that fostering social equality and reducing inequalities in access to resources and opportunities were crucial for the maintenance of Peace within a society. He was critical of hierarchical structures that perpetuated inequalities and argued for the importance of creating a fair and just social order to avoid conflicts and tensions.

Adler's life experiences significantly influenced his understanding of Peace. Born in 1870 in a time of social upheaval and change, he witnessed the challenges faced by individuals and communities in a rapidly evolving society. His personal struggles with physical ailments and his experiences as a medical doctor also informed his views on the interconnectedness of physical and psychological well-being. These experiences motivated him to explore the ways in which individuals and society could better support each other to achieve Peace and harmony.

While Alfred Adler is primarily recognized for his contributions to psychology, his understanding of Peace had far-reaching implications for social work, education, and community development. His ideas on community, social interest, and the role of the individual in creating a more harmonious society continue to resonate with professionals in various fields who work toward the betterment of individuals and their communities.

In conclusion, Alfred Adler's understanding of Peace was rooted in the belief that human beings have a natural inclination toward social harmony and cooperation. He viewed Peace as more than just the absence of conflict; it was a state of mutual respect, social interest, and social equality. His ideas about individual psychology, community, and social dynamics have left an enduring legacy and continue to influence efforts to promote Peace, social cohesion, and well-being.

9   Bertha von Suttner: Lay Down Your Arms!

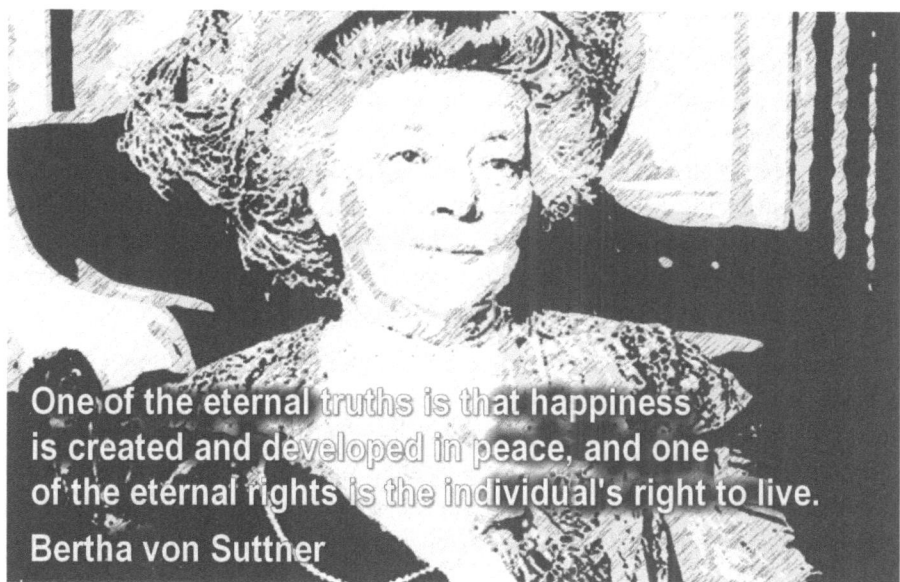

One of the eternal truths is that happiness is created and developed in peace, and one of the eternal rights is the individual's right to live.
Bertha von Suttner

Bertha von Suttner, a trailblazing Austrian pacifist and novelist, emerged as a prominent figure in the late 19th and early 20th centuries, leaving an indelible mark on the burgeoning Peace movement. Her commitment to pacifism was not only a response to the turbulent times she lived in, but also a profound philosophical stance that sought to challenge the prevailing glorification of war and promote alternative paths to resolving conflicts.

Born in 1843 into a noble family, Bertha Kinsky married Arthur Gundaccar von Suttner, a Baron, and became Bertha von Suttner. Her early life was marked by exposure to the military culture of her time, as her husband served in the Austrian navy. However, the experiences of witnessing war, coupled with her insightful reflections on human nature, inspired von Suttner to become a vocal advocate for Peace.

At the core of Bertha von Suttner's pacifism was a rejection of the prevailing romanization of war. In her groundbreaking anti-war novel, "Lay Down Your Arms!" ("*Die Waffen nieder!*"), published in 1889, von Suttner dissected the horrors of armed conflict and the devastating impact it had on individuals, families, and entire societies. Her vivid portrayal of war's grim realities served as a wake-up call to those who idealized militarism and underscored the urgent need for a paradigm shift in international relations.

One of the foundational principles of von Suttner's pacifism was the belief in the power of diplomacy and arbitration as alternatives to war. She ardently advocated for the establishment of international institutions designed to mediate conflicts peacefully. Von Suttner's vision laid the groundwork for the development of the Permanent Court of Arbitration in The Hague and the later creation of the International Court of Justice. Her unwavering belief in the potential for dialogue and negotiation to replace armed confrontation reflected a deep optimism about humanity's capacity for reason and cooperation.

Disarmament was another critical aspect of Bertha von Suttner's pacifist philosophy. She argued that the reduction of military forces and the redirection of resources from arms production to social welfare and education were imperative steps toward creating a more just and peaceful world. Von Suttner's advocacy for disarmament was both practical and ethical, addressing not only the economic toll of militarization but also the moral imperative to prioritize human well-being over the machinery of war.

Strange how blind people are! The torture chambers of the Dark Ages instil disgust in them, but they are proud of their arsenals.

In addition to her emphasis on institutional and structural changes, von Suttner recognized the unique role that women could play in the pursuit of Peace. At a time when women's voices were often marginalized in political discourse, she championed the idea that women, as nurturers and caregivers, had a special responsibility to advocate for Peace. Von Suttner's perspective foreshadowed the later contributions of women to the Peace movement and the recognition of their agency in preventing and resolving conflicts.

Bertha von Suttner's pacifism was not merely an abstract intellectual stance but a lived commitment. She engaged in active efforts to promote Peace, including participating in Peace congresses, delivering lectures, and tirelessly advocating for her beliefs. Her efforts culminated in being awarded the Nobel Peace Prize in 1905, making her the first woman to receive this prestigious honour.

In conclusion, Bertha von Suttner's pacifism was a multifaceted and influential philosophy that challenged the prevailing attitudes towards war and conflict in her time. Her writings, activism, and advocacy for Peace institutions have had a lasting impact on the trajectory of the Peace movement, influencing subsequent generations of pacifists and contributing to the development of international frameworks for conflict resolution. Von Suttner's legacy stands as a testament to the transformative power of individuals who dedicate themselves to the pursuit of a more peaceful and just world.

> *As if killing could make up for anything! As if shed blood could cleanse anything at all, undo anything that has happened! Oh, about the sanctified absurdity under whose rule the stupid world has placed itself.*

10   Bob Marley: One Love

It's time for the world to unite as a human race.

Bob Marley

Bob Marley, the legendary Jamaican musician and cultural icon, is celebrated not only for his groundbreaking reggae music but also for his profound understanding of Peace, unity, and social justice. His perspective on Peace was deeply rooted in his personal experiences, Rastafarian spirituality, and a commitment to using music as a tool for social change. To appreciate Bob Marley's perspective on Peace, it is essential to explore the key elements of his philosophy, his life experiences, and the enduring impact of his work on the pursuit of Peace and justice.

Rastafarianism, the religious and cultural movement that Bob Marley embraced, places a strong emphasis on unity, Love, and the pursuit of a peaceful world. The belief in "One Love," a central tenet of Rastafarian spirituality, underpins Marley's understanding of Peace. The idea that all human beings are interconnected and share a common bond is reflected in many of his songs, such as the iconic "One Love" and "Three Little Birds."

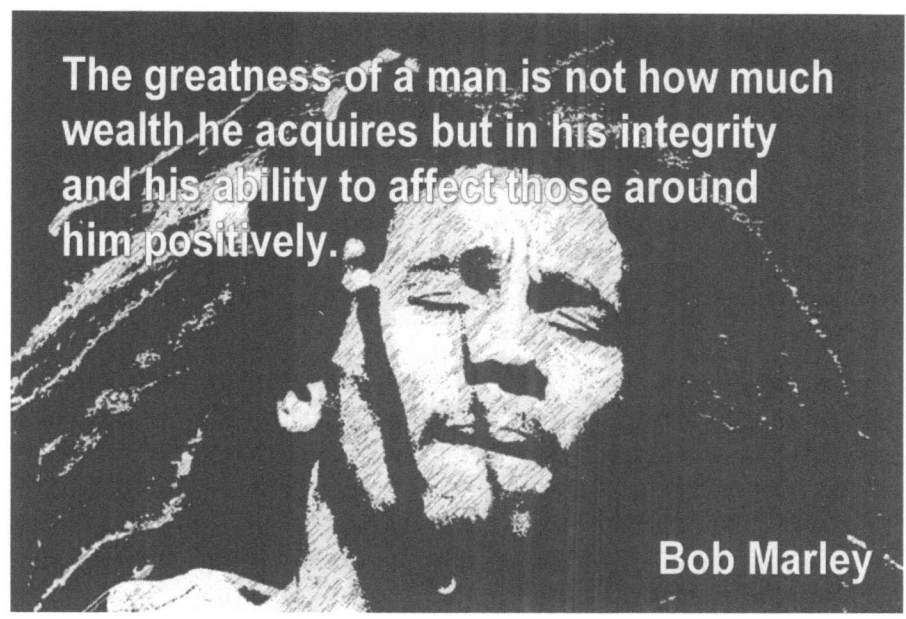

The greatness of a man is not how much wealth he acquires but in his integrity and his ability to affect those around him positively.

Bob Marley

Bob Marley's reggae music became a powerful vehicle for promoting Peace and social change. His lyrics conveyed messages of Love, unity, and resistance to oppression. His songs often addressed issues of social injustice, poverty, and political conflicts. "Get Up, Stand Up," for example, called on people to stand up for their rights and fight for justice, while "Redemption Song" expressed a yearning for freedom and self-determination.

Marley's music had a unifying effect, resonating with people from diverse backgrounds and cultures. He was often described as a "prophet" of Peace because of his ability to transcend borders and bring people together through his music.

Bob Marley's understanding of Peace extended beyond his music. He was deeply committed to using his platform as an artist to advocate for social and political change. His involvement in the "Smile Jamaica" concert in 1978, despite threats to his life, demonstrated his dedication to promoting Peace and unity in his homeland, Jamaica.

Marley's impact on the political landscape of Jamaica was significant. He played a role in brokering a ceasefire between warring political factions and used his influence to encourage non-violence and reconciliation during a turbulent period in the country's history.

Bob Marley's influence on the understanding of Peace, Love, and unity continues to resonate with individuals and movements dedicated to the pursuit of a more peaceful and just world. His music and message have inspired generations of artists, activists, and ordinary people to embrace the values of Peace and social justice. The enduring popularity of his songs, such as "No Woman, No Cry" and "Buffalo Soldier," reflects the timeless relevance of his messages.

In conclusion, Bob Marley's understanding of Peace was deeply rooted in Rastafarian spirituality, a belief in the interconnectedness of all people, and a commitment to using music as a powerful tool for social change. His work serves as a testament to the transformative power of music, spirituality, and activism in the pursuit of Peace and unity. Bob Marley's legacy stands as a reminder of the enduring potential of art and culture to inspire positive change and promote a more peaceful, harmonious world.

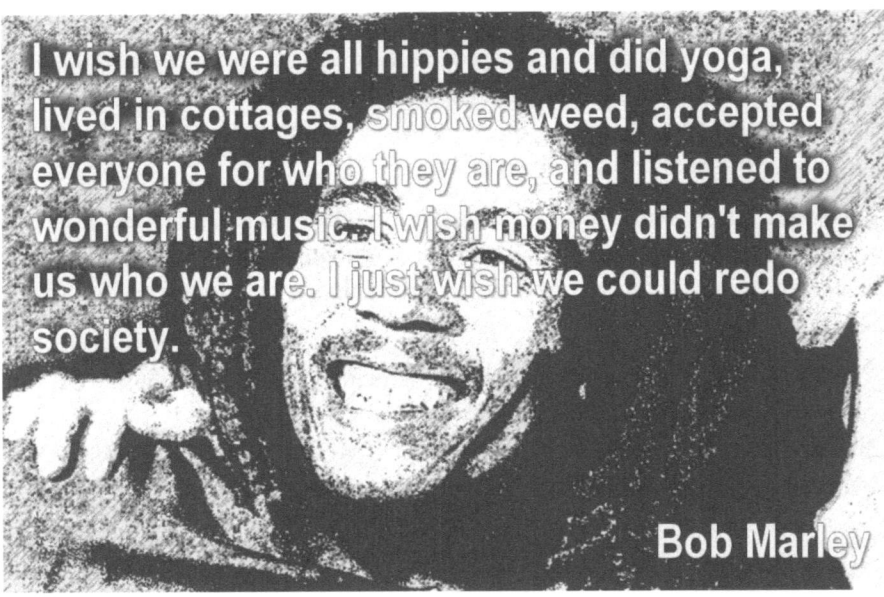

I wish we were all hippies and did yoga, lived in cottages, smoked weed, accepted everyone for who they are, and listened to wonderful music. I wish money didn't make us who we are. I just wish we could redo society.

Bob Marley

11   Black Elk: The Sacred Hoop

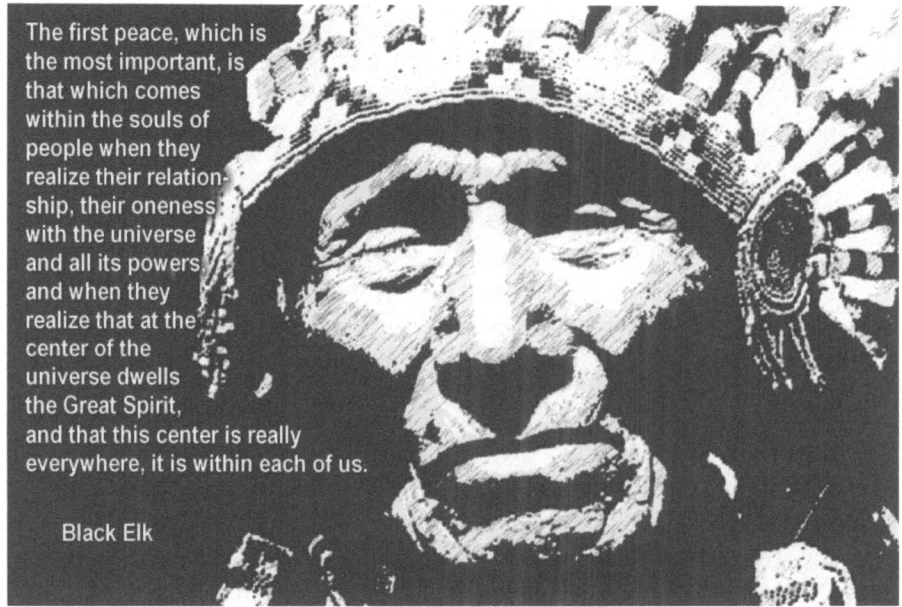

The first peace, which is the most important, is that which comes within the souls of people when they realize their relationship, their oneness with the universe and all its powers, and when they realize that at the center of the universe dwells the Great Spirit, and that this center is really everywhere, it is within each of us.

Black Elk

Black Elk, a prominent figure in the history and spirituality of the Lakota Sioux, offers a unique perspective on Peace that is deeply rooted in his indigenous culture and spiritual beliefs. His understanding of Peace is shaped by his experiences, his connection to the natural world, and his spiritual visions. To appreciate Black Elk's perspective on Peace, it is essential to delve into the key elements of his philosophy, his life experiences, and the enduring legacy of his teachings.

At the heart of Black Elk's understanding of Peace is the concept of the "Sacred Hoop." This sacred circle represents the interconnectedness of all life forms and the unity of the natural world. Black Elk's belief in the interdependence of all living beings emphasizes the importance of harmony, balance, and cooperation in achieving Peace.

Black Elk is renowned for his powerful visions and prophecies, which have significantly shaped his understanding of Peace. His vision on Harney Peak, where he received his great vision, offered a glimpse of a world in which the

Lakota people would find unity and prosperity. This vision conveyed a message of hope, Peace, and a return to spiritual values.

Black Elk's understanding of Peace extends to the relationship between humans and the Earth. He emphasized the need to respect and protect the land, as well as all the creatures that inhabit it. This respect for nature and all its inhabitants is a fundamental component of indigenous approaches to Peace and sustainability.

For Black Elk, Peace is closely tied to the concepts of harmony and balance. He believed that Peace could only be achieved when individuals and communities maintained a sense of balance in their relationships, both with each other and with the natural world. This balance is a key element in preserving the Sacred Hoop and ensuring the well-being of all.

Black Elk's wisdom and teachings continue to resonate with indigenous communities, scholars, and individuals interested in indigenous spirituality and Peace. His book, "Black Elk Speaks," provides valuable insights into Lakota culture, spirituality, and his understanding of Peace. His message of unity, harmony, and respect for the Earth has inspired countless people to reevaluate their relationship with the environment and their fellow human beings.

In conclusion, Black Elk's understanding of Peace is deeply rooted in Lakota spirituality, the Sacred Hoop, and a profound connection to the natural world. His teachings emphasize the importance of unity, balance, and respect for all living beings. His legacy serves as a reminder of the enduring relevance of indigenous wisdom and spirituality in the pursuit of Peace, harmony, and a deeper understanding of the interconnectedness of all life. Black Elk's vision and teachings stand as a testament to the profound potential for Peace and spiritual insight that indigenous cultures offer to the world.

12   Carl von Ossietzky: A Commitment to Peaceful Resistance

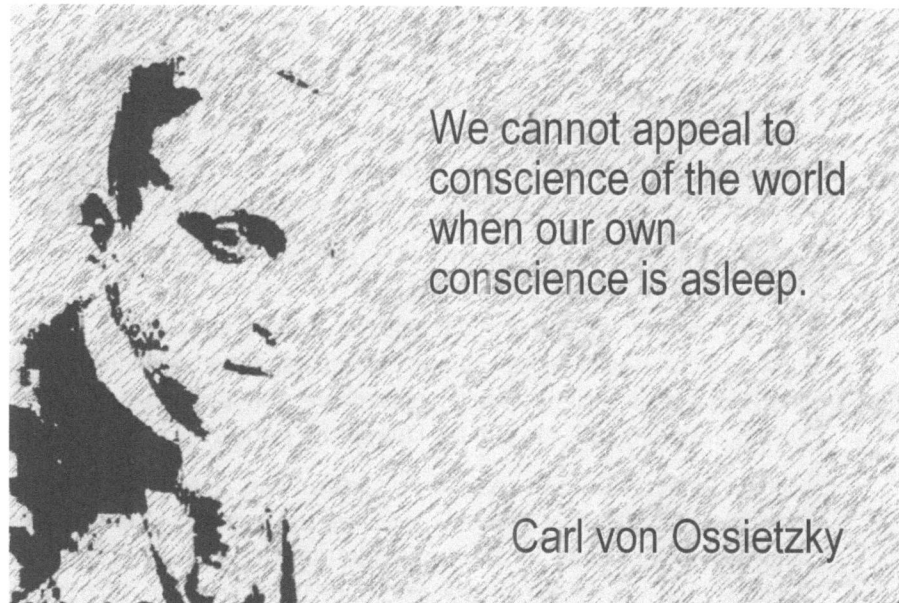

We cannot appeal to conscience of the world when our own conscience is asleep.

Carl von Ossietzky

Carl von Ossietzky, a German journalist, pacifist, and Nobel Peace Prize laureate, played a crucial role in shaping the discourse on pacifism during the tumultuous interwar period. Born on October 3, 1889, Ossietzky's life and work were deeply influenced by the turbulent political climate of his time, particularly the aftermath of World War I and the rise of totalitarian regimes. Ossietzky's concept of pacifism was characterized by a fervent commitment to non-violence, civil resistance, and the defence of human rights.

The period between the two World Wars was marked by political instability, economic crises, and the rise of authoritarian regimes in Europe. Ossietzky, a witness to the devastating consequences of World War I and the emergence of totalitarianism in Germany, became a vocal critic of militarism and an advocate for disarmament. His pacifist stance was rooted in the belief that another war could only lead to further suffering, and he saw the need for a radical shift in international relations.

The idea of pacifism is not the quiet surrender to the injustices of the world but the active struggle to overcome them without violence.

The key elements of Ossietzky's pacifism are:

1. Anti-Militarism: Ossietzky's pacifism was deeply rooted in his opposition to militarism. He saw the military-industrial complex as a major driver of conflict and believed that disarmament was essential for achieving lasting Peace. Ossietzky actively campaigned against the rearmament of Germany, which was taking place in violation of the Treaty of Versailles.

2. Non-violent Resistance: Central to Ossietzky's pacifist philosophy was the principle of non-violent resistance. He rejected the notion that military force could bring about positive change and argued for the power of civil disobedience and peaceful protest. Ossietzky believed that individuals and societies could resist oppression through non-violent means, inspiring others to join the struggle for justice.

3. Human Rights Advocacy: Ossietzky's pacifism was closely linked to his commitment to human rights. He criticized the erosion of civil liberties and democratic values in Germany under the Nazi regime. Ossietzky's advocacy for human rights was not confined to theoretical discussions; he actively engaged in exposing human rights abuses through his journalism, which ultimately led to his imprisonment by the Nazis.

4. Internationalism: Ossietzky's pacifism extended beyond national boundaries. He believed in the importance of international cooperation and the establishment of mechanisms to resolve conflicts peacefully. Ossietzky's vision for a pacifist world was one in which nations would collaborate to address common challenges rather than resorting to military solutions.

Carl von Ossietzky's commitment to pacifism and his unwavering dedication to human rights left a lasting legacy. Despite facing persecution and imprisonment, Ossietzky continued to inspire others to resist oppression through non-violent means. His contributions to the pacifist movement and human rights advocacy were recognized when he was awarded the Nobel Peace Prize in 1935.

His opposition to militarism, advocacy for non-violent resistance, commitment to human rights, and call for international cooperation remain relevant in today's world. Ossietzky's life and work serve as a reminder of the enduring importance of pacifism as a philosophy that seeks to address conflicts through dialogue, understanding, and a commitment to the fundamental dignity of every individual.

War   is a cowardly escape from the problems of peace.

13   Charles Chaplin: The Power of Humbility

You need power, only when you want to do some-thing harmful; otherwise Love is enough to get everything done.

Charles Chaplin

Charles Chaplin, the iconic English actor, comedian, and film-maker, is primarily remembered for his contributions to the world of entertainment. However, beneath the slapstick humour and silent film antics, Chaplin possessed a deep understanding of Peace that was both subtle and profound. His views on Peace were a reflection of the times in which he lived and his commitment to addressing social and political issues. To fully appreciate Chaplin's understanding of Peace, it is crucial to explore the key elements of his philosophy, his life experiences, and the lasting impact of his work.

Chaplin's concept of Peace was intrinsically connected to his keen sense of social justice. He believed that Peace could not exist in a world marked by social inequality, economic disparities, and political oppression. This perspective was most explicitly demonstrated in his 1940 film "The Great Dictator," where he delivered a powerful and timeless speech that conveyed his commitment to the ideals of Peace, liberty, and human dignity.

In "The Great Dictator," Chaplin, in the role of a Jewish barber, delivers a speech that calls for universal brotherhood and the rejection of hate and tyranny. He implores people to unite against the forces of evil and to recognize the inherent value of each individual. The speech was a powerful call for Peace and tolerance, delivered at a time when the world was reeling from the horrors of World War II and the rise of totalitarian regimes.

Chaplin's understanding of Peace was deeply humanitarian. He believed that Peace was not merely the absence of war but the presence of empathy, compassion, and a commitment to alleviating human suffering. In his personal life, Chaplin supported various social causes, including the fight against poverty, the promotion of labour rights, and the protection of civil liberties. He used his fame and fortune to advocate for a more just and compassionate world.

Chaplin's life experiences, too, played a significant role in shaping his understanding of Peace. Born into poverty and orphaned at a young age, he faced his share of personal challenges and hardships. These early experiences likely contributed to his deep empathy for the downtrodden and his conviction that Peace and justice should be accessible to all, regardless of their circumstances.

The impact of Chaplin's understanding of Peace is not limited to the realms of film and entertainment. His timeless speech in "The Great Dictator" continues to inspire individuals and movements worldwide. It has been quoted by political leaders, activists, and artists, emphasizing the enduring power of his message.

In conclusion, Charles Chaplin's understanding of Peace was a reflection of his strong sense of social justice and a belief in the essential dignity of all human beings. He used his platform in the world of entertainment to deliver a powerful message of Peace and tolerance, particularly in the midst of the tumultuous 1940s. His commitment to humanitarian causes and his artistic contributions continue to inspire people to strive for a more just, compassionate, and peaceful world. Charles Chaplin's legacy serves as a reminder that even in the realm of entertainment, profound messages of Peace can resonate across time and place.

Transcription of the final speech in Chaplin's "The Great Dictator":

> I'm sorry, but I don't want to be an emperor. That's not my business. I don't want to rule or conquer anyone. I should like to help everyone - if possible -

Jew, Gentile - black man - white. We all want to help one another. Human beings are like that. We want to live by each other's happiness - not by each other's misery. We don't want to hate and despise one another. In this world there is room for everyone. And the good earth is rich and can provide for everyone. The way of life can be free and beautiful, but we have lost the way.

Greed has poisoned men's souls, has barricaded the world with hate, has goose-stepped us into misery and bloodshed. We have developed speed, but we have shut ourselves in. Machinery that gives abundance has left us in want. Our knowledge has made us cynical. Our cleverness, hard and unkind. We think too much and feel too little. More than machinery we need humanity. More than cleverness we need kindness and gentleness. Without these qualities, life will be violent and all will be lost...

The aeroplane and the radio have brought us closer together. The very nature of these inventions cries out for the goodness in men - cries out for universal brotherhood - for the unity of us all. Even now my voice is reaching millions throughout the world - millions of despairing men, women, and little children - victims of a system that makes men torture and imprison innocent people.

To those who can hear me, I say - do not despair. The misery that is now upon us is but the passing of greed - the bitterness of men who fear the way of human progress. The hate of men will pass, and dictators die, and the power they took from the people will return to the people. And so long as men die, liberty will never perish...

Soldiers! don't give yourselves to brutes - men who despise you - enslave you - who regiment your lives - tell you what to do - what to think and what to feel! Who drill you - diet you - treat you like cattle, use you as cannon fodder. Don't give yourselves to these unnatural men - machine men with machine minds and machine hearts! You are not machines! You are not cattle! You are men! You have the Love of humanity in your hearts! You don't hate! Only the unloved hate - the unloved and the unnatural! Soldiers! Don't fight for slavery! Fight for liberty!

In the 17th Chapter of St Luke it is written: "the Kingdom of God is within man" - not one man nor a group of men, but in all men! In you! You, the people have the power - the power to create machines. The power to create happiness! You, the people, have the power to make this life free and beautiful, to make this life a wonderful adventure.

Then - in the name of democracy - let us use that power - let us all unite. Let us fight for a new world - a decent world that will give men a chance to work - that will give youth a future and old age a security. By the promise of these things, brutes have risen to power. But they lie! They do not fulfil that promise. They never will!

Dictators free themselves but they enslave the people! Now let us fight to fulfil that promise! Let us fight to free the world - to do away with national barriers - to do away with greed, with hate and intolerance. Let us fight for a world of reason, a world where science and progress will lead to all men's happiness. Soldiers! in the name of democracy, let us all unite!

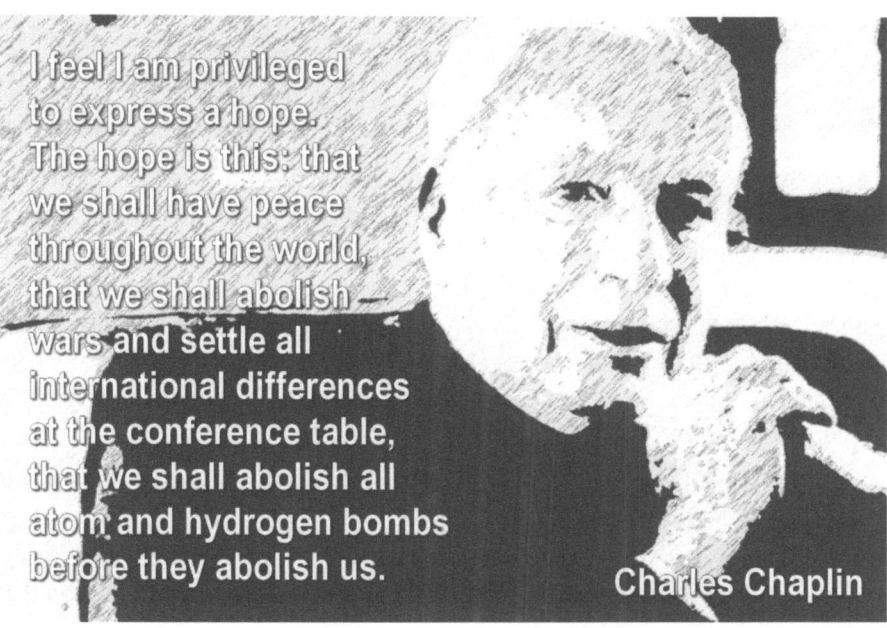

I feel I am privileged to express a hope. The hope is this: that we shall have peace throughout the world, that we shall abolish wars and settle all international differences at the conference table, that we shall abolish all atom and hydrogen bombs before they abolish us.

Charles Chaplin

14 Dalai Lama 14 (Tenzin Gyatso): Peace Through Compassion

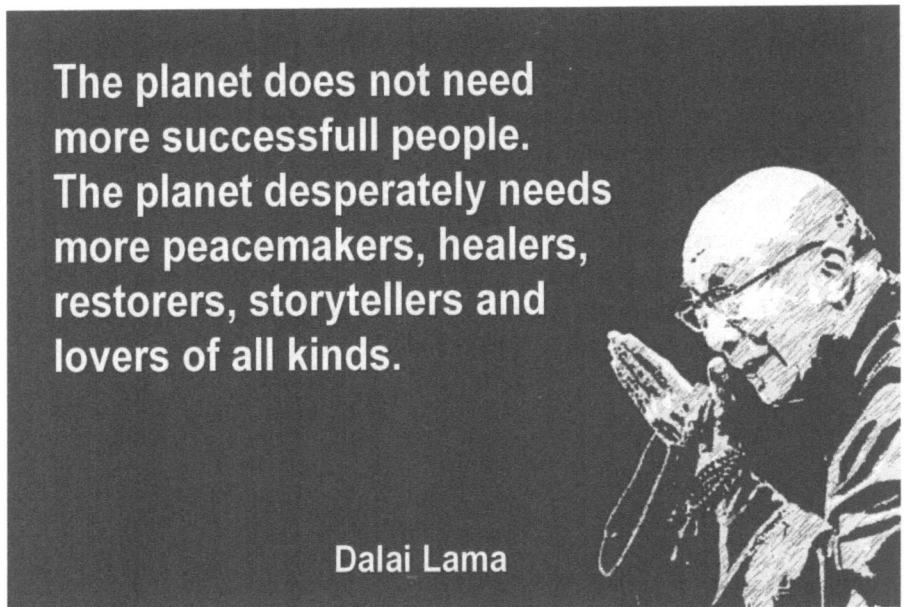

The planet does not need more successfull people. The planet desperately needs more peacemakers, healers, restorers, storytellers and lovers of all kinds.

Dalai Lama

Tenzin Gyatso, the 14th Dalai Lama, is not only the spiritual leader of Tibetan Buddhism but also a global symbol of Peace and compassion. His understanding of Peace is deeply rooted in Buddhist principles, compassion, and a commitment to non-violence. Throughout his life, he has worked tirelessly to promote these values, both in his spiritual teachings and his advocacy for the Tibetan people. To understand the Dalai Lama's perspective on Peace, one must delve into the core principles that underpin his philosophy, his life experiences, and his contributions to global Peace.

Central to the Dalai Lama's understanding of Peace is the Buddhist concept of compassion, which he often refers to as "*Karuna*." Compassion, in this context, is not just a feeling of empathy but a force that drives individuals to alleviate suffering and promote the well-being of others. The Dalai Lama believes that Peace is intimately connected to compassion because it entails the absence of harm and the presence of well-being, not just for oneself but for all sentient beings.

Non-violence, or "*Ahimsa*," is another fundamental aspect of the Dalai Lama's philosophy of Peace. He draws from the teachings of Mahatma Gandhi and other proponents of non-violence, emphasizing that true Peace can only be achieved by eschewing physical, verbal, and mental harm. His commitment to non-violence is evident in his approach to the Tibetan struggle for autonomy and his advocacy for peaceful dialogue and negotiation with the Chinese government.

The Dalai Lama's vision of Peace extends beyond individual well-being and encompasses societal and global dimensions. He believes that Peace is contingent on justice, freedom, and human rights. His unwavering commitment to the rights of the Tibetan people and their right to preserve their culture and religious traditions is a testament to this principle. He consistently advocates for peaceful resolutions to conflicts and the importance of dialogue and reconciliation.

The Dalai Lama's approach to Peace is deeply spiritual, as it is grounded in his Buddhist beliefs and his conviction that inner Peace is a prerequisite for external Peace. He encourages individuals to cultivate inner Peace through mindfulness, meditation, and self-awareness, which, in turn, can contribute to a more peaceful world. His message of inner transformation aligns with Gandhi's famous phrase, "You must be the change you want to see in the world."

The Dalai Lama's life experiences have profoundly influenced his understanding of Peace. Forced into exile from Tibet in 1959 following the Chinese occupation, he has faced personal hardship and persecution. Despite these challenges, he has consistently advocated for non-violence and peaceful resistance as the means to address the Tibetan issue and global conflicts. His resilience and commitment to his principles have made him an international symbol of Peace and justice.

The Dalai Lama's contributions to Peace extend beyond the spiritual realm. He is a Nobel Peace Prize laureate, and his tireless efforts to promote interfaith dialogue, human rights, and environmental sustainability have earned him worldwide recognition. His engagement in promoting a secular ethics based on common values further underscores his commitment to global Peace.

In conclusion, Tenzin Gyatso, the 14th Dalai Lama, offers a profound understanding of Peace that is rooted in compassion, non-violence, and a commitment to justice and human rights. His philosophy emphasizes the interconnectedness of all beings and the importance of inner Peace as a catalyst for external Peace. The Dalai Lama's life experiences and contributions to global Peace have made him a revered figure, inspiring individuals and nations to strive for a more peaceful and harmonious world.

> In fact, we have all been brainwashed.
> Since armies are legal, we believe that
> war is acceptable and legal.
> No one has the feeling that war
> is a crime and that his acceptance
> is equal to a criminal attitude.
> War is monstrous, its nature
> is tragedy and suffering.
>
> Dalai Lama

15 Daniele Ganser: Transparency and Self-Thinking

Let's resolve conflicts without violence and communicate without devaluation. Devaluing, killing ... that is the system, that we as a human family must overcome. If the values of courage, love and truthguide us, we cannot lose our way.

Daniele Ganser

Dr. Daniele Ganser, a Swiss historian with a focus on covert operations and geopolitics, offers a unique perspective on conflict and Peace that intertwines historical analysis with an understanding of the intricate dynamics of global power. This essay aims to delve into the core elements of Ganser's concept of Peace, exploring how his research sheds light on the challenges and opportunities for fostering a more harmonious world.

Ganser's extensive research on covert warfare highlights a crucial aspect of international relations often overlooked in discussions about Peace. He emphasizes the role of clandestine operations, secret services, and geopolitical manoeuvring in shaping the global landscape. According to Ganser, Peace cannot be fully comprehended without acknowledging and addressing the hidden forces that contribute to conflict.

The concept of Peace, from Ganser's perspective, involves not only the absence of overt warfare but also the dismantling of covert strategies that perpetuate instability. By uncovering historical instances of covert operations and secret interventions, Ganser underscores the importance of transparency and accountability in fostering lasting Peace. Another dimension of Ganser's concept of Peace lies in the examination of energy politics and economic interests. Ganser's work often explores how resource competition, particularly in the context of energy, can be a driver of conflict. He posits that achieving a sustainable and lasting Peace requires a reevaluation of global economic structures and a move towards equitable resource distribution.

Ganser's vision of Peace extends beyond the absence of military hostilities to encompass economic justice and the fair allocation of resources. By addressing the root causes of economic disparity and resource-driven conflicts, Ganser advocates for a holistic approach to Peace that goes beyond conventional diplomatic efforts. His perspective on Peace also recognizes the pivotal role of civil society and grassroots movements in shaping the global narrative. He contends that genuine and lasting Peace cannot be achieved solely through top-down diplomatic initiatives but requires the active participation of informed and engaged citizens.

By emphasizing the agency of individuals and communities, Ganser encourages a bottom-up approach to Peacebuilding. Grassroots movements, in his view, play a vital role in holding governments and institutions accountable, fostering social justice, and promoting a culture of Peace that transcends national borders.

Let's resolve conflicts without violence and communicate without devaluing judgement.

Daniele Ganser has extensively researched and written about the role of media and propaganda in wars. He argues that the media, often influenced by political agendas, can play a significant role in shaping public opinion and perception during times of conflict. Ganser's analysis emphasizes several key points regarding the media's involvement in wars:

1. Propaganda as a Tool of War: Ganser contends that propaganda is not only a consequence of war but also a deliberate tool employed by governments and other actors to control information and manipulate public sentiment. This manipulation can involve shaping narratives,

controlling the flow of information, and influencing how events are portrayed to serve specific political goals.

2. Manufacturing Consent: Drawing on the ideas of media scholar Noam Chomsky, Ganser argues that media outlets often participate in manufacturing consent—a process where the media, intentionally or unintentionally, aligns with government narratives and interests. This alignment can create a distorted view of events, influencing public opinion and garnering support for government actions, even in the absence of comprehensive or accurate information.

3. Selective Reporting and Bias: Ganser highlights the selective reporting of events during conflicts, where media outlets may prioritize or omit certain information to support a particular narrative. This selectivity can contribute to a skewed understanding of the reasons for and consequences of war, potentially masking the true motivations behind military interventions.

4. Role of Embedded Journalists: Ganser explores the phenomenon of embedded journalism, where reporters are given access to military units and operations with the understanding that their reporting will be favorable to the military's perspective. While embedded journalism can provide a close-up view of the front lines, it also raises concerns about the independence and objectivity of the reporting.

5. Media's Influence on Public Perception: According to Ganser, the media's portrayal of wars can significantly influence public perception and, consequently, public support for military actions. By framing conflicts in certain ways, media outlets can shape the narrative, either justifying or criticizing military interventions.

6. Information Control and Secrecy: Ganser discusses how governments, particularly in times of war, may seek to control information and maintain secrecy. This can involve limiting access to certain areas, controlling the dissemination of information, and even engaging in disinformation campaigns to confuse and mislead the public.

In summary, Daniele Ganser argues that the media and propaganda play crucial roles in the context of wars. He emphasizes the need for critical media literacy and an awareness of potential biases, urging the public to question the information presented during times of conflict and to seek a more comprehensive and nuanced understanding of the complex factors at play.

> *If you blindly accept all this war propaganda, then you hate people who don't know it and are in favour of wars you don't understand. That is a sad state of affairs. It would be much better if we remember that every human being belongs to the human family.*

Daniele Ganser repeatedly emphasises that the whole of humanity is a single "human family" ("*Menschenfamilie*"). Accepting this and behaving accordingly is essential. Propaganda destroys this feeling of a human family, which is why it is important to expose the lies that wars require and to rediscover ourselves as a human family, which promotes Peace.

> *We certainly have a problem in the world with hostilities that get out of control. The word 'human family' helps to overcome these pervasive divisions and promote Peace.*

Daniele Ganser's concept of Peace emerges as a multifaceted and dynamic framework that addresses both the visible and hidden dimensions of global conflict. His emphasis on transparency, economic justice, and the active involvement of civil society reflects a holistic understanding of Peace that extends beyond the traditional confines of diplomatic negotiations. As the world continues to grapple with complex geopolitical challenges, Ganser's insights provide valuable perspectives on the interconnectedness of historical events, covert operations, and the pursuit of a more harmonious future.

> *If the words courage, love and truth and guide us, we cannot go astray.*

Although Daniele Ganser is not an outspoken pacifist, his work helps to uncover the true causes and dynamics of armed conflicts and to understand the resulting clear demands and conditions for a policy of Peace. His motivation is ground on a positive human image and aims to empower Peace movements.

16 Desmond Tutu: Forgiving for the Sake of Peace

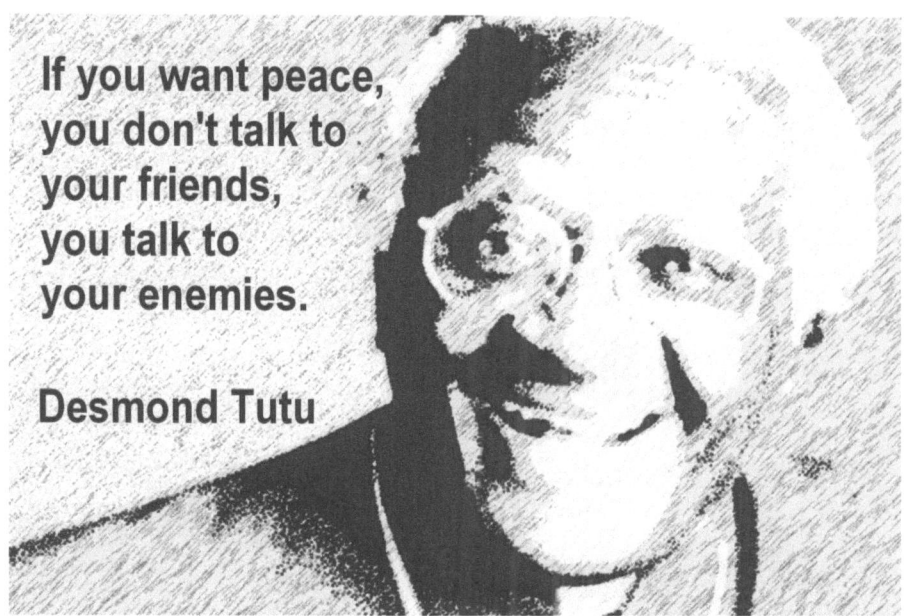

If you want peace, you don't talk to your friends, you talk to your enemies.

Desmond Tutu

Desmond Tutu, the South African Anglican bishop, theologian, and Nobel Peace Prize laureate, is a towering figure in the pursuit of Peace, justice, and reconciliation. His understanding of Peace is deeply rooted in his experiences in apartheid-era South Africa and his tireless efforts to combat oppression and promote reconciliation. To appreciate Desmond Tutu's perspective on Peace, it is essential to explore the key elements of his philosophy, his role in the anti-apartheid struggle, and the enduring impact of his work on the pursuit of Peace and human rights.

Desmond Tutu's understanding of Peace centres on the concepts of reconciliation and forgiveness. He firmly believed that genuine Peace could only be achieved through the acknowledgment of past wrongs, forgiveness, and the restoration of human dignity. As the chairperson of South Africa's Truth and Reconciliation Commission, he played a pivotal role in facilitating dialogue and forgiveness between victims and perpetrators of apartheid-era atrocities.

Tutu was a proponent of non-violent resistance against the apartheid regime. He, alongside figures like Nelson Mandela, advocated for peaceful means of challenging oppression and injustice. His commitment to non-violence as a tool for achieving social change is a fundamental element of his understanding of Peace.

The concept of "*ubuntu*" plays a significant role in Tutu's philosophy. Ubuntu, an African philosophical idea, emphasizes the interconnectedness of humanity. It underscores the belief that our well-being is intricately linked to the well-being of others. Tutu's understanding of Peace is deeply rooted in the idea that we are all bound together and, therefore, must strive for justice and harmony.

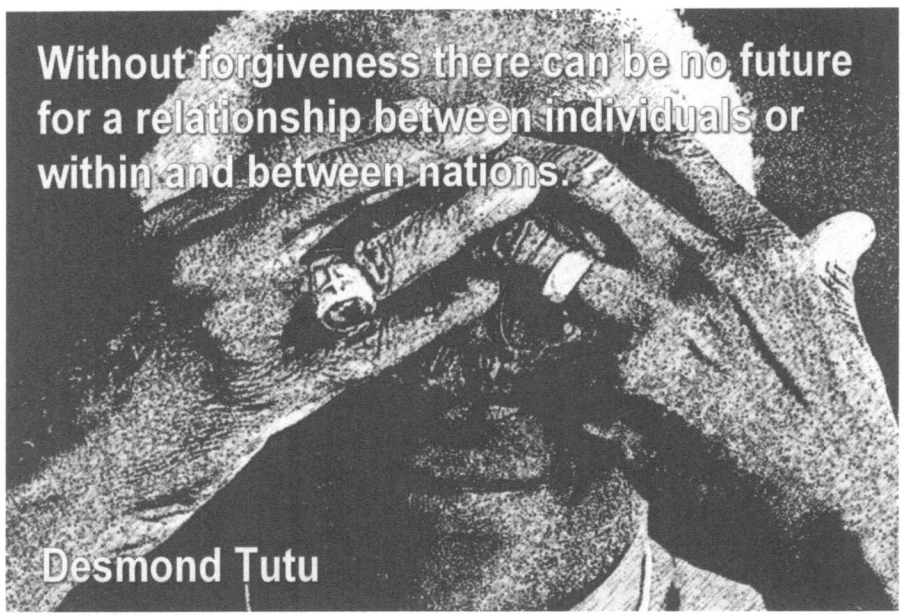

Without forgiveness there can be no future for a relationship between individuals or within and between nations.

Desmond Tutu

Desmond Tutu's perspective on Peace extends beyond the absence of violence. He advocates for social justice, equality, and human rights. He recognizes that lasting Peace cannot exist without addressing the structural injustices that perpetuate conflict and inequality. As a moral leader and clergyman, Tutu's commitment to Peace is intertwined with his deep religious convictions. He believed that religion had a central role to play in promoting values of Love, compassion, and justice. His theological background informed his approach to reconciliation and his unwavering belief in the potential for redemption and transformation.

Desmond Tutu's impact on the understanding of Peace is profound and continues to inspire people worldwide. His leadership in the struggle against apartheid, his work with the Truth and Reconciliation Commission, and his tireless advocacy for human rights have left an incelible mark on the pursuit of Peace, justice, and reconciliation. His legacy serves as a testament to the enduring potential of individuals and nations to heal deep wounds, acknowledge past injustices, and work together to build a more just and peaceful world.

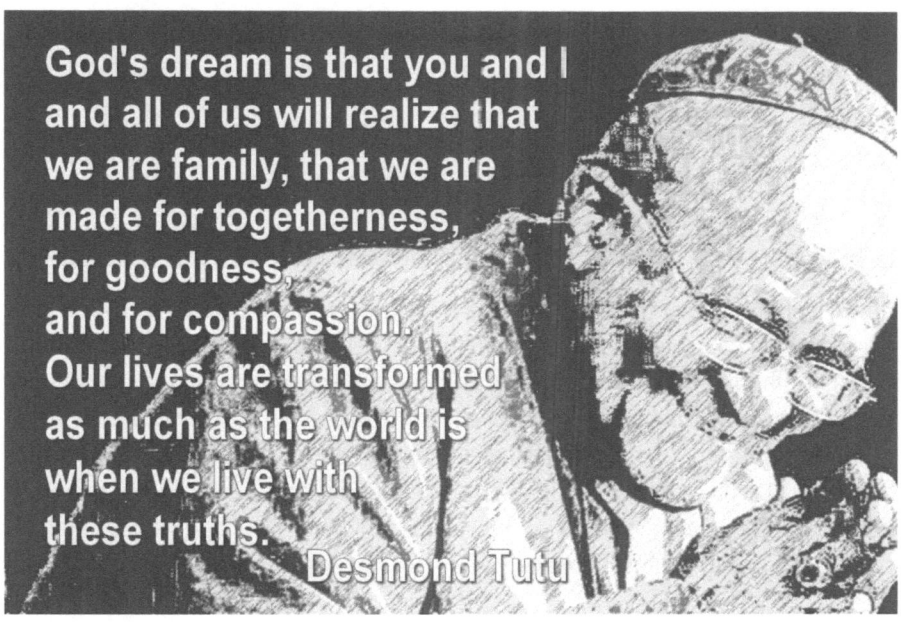

God's dream is that you and I and all of us will realize that we are family, that we are made for togetherness, for goodness, and for compassion. Our lives are transformed as much as the world is when we live with these truths. Desmond Tutu

In conclusion, Desmond Tutu's understanding of Peace is characterized by a commitment to reconciliation, forgiveness, non-violence, *ubuntu*, social justice, and moral leadership. His life and work exemplify the transformative power of forgiveness and the pursuit of justice as essential elements in achieving lasting Peace. Tutu's legacy stands as a reminder of the profound potential for individuals to drive positive change, heal divisions, and work towards a more peaceful and equitable global community.

17   Dietrich Bonhoeffer: Peace Must be Dared

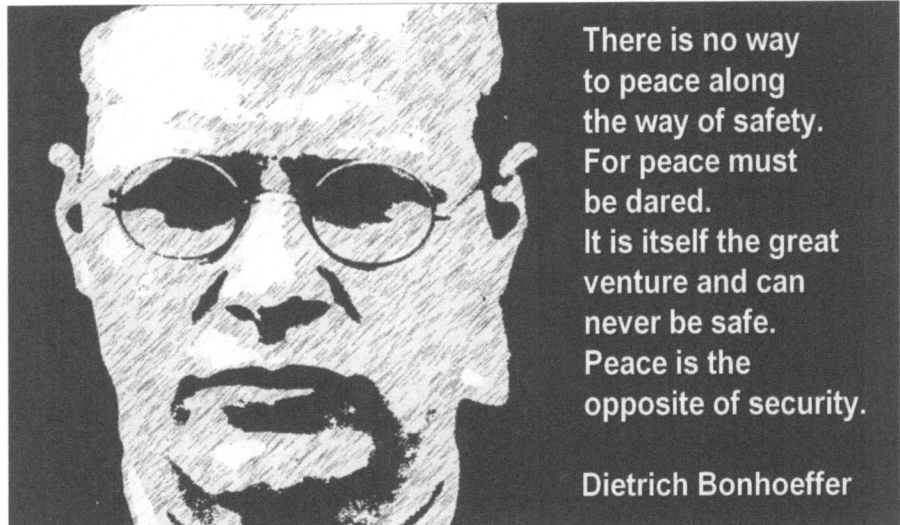

There is no way
to peace along
the way of safety.
For peace must
be dared.
It is itself the great
venture and can
never be safe.
Peace is the
opposite of security.

Dietrich Bonhoeffer

Dietrich Bonhoeffer, a German Lutheran pastor, theologian, and anti-Nazi dissident, had a profound understanding of Peace that was deeply rooted in his Christian faith, ethical convictions, and his experiences during a tumultuous period in history. Bonhoeffer's perspective on Peace was notably complex, as he grappled with the moral dilemmas posed by the rise of Nazism and the atrocities of World War II. To comprehend Bonhoeffer's understanding of Peace, one must delve into the core elements of his philosophy, his life experiences, and his courageous stand against injustice.

Bonhoeffer's concept of Peace was deeply informed by his Christian faith. He believed that true Peace, or "Shalom" in Hebrew, was more than just the absence of conflict; it was a state of wholeness, justice, and reconciliation with God. For him, Peace was inseparable from righteousness and required individuals to actively pursue justice and confront evil. His faith provided the foundation for his unwavering commitment to Peace, even in the face of severe moral dilemmas.

Central to Bonhoeffer's understanding of Peace was the idea that Peace and justice were interdependent. He famously wrote, "Silence in the face of evil is itself evil: God will not hold us guiltless. Not to speak is to speak. Not to act is to act." These words underscored his belief that individuals had a moral responsibility to stand up against oppression and injustice. He contended that Peace could not be achieved by appeasing or accommodating evil, but rather by confronting it with ethical action.

Bonhoeffer's approach to Peace was further complicated by his active resistance against the Nazi regime. He was part of the Confessing Church, a faction of German Protestants who opposed the Nazis' efforts to co-opt the church for their own purposes. Bonhoeffer's involvement in a plot to assassinate Adolf Hitler was a morally fraught decision, as he grappled with the tension between his commitment to Peace and the necessity of ending a regime that was perpetrating unspeakable horrors. This internal struggle highlighted the complexity of his understanding of Peace.

Furthermore, Bonhoeffer's life experiences were profoundly shaped by the historical context in which he lived. He witnessed the erosion of civil liberties, the persecution of Jews, and the horrors of the Holocaust. These experiences reinforced his belief that Peace required active opposition to tyranny and a commitment to protect the vulnerable. His participation in the resistance movement was driven by his unwavering commitment to preserving human dignity and opposing the forces of darkness.

The impact of Dietrich Bonhoeffer's understanding of Peace transcends his lifetime. His writings, including "The Cost of Discipleship" and "Letters and Papers from Prison," continue to inspire individuals worldwide. His emphasis on the moral responsibility to stand against injustice and his belief in the inseparable link between Peace and justice have left an enduring legacy.

In conclusion, Dietrich Bonhoeffer's understanding of Peace was complex, rooted in his Christian faith, and characterized by a profound commitment to justice. He grappled with moral dilemmas and the necessity of active resistance against evil during a dark period in history. His courageous stand against the Nazi regime and his writings continue to serve as a testament to the ethical imperative of pursuing Peace through active opposition to injustice. Bonhoeffer's legacy remains a source of inspiration for those who seek to confront evil and work toward a more just and peaceful world.

18   Dorothy Day: Peace Through Social Justice

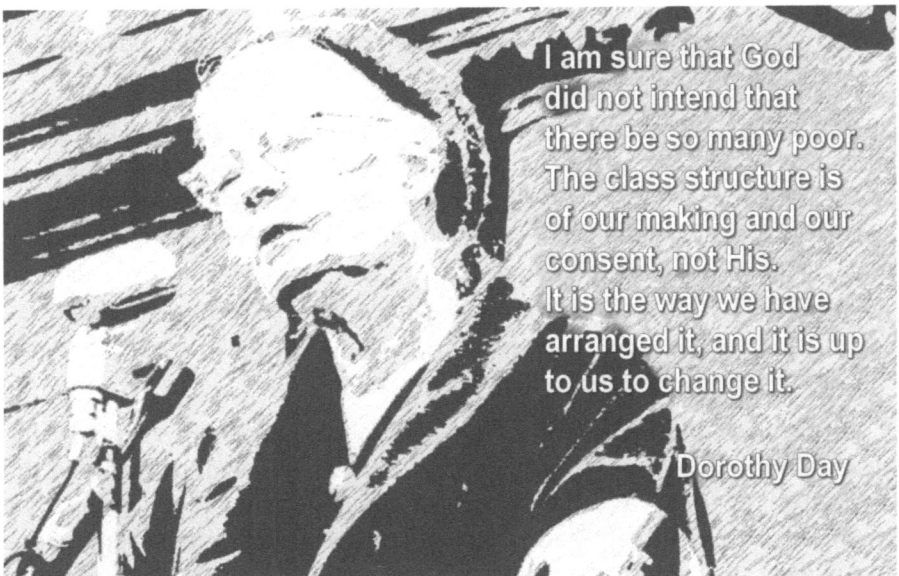

I am sure that God did not intend that there be so many poor. The class structure is of our making and our consent, not His. It is the way we have arranged it, and it is up to us to change it.

Dorothy Day

Dorothy Day, a prominent American social activist, journalist, and co-founder of the Catholic Worker Movement, is celebrated for her unwavering commitment to pacifism. Born in 1897, Day's life unfolded against the backdrop of two World Wars, the Great Depression, and significant social and political upheaval. Her pacifist philosophy was deeply intertwined with her Catholic faith and her dedication to social justice.

At the heart of Dorothy Day's pacifism was a profound adherence to the teachings of Jesus Christ, particularly the principles of Love, forgiveness, and non-violence. Influenced by the Catholic Church's teachings on social justice and the sanctity of human life, Day vehemently opposed war and violence in all its forms. Her commitment to pacifism was not a passive ideology but an active and lived practice, influencing both her personal life and her work as a social activist.

One of the key elements of Day's pacifism was her critique of the institutionalization of violence. She argued that governments, by resorting to war and military interventions, perpetuated a cycle of destruction and dehumanization. Day's pacifism, therefore, extended beyond individual actions to a systemic critique of the structures that led to violence. This perspective aligned with her broader advocacy for a more just and compassionate society.

Dorothy Day was a vocal opponent of war, consistently speaking out against U.S. involvement in conflicts such as World War II and the Vietnam War. Her activism was rooted in a belief that war contradicted the Christian principles of Love and mercy. Day believed in addressing the root causes of conflict through social and economic justice, rather than resorting to militarism as a solution.

Integral to Day's pacifist philosophy was her commitment to voluntary poverty and simplicity of life. In founding the Catholic Worker Movement with Peter Maurin in 1933, she sought to create a community that embodied the principles of hospitality, non-violence, and self-sufficiency. The movement established "houses of hospitality" where those in need could find food, shelter, and support. Through these efforts, Day demonstrated the practical application of her pacifist beliefs by creating spaces of compassion and solidarity in the midst of societal challenges.

The concept of personalism was also central to Day's pacifist philosophy. She emphasized the inherent dignity of every individual and believed in the transformative power of personal relationships. Day's approach to pacifism was not solely about protesting against war but also about building a culture of encounter, understanding, and empathy. By living among and serving the marginalized and impoverished, she aimed to foster a sense of community that transcended divisions.

Dorothy Day's pacifism was deeply rooted in her understanding of Christianity as a radical call to Love and service. Her commitment to non-violence was not passive; it was an active engagement with the world's injustices, a refusal to accept violence as a solution, and a persistent call for social transformation. Day's legacy continues to inspire contemporary pacifists and social justice advocates, illustrating the enduring power of a philosophy grounded in Love, compassion, and a relentless pursuit of Peace.

19   Edmond Bordeaux Székely: In Quest of Wisdom

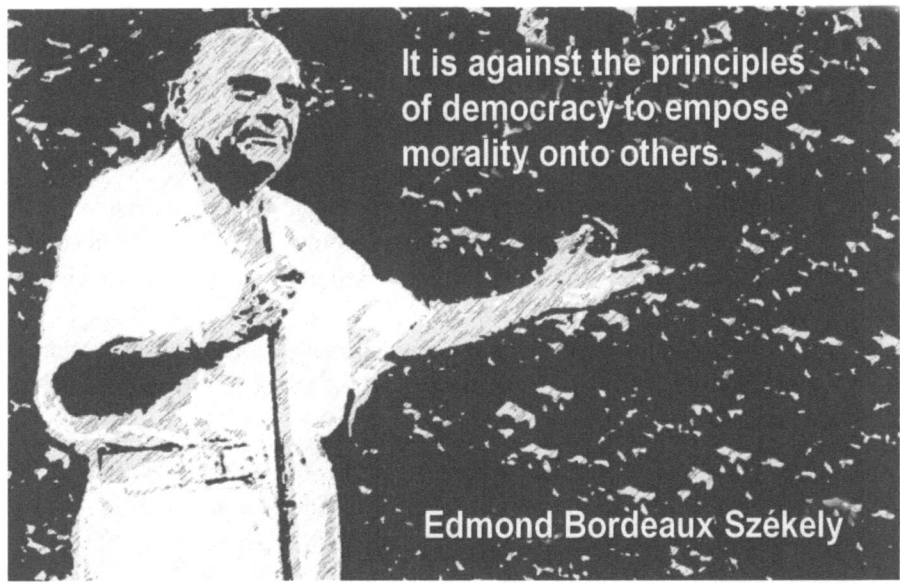

It is against the principles of democracy to empose morality onto others.

Edmond Bordeaux Székely

Edmond Bordeaux Székely, a renowned scholar, philosopher, and translator, had a unique understanding of Peace that was deeply rooted in his explorations of ancient texts, natural health, and spirituality. His perspective on Peace emphasized the interconnectedness of humanity with the natural world, the pursuit of physical and spiritual well-being, and the importance of conscious living. To appreciate Edmond Bordeaux Székely's perspective on Peace, it is essential to explore the key elements of his philosophy, his contributions to natural living, and the enduring impact of his work on the pursuit of a harmonious and healthy existence.

Edmond Bordeaux Székely is best known for his translations and interpretations of the Essene Gospel of Peace, a collection of ancient texts attributed to a Jewish sect known as the Essenes. These teachings emphasized a holistic approach to life, including natural living, plant-based nutrition, and a deep respect for the Earth. The Essenes' way of life served as the foundation for Székely's understanding of Peace.

Székely believed in the profound connection between humanity and the natural world. He saw nature as a source of wisdom, healing, and Peace. His philosophy emphasized living in harmony with the Earth and embracing sustainable practices to nurture both the environment and human well-being.

Edmond Bordeaux Székely was a proponent of plant-based nutrition and believed that a diet centred around fresh fruits, vegetables, and whole foods was essential for physical and spiritual health. He saw the consumption of natural, unprocessed foods as a means to achieve vitality and inner Peace.

Székely's perspective on Peace also encompassed the idea of conscious living. He encouraged individuals to be mindful of their choices, actions, and the impact they had on themselves and the world around them. He believed that a conscious approach to life could lead to greater Peace and harmony.

Edmond Bordeaux Székely was a pioneer in the field of natural healing and holistic medicine. He advocated for alternative therapies, such as fasting and herbal remedies, as ways to restore health and vitality. His emphasis on physical well-being was closely tied to his understanding of Peace as a state of balance and health.

Edmond Bordeaux Székely's impact on the understanding of Peace is evident in his contributions to natural living, holistic health, and spiritual well-being. His interpretations of the Essene teachings continue to inspire individuals seeking a deeper connection with nature, a plant-based lifestyle, and an approach to health that considers the physical, mental, and spiritual aspects of human existence. Székely's work serves as a reminder of the potential for conscious and holistic living to lead to personal and global Peace and well-being.

In conclusion, Edmond Bordeaux Székely's understanding of Peace was characterized by his commitment to natural living, unity with nature, plant-based nutrition, conscious living, and holistic well-being. His philosophy emphasizes the importance of living in harmony with the Earth, nurturing both physical and spiritual health, and embracing a lifestyle that supports inner and outer Peace. Székely's legacy stands as a testament to the potential for individuals to achieve Peace through a holistic and balanced way of life.

20   Eugen Drewermann: Pacifism as Fundamental Principle of Christian Faith

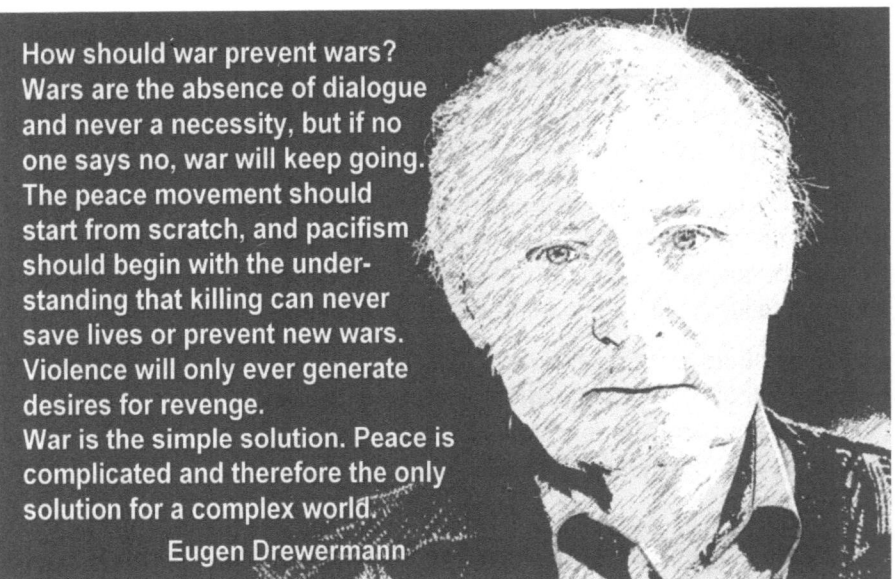

How should war prevent wars? Wars are the absence of dialogue and never a necessity, but if no one says no, war will keep going. The peace movement should start from scratch, and pacifism should begin with the understanding that killing can never save lives or prevent new wars. Violence will only ever generate desires for revenge.
War is the simple solution. Peace is complicated and therefore the only solution for a complex world.
Eugen Drewermann

Eugen Drewermann, the German theologian, psychotherapist, and prolific writer, possesses a unique and multifaceted understanding of Peace that is deeply rooted in his exploration of psychology, spirituality, and the human condition. Drewermann's perspective on Peace encompasses both personal and global dimensions, emphasizing the importance of inner harmony, compassion, and social justice. To appreciate Eugen Drewermann's perspective on Peace, it is essential to explore the key elements of his philosophy, his life experiences, and the enduring impact of his work on the pursuit of Peace and well-being.

Eugen Drewermann's understanding of Peace is closely intertwined with his expertise in psychotherapy. He recognizes the significance of inner Peace as a prerequisite for a peaceful world. Drewermann's work often delves into the human psyche, exploring the roots of conflict, violence, and suffering. He believes that addressing inner turmoil and psychological wounds is essential for achieving personal Peace and, by extension, Peace in society.

Drewermann's understanding of Peace draws from spiritual traditions, especially Christian theology. He emphasizes the importance of compassion, empathy, and Love as foundational principles for Peace. In his view, connecting with the spiritual dimension of life can lead individuals and societies toward a more harmonious existence.

| *People* have no right to kill other people! Neither with the Colt nor with the pickaxe nor with drones.

Drewermann is critical of religious dogma and institutionalized religion that has been used to justify violence and oppression. He believes that religion should be a force for Peace and social justice, advocating for the liberation theology movement and the role of religion in addressing societal inequalities and advocating for the marginalized.

Eugen Drewermann extends his understanding of Peace to include human rights and environmental concerns. He recognizes that Peace is not solely about the absence of conflict but also about addressing injustices, protecting human rights, and ensuring the well-being of all people. His perspective on Peace thus encompasses a commitment to environmental stewardship and social justice.

Drewermann has also spoken about the power of non-violence as a means of resolving conflicts and achieving Peace. He draws inspiration from figures like Mahatma Gandhi and Martin Luther King Jr., who demonstrated that peaceful resistance can bring about significant social change.

Eugen Drewermann theologically grounds pacifism in various ways:

1. The Commandment of Love and Non-violence: Drewermann emphasizes the central commandment of Love in the Christian faith, as found in the teachings of Jesus Christ. This commandment includes the call to Love one's enemies and to practice non-violence. He argues that the teachings of Jesus form the basis for a non-violent and peaceful coexistence, constituting the theological core of pacifism.

2. Advocacy for Justice: The theologian sees the theological foundation of pacifism in the church's mission to work for justice and the well-being of the oppressed. He interprets the Christian message as a call to social justice, and views violence and wars as a departure from this mission.

3. Rejection of Violence in the Name of God: Drewermann criticizes the misuse of religions and belief systems to justify violence and wars. He argues that theology has a responsibility to prevent the alienation of religion and violence by emphasizing the ethical and moral principles of faith.

4. Critique of Structural Violence: The theologian points out the importance of overcoming structural violence, which exists in the form of social, economic, and political injustices in the world. He argues that theology should show the way to prevent wars and conflicts by addressing and eliminating this structural violence.

Overall, Drewermann theologically grounds pacifism in the fundamental principles of the Christian faith, as found in the Bible and the teachings of Jesus. His theological perspective emphasizes the rejection of violence, the promotion of non-violence, and active work for justice and Peace as central elements of the Christian faith and pacifism.

21   St. Francis of Asisi: Peace as a Fundamental Demand for Creation

St. Francis of Assisi (1181/1182–1226), the medieval Italian Catholic friar and preacher, is often regarded as a symbol of Peace and compassion. While the term "pacifist" may not directly apply to figures from the medieval period in the same way it does in modern contexts, St. Francis is widely recognized for his commitment to Peace, humility, and harmony with all creation.

St. Francis' approach to Peace was deeply rooted in his interpretation and embodiment of Christian teachings. One of the most well-known episodes in his life is the encounter with the Sultan Malik al-Kamil during the Fifth Crusade in 1219. Despite the ongoing conflict between Christians and Muslims, St. Francis sought to engage in peaceful dialogue with the Sultan. The meeting is often characterized by mutual respect, and it is said that St. Francis and the Sultan exchanged gifts as a sign of goodwill.

St. Francis' commitment to Peace extended beyond human interactions to encompass all creation. His famous Canticle of the Sun, also known as the Canticle of the Creatures, praises God for the beauty and interconnectedness of the natural world. This deep reverence for all living beings, including animals and the environment, reflects his holistic understanding of Peace.

While St. Francis did not explicitly articulate a systematic theology of non-violence, his lifestyle and teachings emphasized the virtues of humility, simplicity, and non-possession. His followers, known as Franciscans, have historically embraced these values and have often been associated with efforts to promote Peace and social justice.

It's important to note that St. Francis lived in a medieval context, shaped by different cultural and religious dynamics than those of the modern world. The concept of pacifism, as understood in contemporary terms, may not be a precise fit for describing figures from this period. However, St. Francis' emphasis on Love, compassion, and a harmonious relationship with others and the natural world aligns with principles often associated with pacifism.

In summary, while St. Francis of Assisi may not have identified explicitly as a pacifist in the contemporary sense, his life, actions, and teachings demonstrate a profound commitment to Peace, reconciliation, and a harmonious coexistence with all the creation. His legacy continues to inspire individuals who seek a path of compassion, simplicity, and non-violence.

Most High, all-powerful, all-good Lord, All praise is Yours, all glory, all honour and all blessings.

To you alone, Most High, do they belong, and no mortal lips are worthy to pronounce Your Name.

Praised be You my Lord with all Your creatures, especially Sir Brother Sun, Who is the day through whom You give us light. And he is beautiful and radiant with great splendour, Of You Most High, he bears the likeness.

Praised be You, my Lord, through Sister Moon and the stars, In the heavens you have made them bright, precious and fair.

Praised be You, my Lord, through Brothers Wind and Air, And fair and stormy, all weather's moods, by which You cherish all that You have made.

Praised be You my Lord through Sister Water, So useful, humble, precious and pure.

Praised be You my Lord through Brother Fire, through whom You light the night and he is beautiful and playful and robust and strong.

Praised be You my Lord through our Sister, Mother Earth who sustains and governs us, producing varied fruits with coloured flowers and herbs. Praise be You my Lord through those who grant pardon for Love of You and bear sickness and trial.

Blessed are those who endure in Peace, By You Most High, they will be crowned.

Praised be You, my Lord through Sister Death, from whom no-one living can escape. Woe to those who die in mortal sin! Blessed are they She finds doing Your Will.

No second death can do them harm. Praise and bless my Lord and give Him thanks, And serve Him with great humility.

22 Hannah Arendt: The Role of Self-Responsibility for Peace

There is no right to obedience.

Hannah Arendt

Hannah Arendt, a prominent political theorist and philosopher of the 20th century, made significant contributions to the understanding of politics, human rights, and the concept of Peace. Her thoughts on the role of self-responsibility in the pursuit of Peace are especially relevant in today's complex global landscape. Arendt's ideas emphasize the individual's capacity to influence Peace through self-responsibility, which involves an active and thoughtful engagement with the political world.

Arendt's exploration of the "human condition" emphasizes the fundamental aspects of human existence. In her book "The Human Condition," she discusses three activities that define the human experience: labour, work, and action. Labour relates to the necessity of sustaining one's life through biological processes, work pertains to the creation of durable things in the world, and action concerns the interactions, deeds, and words that form the public realm.

Arendt suggests that Peace is not simply the absence of war, but rather a state in which people can engage in the public realm without fear or oppression.

For her, action, as a political activity, is central to the human condition and essential for maintaining Peace.

Arendt argues that the public realm, where action takes place, is characterized by "plurality." This concept highlights the diversity of human perspectives and the uniqueness of each individual. Plurality means that no one perspective should dominate the public realm. Instead, individuals should engage in dialogue and deliberation to reach common understandings and decisions.

This idea of plurality emphasizes the need for self-responsibility in upholding Peace. Individuals must take responsibility for engaging in the public realm, listening to others, and participating in the political process.

Arendt's reporting on the trial of Adolf Eichmann, a high-ranking Nazi official responsible for the logistics of the Holocaust, offers an important perspective on self-responsibility for Peace. Arendt's description of Eichmann as an ordinary bureaucrat who merely followed orders raised questions about individual responsibility in a political context.

Arendt argued that individuals should not evade their moral and ethical responsibility by blindly following orders. Instead, they should actively engage their moral judgment and refuse to participate in actions that violate human rights and principles of justice. This is a significant aspect of self-responsibility for Peace – the willingness to resist and oppose actions that lead to violence and conflict.

Arendt's philosophy encourages critical thinking and active citizenship as a means of achieving Peace. She believed that individuals should exercise their political agency by participating in public discussions, challenging oppressive systems, and promoting values that uphold human dignity.

By fostering a culture of self-responsibility, where individuals actively seek to understand and shape the world around them, we can work towards a more just and peaceful society. Arendt's ideas serve as a reminder that individuals have the capacity and the moral duty to contribute to the maintenance of Peace.

Hannah Arendt's insights on self-responsibility for Peace emphasize the importance of individual engagement in the political realm. She encourages active citizenship, critical thinking, and moral judgment as essential tools in the pursuit of Peace. Arendt's philosophy challenges individuals to take responsibility for their actions, to resist participation in oppressive systems, and to actively contribute to the establishment of a just and peaceful society. In a world marked by complex global challenges, her ideas remain relevant and serve as a call to action for those who aspire to build a more peaceful and just world.

> *In* *an ever-changing, incomprehensible world the masses had reached the point where they would, at the same time, believe everything and nothing, think that everything was possible and that nothing was true. ... Mass propaganda discovered that its audience was ready at all times to believe the worst, no matter how absurd, and did not particularly object to being deceived because it held every statement to be a lie anyhow. The totalitarian mass leaders based their propaganda on the correct psychological assumption that, under such conditions, one could make people believe the most fantastic statements one day, and trust that if the next day they were given irrefutable proof of their falsehood, they would take refuge in cynicism; instead of deserting the leaders who had lied to them, they would protest that they had known all along that the statement was a lie and would admire the leaders for their superior tactical cleverness." (Hannah Arendt, The Origins of Totalitarianism)*

23   Harry Patch: War is Organised Murder

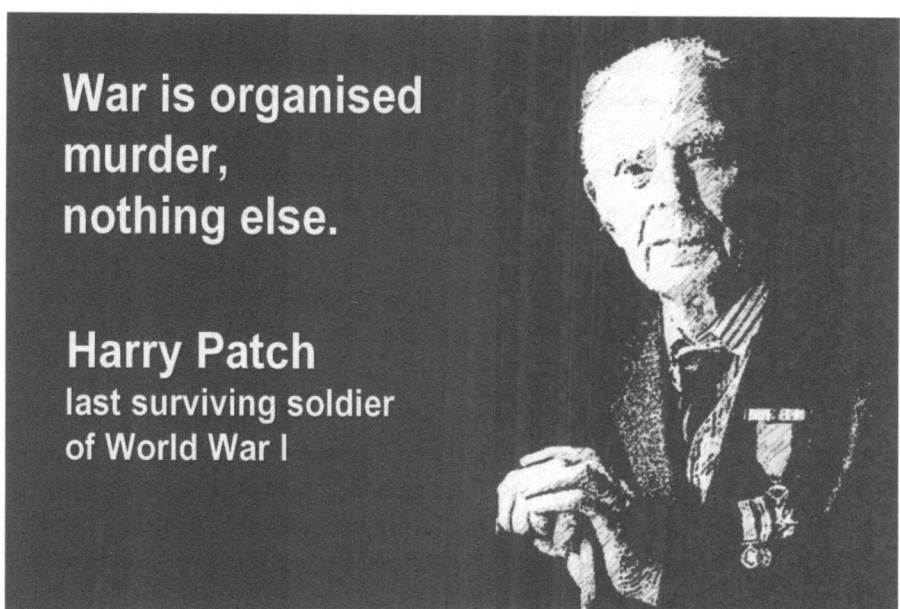

War is organised murder, nothing else.

Harry Patch
last surviving soldier of World War I

Harry Patch, often known as "The Last Tommy,' was a remarkable individual who came to symbolize the enduring human quest for Peace. As one of the last surviving veterans of World War I, he witnessed the horrors of war first-hand. His understanding of Peace was profoundly shaped by the harrowing experiences he endured on the battlefield. This chapter delves into Harry Patch's unique perspective on Peace, drawing from his own words and his role as a living testament to the cost of war.

Harry Patch's perspective on Peace was fundamentally shaped by his service during World War I, which he described as "legalized mass murder." He fought in the trenches and experienced the horrors of the conflict, losing many comrades and witnessing the devastating consequences of warfare. This first-hand experience of war, including the Battle of Passchendaele, contributed to his deep commitment to Peace.

Patch's reflections on the brutality of war led him to become an advocate for pacifism. He believed that the sacrifices made by soldiers like himself should serve as a reminder of the profound importance of avoiding future conflicts.

One of the remarkable aspects of Harry Patch's perspective on Peace was his commitment to forgiveness and reconciliation. Despite the tremendous suffering he endured during the war, he advocated for understanding and healing in the post-war era. He participated in commemorations and met with German veterans, emphasizing the need for reconciliation and acknowledging that both sides had suffered.

Patch's willingness to reconcile with former enemies exemplifies his belief in the transformative power of forgiveness and the importance of healing the wounds of war to achieve lasting Peace.

Harry Patch was a strong advocate for educating future generations about the horrors of war. He believed that by learning about the past, particularly the devastating consequences of armed conflict, young people could be inspired to work for Peace and to prevent the recurrence of such suffering. Patch's involvement in educational initiatives and his willingness to share his experiences with students exemplified his commitment to passing on the lessons of history to ensure a more peaceful future.

In the latter years of his life, Harry Patch became an outspoken critic of war and an advocate for Peace. He often spoke out against the futility and destructiveness of war, using his platform and his own experiences to convey a powerful anti-war message. His advocacy underscored his belief that the human race must do everything in its power to prevent the horrors he witnessed from happening again.

Harry Patch's perspective on Peace, born from his experiences as a soldier in World War I, was deeply rooted in the horrors of armed conflict and the profound suffering it caused. His commitment to pacifism, forgiveness, reconciliation, and education exemplified his belief in the power of understanding and compassion to prevent future wars. As "The Last Tommy," Harry Patch served as a living reminder of the cost of war and an inspirational advocate for a more peaceful world. His legacy continues to influence those who believe in the importance of Peace and the pursuit of a future free from the horrors of war.

24   Hugh Mundell: Rastafarian Advocacy for Social and Spiritual Change

Jah say the time has now come
For all his people to live as one
Jah say the time has now come
For I and I to live as one

Hugh Mundell

Hugh Mundell, born as Hugh Anthony Holmes in 1962, was a talented Jamaican reggae artist whose life was tragically cut short. Despite his relatively brief life, he made significant contributions to the world of reggae music and left an indelible mark on the genre. Mundell's life was characterized by both musical achievements and personal challenges.

Mundell's early life was immersed in the vibrant reggae culture of Jamaica. He was discovered by the legendary producer Augustus Pablo when he was just a teenager. His breakthrough came with the release of the album "Africa Must Be Free by 1983," produced by Pablo and released when Mundell was only 16. The album received critical acclaim and solidified Mundell's reputation as a promising reggae artist.

Mundell's music was known for its conscious and spiritual themes, often rooted in his Rastafarian faith. His lyrics conveyed messages of Peace, unity, and the rejection of violence, which resonated with the cultural and spiritual ethos of reggae. Songs like "Jah Fire" and "Let's All Unite" remain emblematic of his commitment to these themes.

Despite his early success, Mundell faced personal challenges, including issues with drug addiction, which affected his career and personal life. Tragically, his life was cut short in 1983 when he was fatally shot at the age of 21 during a confrontation in Kingston, Jamaica. His untimely death marked a tragic loss to the reggae music world and to those who admired his talent and messages of Peace.

Hugh Mundell's life serves as a reminder of the complex and often turbulent nature of the reggae music scene in Jamaica. While he faced personal challenges, his contributions to the genre were significant, and his music continues to inspire reggae enthusiasts and those who appreciate the genre's messages of Peace, Love, and unity. His legacy endures through his music, which remains a testament to the power of reggae as a means of promoting social and spiritual change.

Hugh Mundell, possessed a deep understanding of Peace, rooted in the cultural and spiritual context of reggae music. His perspective on Peace was shaped by his experiences growing up in Jamaica, the Rastafarian faith, and a commitment to using his music to advocate for social and spiritual change. To appreciate Hugh Mundell's perspective on Peace, it is essential to explore the key elements of his philosophy, his life experiences, and the impact of his work on the promotion of Peace and unity.

Reggae music has long been a vehicle for conveying messages of Peace, Love, and unity, and Hugh Mundell was a notable contributor to this tradition. His lyrics and melodies often carried messages of hope, harmony, and the rejection of violence. Songs like "Jah Fire" and "Let's All Unite" exemplify his commitment to using music as a tool for promoting Peace and spiritual awakening.

Lyrics of his song "Africa must be free", 1983:

No *more war*
No more beating
No more slavery
No more brutality, yeah

Hugh Mundell was a devoted Rastafarian, and the Rastafarian faith, deeply rooted in Jamaican culture, played a central role in shaping his understanding of Peace. Rastafarianism emphasizes a reverence for the divine, a connection to nature, and a rejection of materialism. These principles are closely tied to the pursuit of inner Peace and the belief in a better world through faith and righteousness.

While many reggae artists, including Bob Marley, used their music to address social and political issues, Hugh Mundell's songs often carried messages of Peace and unity in the face of violence and political unrest. In a tumultuous period of Jamaican history marked by social and political tensions, his music provided a sense of hope and a call for reconciliation.

Hugh Mundell's impact on the understanding of Peace, Love, and unity continues to inspire individuals and reggae enthusiasts dedicated to these principles. His work serves as a reminder of the power of music to promote social and spiritual change, even in challenging and turbulent environments.

Never you cheat or back-bite

Put a stop to fuss and fight

Let us live upright

And walk the path that is right

And your name will be written

In the book of life

Watch every step you make

You surely can't afford to make a mistake

Then let Jah in your heart

And throw away your evil thought

Love your brother as yourself

And your name will be written

In the book of life

So do the right and not the wrong

And Jah will give you a helping hand

And walk in the counsel of the righteous

And do the things of the righteous man

And your name will be written

In the book of life

(Lyrics of Mundell's song "Book of Life")

In conclusion, Hugh Mundell's understanding of Peace was deeply rooted in the reggae music tradition, his Rastafarian faith, and his commitment to using music as a means of conveying messages of Peace, Love, and unity. His work reminds us of the enduring potential of music to inspire positive change and promote a more peaceful and harmonious world. Hugh Mundell's legacy stands as a testament to the transformative power of music and spirituality in the pursuit of Peace and unity.

25 Immanuel Kant: The Categorical Imperative

Freedom is the alone unoriginated birthright of man, and belongs to him by force of his humanity.

Immanuel Kant

Immanuel Kant, an influential figure in the Enlightenment era, is renowned for his extensive contributions to philosophy, including his profound insights into the concept of Peace. Kant's ideas on Peace, encapsulated in his essays and works such as "Perpetual Peace" and "Idea for a Universal History with a Cosmopolitan Purpose," continue to influence the fields of political philosophy and international relations. In this essay, we will delve into Kant's understanding of Peace, examining the principles he laid out and their enduring significance.

At the core of Kant's vision of Peace lies his moral philosophy, particularly the notion of moral autonomy. Kant argued that individuals possess the capacity for rational moral judgment and should be guided by the moral law, which he formulated as the "categorical imperative." This principle essentially states that individuals should act according to principles that could be universalized, treating others as ends in themselves rather than means to an end. Kant believed that Peace could be realized through the moral autonomy of individuals and nations alike.

Kant was a proponent of the idea that the establishment of a system of international law was essential for achieving and maintaining Peace among nations. He envisioned a world where nations would be bound by a shared set of laws that regulated their interactions. Kant's "Perpetual Peace" essay introduces the idea of a "Federation of Free States," where nations voluntarily come together to form a confederation based on shared principles of republican government and respect for individual rights. This federation would serve as a means of preventing war and fostering Peace between states.

> *The* universal and lasting establishment of Peace constitutes not merely a part, but the whole final purpose and end of the science of right as viewed within the limits of reason.

Kant's cosmopolitanism was rooted in the idea that individuals, regardless of their nationality, shared a common humanity. He believed that a global federation of states should be established to promote Peace, safeguard human rights, and prevent conflicts. Although Kant's vision predated the formation of the United Nations by over a century, his ideas resonate strongly with the principles underpinning international organizations like the UN.

> *The* notion that the rights of nations contain a right to make war is truly unintelligible, for that would be a right to determine what is legitimate, not in accordance with the universally valid laws restricting the freedom of every individual, but by using one-sided maxims driven home by force.

Kant considered the pursuit of Peace to be a moral duty, both for individuals and nations. He argued that while the ideal of perpetual Peace might seem distant and unattainable, it was a moral imperative to strive towards it. For Kant, the pursuit of Peace was not merely a pragmatic or political objective, but a reflection of the ethical duty to respect the rights and dignity of all individuals.

Kant believed that Peace could only be realized in a world where reason and enlightenment prevailed. He saw the Enlightenment as a force that would lead to greater understanding, tolerance, and the rejection of irrational, divisive beliefs. In this context, education and the promotion of reason were seen as crucial components of achieving lasting Peace

For Peace to reign on Earth, humans must evolve into new beings who have learned to see the whole first.

Immanuel Kant formulated the "categorical imperative" as a fundamental concept in his moral philosophy. The categorical imperative is a universal principle that serves as the foundation for his ethical system. Kant presented several formulations of the categorical imperative, but the most well-known and frequently discussed one is the Formula of Universal Law, which can be expressed as follows:

Act only according to that maxim, whereby you can at the same time will that it should become a universal law.

In simpler terms, the categorical imperative instructs individuals to evaluate their actions by considering whether the principle (or maxim) guiding their action could be consistently applied as a universal law, without leading to logical contradictions or moral inconsistencies. In other words, one should act based on principles that can be universally applied without generating any logical or ethical conflicts.

Kant's categorical imperative is a deontological ethical framework, which means that it emphasizes the moral duty inherent in actions themselves rather than the consequences of those actions. It prioritizes the idea that individuals have an inherent moral duty to act in a way that is justifiable by universalizable principles, regardless of the specific circumstances or outcomes.

Kant believed that the categorical imperative provided a rational and objective basis for ethics, where moral principles could be determined through reason and applied universally, rather than relying on subjective emotions or desires. This concept has had a profound influence on modern moral philosophy and remains a central component of Kant's ethical system.

Immanuel Kant's understanding of Peace is grounded in a profound moral philosophy that places human autonomy and reason at its core. He envisioned a world where individuals and nations would come together under the rule of law, respecting each other's rights and promoting the greater good. Kant's ideas on Peace continue to be influential in contemporary discussions of international relations and the pursuit of a more peaceful world.

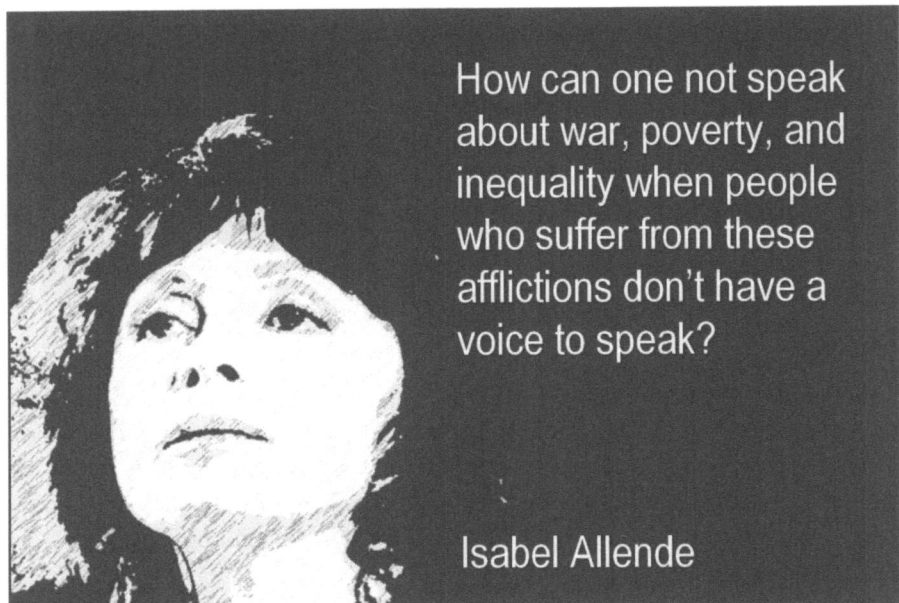

How can one not speak about war, poverty, and inequality when people who suffer from these afflictions don't have a voice to speak?

Isabel Allende

Isabel Allende, the renowned Chilean-American author, is best known for her literary works that blend history, magical realism, and deeply human narratives. Her understanding of Peace is intricately woven into her storytelling, reflecting a unique perspective that is shaped by her own experiences, the history of her native Chile, and her commitment to social justice. To grasp Isabel Allende's perspective on Peace, one must delve into the core elements of her philosophy, her life experiences, and the recurring themes in her literature that speak to the pursuit of Peace and justice.

Isabel Allende's understanding of Peace is rooted in a multifaceted approach that encompasses both personal and collective dimensions. Her novels frequently explore the themes of resilience, Love, and reconciliation in the face of adversity, reflecting a deep belief in the capacity of individuals to find Peace within themselves and with others. Her characters often grapple with personal traumas and social upheaval, and they seek solace and harmony through connection and understanding.

Allende's commitment to social justice and human rights is a defining aspect of her understanding of Peace. Born in Chile in 1942, she witnessed the tumultuous events of the 20th century in her homeland, including the 1973 coup that overthrew the democratically elected government of Salvador Allende, her uncle. Her family's exile following the coup and her personal connection to the political struggle deeply influenced her perspective on Peace. She understood that true Peace could only be achieved through justice and the protection of human rights. In her literature, Allende frequently addresses political and social issues, particularly in the context of Latin American history and contemporary events. Her novels, such as "The House of the Spirits" and "Of Love and Shadows," explore the impact of dictatorship, human rights abuses, and social inequality. Through her characters and narratives, she highlights the importance of confronting social injustices and working toward a more equitable and peaceful society.

The theme of reconciliation is another crucial element of Isabel Allende's understanding of Peace. Her characters often grapple with painful pasts and seek reconciliation with themselves and with others. Through their journeys, she underscores the power of forgiveness and the healing potential of human relationships. This theme is not limited to her fiction; in her memoir "Paula," she explores her own process of healing and reconciliation following personal tragedy.

Allende's impact on the understanding of Peace goes beyond her literary works. She has been a vocal advocate for social justice, women's rights, and the plight of refugees and immigrants. Her commitment to addressing issues such as gender equality and the rights of marginalized communities demonstrates her belief in the importance of working for Peace and justice in the real world.

In conclusion, Isabel Allende's understanding of Peace is multifaceted, encompassing personal, societal, and global dimensions. Her literature reflects a deep belief in the capacity of individuals to find Peace and reconciliation, even in the face of great adversity. Moreover, her commitment to social justice and human rights underscores her understanding that true Peace can only be achieved through justice and equity. Isabel Allende's impact on literature and her advocacy for a more just and peaceful world make her a significant voice in the ongoing quest for Peace and harmony.

27.   Jeannette Rankin: The Unwavering Voice for Peace

You can no more win a war
than you can win an earthquake.

Jeannette Rankin

Jeannette Rankin, a Republican from Montana, holds a unique place in American history as the first woman elected to the U.S. Congress in 1916. A lifelong pacifist and advocate for women's rights, Rankin became famous – and controversial – for her unwavering stance against war. She cast her votes against U.S. involvement in both World War I and World War II, the latter making her the only member of Congress to oppose the war declaration against Japan following the dubious attack on Pearl Harbor.

There *can be no compromise with war; it cannot be reformed or controlled; it cannot be disciplined into decency or codified into common sense, for war is the slaughter of human beings, temporarily regarded as enemies, on as large a scale as possible.*

Rankin's pacifism was deeply rooted in her beliefs about justice and the value of human Life. During her first term in Congress, she was one of 50 members to vote against entering World War I, a position that sparked public outrage but underscored her steadfast conviction.

In 1941, Rankin returned to Congress, just in time for one of the most pivotal votes in U.S. history. After the bombing of Pearl Harbor, which Roosevelt provoked and let happen, Congress overwhelmingly supported a declaration of war against Japan. Rankin, however, stood alone in opposition. "As a woman, I can't go to war, and I refuse to send anyone else," she declared. Her solitary "no" vote made her a symbol of pacifism but also a target of public scorn.

Rankin's vote against World War II was met with widespread outrage. She was booed and jeered in Congress, and angry mobs gathered outside her office. She had to be escorted by police for her safety. Many newspapers and commentators accused her of cowardice and treason. Her political career effectively ended after the vote, and she chose not to seek re-election.

Despite the backlash, Rankin never wavered in her principles. She spent the rest of her Life advocating for Peace and social justice, travelling extensively and participating in anti-war protests, including opposition to the Vietnam War in the 1960s. In 1968, at the age of 87, she led the "Jeannette Rankin Brigade" of 5'000 women in a march on Washington to protest U.S. involvement in Vietnam.

Jeannette Rankin's courage in standing by her beliefs, even in the face of overwhelming opposition, has made her a symbol of integrity and conviction. While she faced immense criticism during her lifetime, her legacy has grown in stature over the years. Today, she is celebrated as a trailblazer for women in politics and a champion of Peace.

What one decides to do in crisis depends on one's philosophy of life, and that philosophy cannot be changed by an incident.

Rankin's Life serves as a reminder of the power of principle, even when it comes at great personal cost. Her unwavering commitment to non-violence continues to inspire those who strive for a more peaceful world.

Blessed I dare to call those, who in this world have the courage to remain peaceful.

Jesus

Jesus of Nazareth, a central figure in Christianity and a prophet in Islam, is widely recognized for his teachings on Love, compassion, and Peace. His understanding of Peace, deeply rooted in his spiritual and ethical principles, has left a lasting legacy that transcends religious boundaries. To appreciate Jesus's perspective on Peace, it is crucial to delve into the core elements of his teachings, his life experiences, and the enduring impact of his message.

At the heart of Jesus's understanding of Peace is the concept of inner Peace. He emphasized the importance of inner transformation, teaching that true Peace begins within the individual. One of the most well-known passages in the New Testament is the Sermon on the Mount, where Jesus delivers the Beatitudes. Among these, "Blessed are the Peacemakers, for they shall be called the children of God," underscores the significance of those who actively work to create Peace, both within themselves and in their communities.

Jesus advocated for Love and forgiveness as fundamental principles for achieving Peace. He encouraged his followers to Love their enemies and to turn the other cheek in the face of aggression. This message challenged the prevailing cultural norms and reflected Jesus's belief in the power of Love to overcome conflict and hostility.

Jesus's understanding of Peace extended beyond personal relationships to a vision of societal and global harmony. He emphasized social justice, calling for the fair treatment of the marginalized, the oppressed, and the poor. He challenged economic inequalities and the exploitation of the vulnerable. His cleansing of the temple in Jerusalem, where he overturned the tables of moneychangers, illustrated his commitment to justice and opposition to practices that harmed the disadvantaged.

A central component of Jesus's vision of Peace was reconciliation and the resolution of conflicts. He provided guidance on how to address grievances within the community, emphasizing the importance of reconciliation and forgiveness as essential steps toward Peace. His teachings laid the foundation for conflict resolution and restorative justice principles.

The crucifixion of Jesus is a powerful testament to his commitment to Peace. When faced with suffering and death, he maintained a message of forgiveness and compassion. His words on the cross, "Father, forgive them, for they do not know what they are doing," exemplified his unwavering commitment to non-violence and forgiveness even in the face of extreme adversity.

The enduring impact of Jesus's understanding of Peace is profound. His teachings have influenced the development of Christian theology, ethics, and practices. Throughout history, numerous individuals and movements have been inspired by his message of Love, forgiveness, and non-violence, and they have worked toward Peace and social justice in his name.

In conclusion, Jesus's understanding of Peace was multifaceted, encompassing inner transformation, Love, forgiveness, social justice, and reconciliation. His message continues to inspire individuals and communities to strive for a more peaceful and just world. His enduring legacy as a Peacemaker and spiritual guide reminds us of the profound potential of Love and compassion in resolving conflicts and fostering harmony in our lives and societies.

29   Jim Wallis: Believe in Righteousness

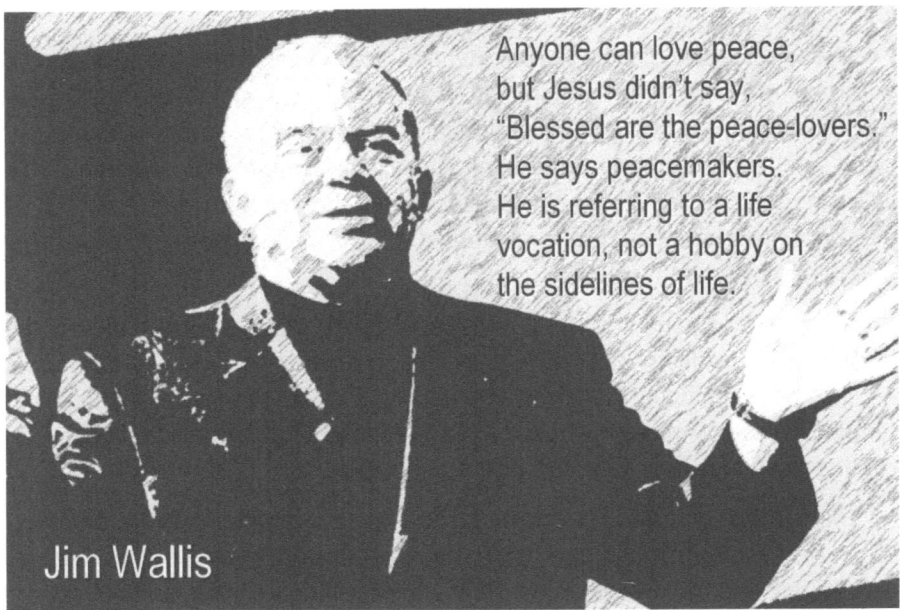

Anyone can love peace, but Jesus didn't say, "Blessed are the peace-lovers." He says peacemakers. He is referring to a life vocation, not a hobby on the sidelines of life.

Jim Wallis

Jm Wallis, an American Christian writer, theologian, and social activist, has long been a prominent voice in discussions about faith, justice, and Peace. His understanding of Peace is deeply rooted in his Christian faith and his commitment to social justice. Wallis's perspective on Peace reflects a holistic approach that considers the personal, social, and global dimensions of harmony and tranquillity. To grasp Jim Wallis's perspective on Peace, it is essential to explore the key elements of his philosophy, his life experiences, and his contributions to the pursuit of a more peaceful world.

At the heart of Jim Wallis's understanding of Peace is the recognition that Peace is more than just the absence of war or conflict. He emphasizes the importance of "shalom," a Hebrew word often translated as "Peace," which signifies wholeness, well-being, and the right relationships between individuals and communities. For Wallis, Peace is inseparable from justice and social righteousness. His faith informs his belief that true Peace can only be achieved when individuals and societies actively work to address systemic injustices and create equitable and inclusive communities.

Social justice is a central component of Wallis's understanding of Peace. He argues that Peace is not just a matter of personal tranquillity but also the result of a just and equitable society. He advocates for policies and practices that prioritize the needs of the most vulnerable and marginalized members of society. His commitment to social justice encompasses issues such as poverty, racial inequality, and environmental stewardship. Wallis sees Peace as the natural outcome of a society that embraces fairness and compassion.

Jim Wallis's life experiences have profoundly shaped his perspective on Peace. He grew up in a racially divided America and witnessed the civil rights movement's struggle for justice and equality. These experiences instilled in him a deep sense of the moral imperative of social activism. As a young man, he became involved in the anti-Vietnam War movement, further solidifying his commitment to issues of Peace and justice.

Wallis's Christian faith has been a driving force in his understanding of Peace. He is the founder of Sojourners, a Christian organization that emphasizes faith-based social justice. His approach to Peace is deeply influenced by Christian teachings on Love, compassion, and the call to care for the least among us. He believes that the Church has a vital role to play in addressing societal injustices and promoting Peace, and he has been a leading advocate for the integration of faith and activism.

Jim Wallis's impact on the understanding of Peace extends beyond his writings and advocacy. He has been a prominent voice in American public discourse, engaging with policymakers, faith leaders, and activists on critical issues related to Peace and social justice. His work encourages individuals and communities to take action, address systemic problems, and build a more just and peaceful society.

In conclusion, Jim Wallis's understanding of Peace is grounded in his Christian faith and his unwavering commitment to social justice. He sees Peace as the natural outcome of a just and equitable society that addresses the needs of the marginalized and vulnerable. His life experiences and advocacy have left an enduring mark on the pursuit of Peace and social justice, reminding us of the profound connection between faith, compassion, and the quest for a more peaceful and just world.

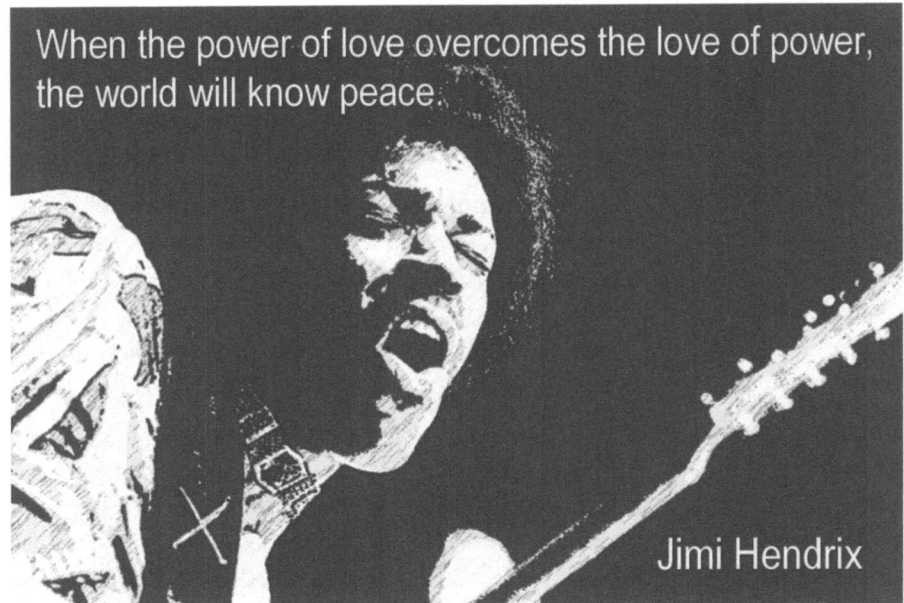

When the power of love overcomes the love of power, the world will know peace.

Jimi Hendrix

James Marshall "Jimi" Hendrix, the legendary American guitarist and songwriter, is primarily celebrated for his groundbreaking contributions to rock music and his iconic performances at Woodstock and other major music festivals. While Hendrix may not be a philosopher or a Peace activist in the traditional sense, his understanding of Peace, deeply rooted in the counterculture of the 1960s, is worth exploring. To appreciate Jimi Hendrix's perspective on Peace, one must delve into the core elements of his philosophy, his life experiences, and the cultural context that informed his music and message.

Hendrix emerged as a cultural icon during the 1960s, a decade marked by significant social and political upheaval, particularly in the United States. The era was characterized by the civil rights movement, the anti-Vietnam War protests, and the counterculture movement, which sought to challenge traditional norms and promote Peace, Love, and a rejection of militarism. It was in this context that Hendrix's music and message found resonance.

Jimi Hendrix's music was a fusion of rock, blues, and psychedelic elements, but his lyrics often carried profound messages related to Peace, Love, and unity. His iconic song "Purple Haze" is often interpreted as a call for transcendence and the exploration of consciousness. The lyrics invite listeners to "excuse me while I kiss the sky," which can be seen as a metaphor for rising above conflict and seeking higher states of consciousness.

Hendrix's song "The Wind Cries Mary" is often seen as a more direct commentary on the quest for Peace. The melancholic lyrics convey a sense of longing and reconciliation. The message is that Love and understanding can help repair damaged relationships and, by extension, contribute to a more peaceful world.

Hendrix's experiences as a black musician in the United States during the civil rights era deeply influenced his perspective. He faced racial discrimination and witnessed the struggle for civil rights, which was a significant part of the broader push for Peace and equality in the 1960s.

His performances at Woodstock in 1969 and other music festivals of the era were not only musical milestones but also cultural moments that represented the counterculture's ethos of Peace, Love, and unity. The iconic image of Hendrix playing his guitar at Woodstock in a sea of people has become synonymous with the Peace and Love movement of the 1960s.

Jimi Hendrix's music and message continue to inspire individuals and movements that advocate for Peace and social change. While he may not have been a traditional Peace activist, his artistic expression and countercultural influence played a role in fostering a sense of unity and harmony during a time of great societal change and upheaval.

In conclusion, Jimi Hendrix's understanding of Peace was a product of his time, rooted in the countercultural movement of the 1960s. While he may be best known for his groundbreaking guitar skills and iconic performances, his music and message carried profound themes related to Peace, Love, and unity. Hendrix's legacy reminds us of the power of music and cultural expression to convey messages of Peace and to inspire social change, even in the midst of societal turbulence.

John Lennon, the iconic musician, songwriter, and Peace activist, had a profound and influential understanding of Peace that transcended both his music and his activism. His perspective on Peace was deeply rooted in his personal experiences, the tumultuous times in which he lived, and his unwavering commitment to promoting Love, unity, and non-violence. To appreciate John Lennon's perspective on Peace, it is essential to explore the key elements of his philosophy, his role as an advocate for Peace, and the enduring impact of his work on the pursuit of a more peaceful and just world.

John Lennon recognized the unifying power of music as a means to convey messages of Peace, Love, and understanding. He often used his music to advocate for these ideals. Iconic songs like "Imagine" and "Give Peace a Chance" continue to inspire people with their messages of hope and unity.

Lennon was a vocal advocate against the Vietnam War and other conflicts of his time. He and his wife, Yoko Ono, conducted several high-profile Peace protests, including their famous "Bed-Ins for Peace." These events were designed to raise awareness and promote non-violent resistance to war.

Lennon's understanding of Peace was also a result of his personal journey. He went through a period of self-discovery and transformation, which led him to embrace Peace, Love, and spirituality. His own evolution played a significant role in shaping his advocacy for a more peaceful world.

If everyone demanded peace instead of another television set, then there'd be peace.

John Lennon

In addition to his anti-war efforts, John Lennon was an advocate for social justice and civil rights. He believed that Peace extended beyond the absence of war and included the elimination of discrimination, poverty, and inequality.

Perhaps the most iconic expression of Lennon's understanding of Peace is the song "Imagine." The lyrics envision a world without borders, religion, or possessions, where people live in harmony. This song continues to be a powerful anthem for Peace and unity.

John Lennon's impact on the understanding of Peace is profound and enduring. His commitment to Love, non-violence, and unity continues to inspire generations of individuals who seek a more peaceful and just world. His work, both as a musician and an activist, demonstrates the potential of art and personal conviction to drive social change.

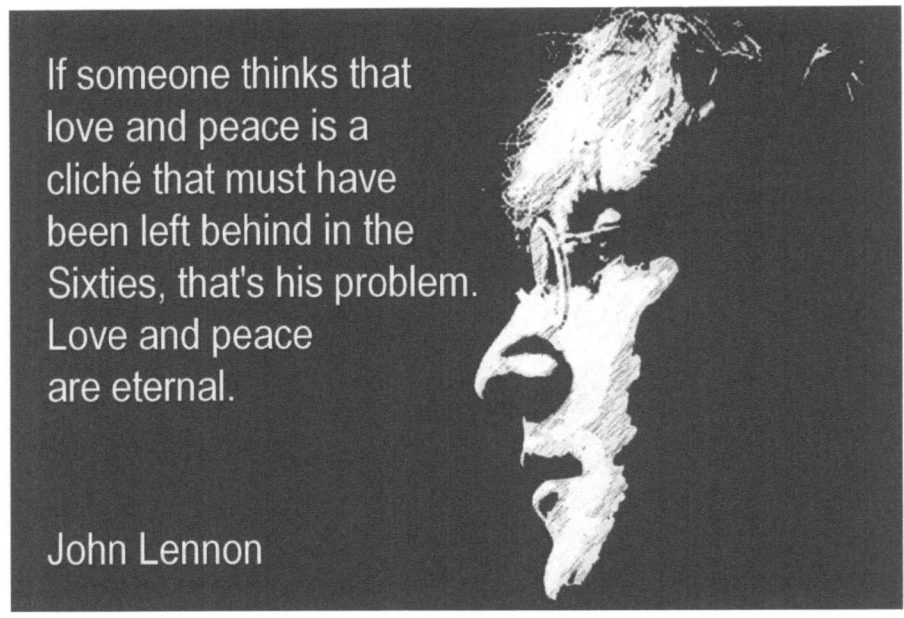

If someone thinks that love and peace is a cliché that must have been left behind in the Sixties, that's his problem. Love and peace are eternal.

John Lennon

In conclusion, John Lennon's understanding of Peace was characterized by a belief in the power of music, a commitment to anti-war activism, personal transformation, advocacy for social justice, and the iconic vision of a world without divisions. His life and work serve as a reminder of the profound impact that a single individual can have in advocating for Peace and a world where Love and understanding prevail over conflict and division. John Lennon's legacy is an enduring testament to the potential for art and activism to inspire positive change in the pursuit of Peace.

Imagine there's no countries — It isn't hard to do

Nothing to kill or die for — And no religion, too

Imagine all the people — Livin' life in Peace

You may say I'm a dreamer — But I'm not the only one

I hope someday you'll join us — And the world will be as one

32　Joan Baez: The Intersection of Music and Activism

That's all nonviolence is — organized love.

Joan Baez

Joan Baez, the iconic American folk singer, songwriter, and activist, has been a prominent voice in the realms of music and social justice for more than six decades. Her understanding of Peace is deeply intertwined with her commitment to civil rights, non-violence, and humanitarianism. Baez's perspective on Peace is a reflection of her personal journey, her contributions to social and political movements, and her belief in the power of music to inspire positive change.

Joan Baez's understanding of Peace is inherently linked to her unwavering commitment to non-violence. Throughout her career, she has been a vocal advocate for pacifism and the use of peaceful means to address conflicts and promote social change. Her involvement in the civil rights movement and the anti-Vietnam War movement of the 1960s was a testament to her dedication to Peace and justice.

Joan Baez firmly believes in the power of music to convey messages of Peace and inspire social change. Her folk songs, particularly those with protest and anti-war themes, have served as anthems for movements striving for Peace and equality. Her rendition of songs like "We Shall Overcome" during the civil rights era and her adaptation of Bob Dylan's "Blowin' in the Wind" became rallying cries for Peace and justice.

Baez's live performances, often accompanied by her ethereal voice and acoustic guitar, have created a sense of collective purpose and unity among her audiences. Her concerts have been a gathering point for activists and advocates of Peace, providing a space for like-minded individuals to come together and amplify their voices for change.

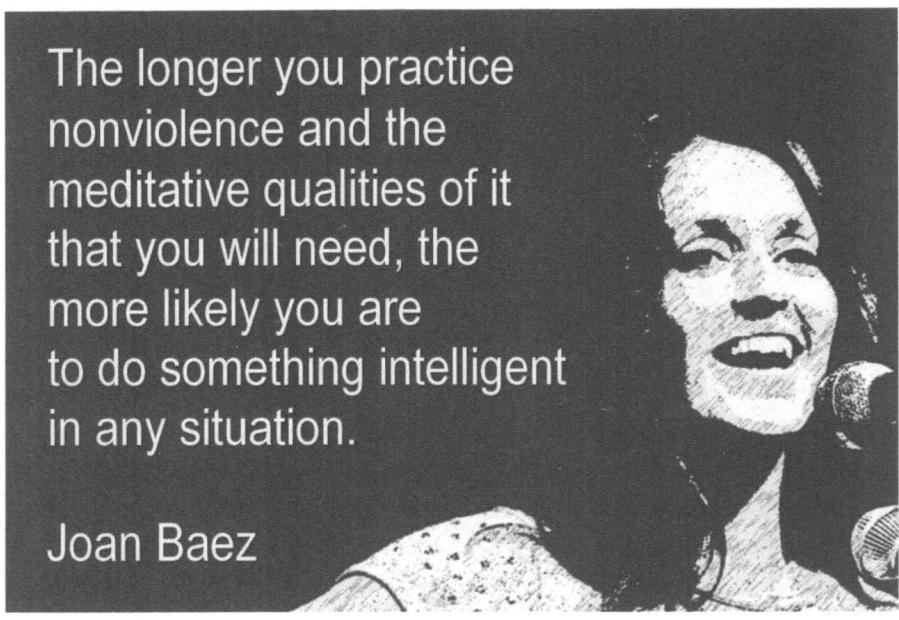

The longer you practice nonviolence and the meditative qualities of it that you will need, the more likely you are to do something intelligent in any situation.

Joan Baez

Joan Baez's activism extends far beyond her music. She has been actively engaged in numerous social and political causes, using her platform to address issues related to civil rights, anti-war efforts, human rights, and environmental protection. Baez's participation in non-violent protests, civil disobedience, and human rights campaigns underscores her belief in the importance of taking direct action to promote Peace and justice.

Joan Baez's understanding of Peace is also a reflection of her personal commitment to living a life in accordance with her principles. She has consistently aligned her actions with her advocacy for Peace, often at great personal risk. Her activism has led to multiple arrests, but she has remained steadfast in her commitment to non-violence and the pursuit of a more just and peaceful world.

Joan Baez's influence extends to subsequent generations of musicians and activists who share her passion for Peace and justice. Her legacy serves as a reminder of the enduring power of music and the role of artists in advancing social change and promoting Peace. She has been recognized for her contributions with numerous awards and honours, including the Kennedy Center Honours and the Rock and Roll Hall of Fame induction.

In conclusion, Joan Baez's understanding of Peace is deeply rooted in her lifelong commitment to non-violence, activism, and the power of music to inspire positive change. Her journey as a folk singer, songwriter, and humanitarian has left an indelible mark on the world, demonstrating that Peace and justice can be advanced through the transformative power of art and activism. Joan Baez's life and work stand as a testament to the enduring relevance of Peace as a guiding principle in the face of societal challenges and conflicts.

33 John Greenleaf Whittier: Quaker's Abolitionism and Poetry

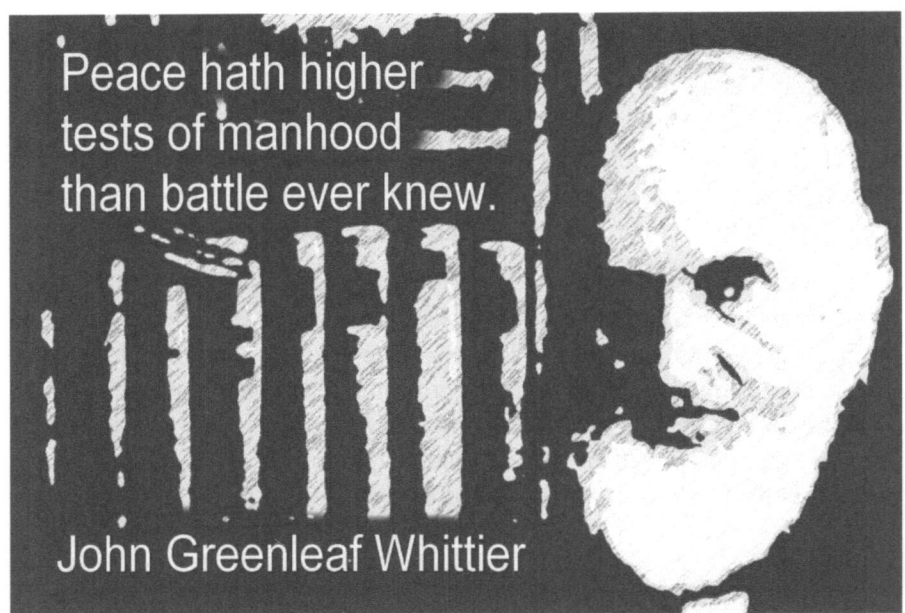

Peace hath higher tests of manhood than battle ever knew.

John Greenleaf Whittier

John Greenleaf Whittier, the American Quaker poet and advocate for social reform, held a profound and enduring understanding of Peace. His perspective on Peace was deeply rooted in his Quaker faith, his passionate advocacy for abolitionism and social justice, and his ability to express his beliefs through the power of poetry. To appreciate John Greenleaf Whittier's perspective on Peace, it is essential to explore the key elements of his philosophy, his life experiences, and the enduring impact of his work on the pursuit of Peace and social reform.

Whittier's Quaker faith played a pivotal role in shaping his understanding of Peace. Quakers, known for their commitment to non-violence, equality, and simplicity, deeply influenced Whittier's beliefs. The Quaker tradition emphasizes the "Inner Light" within every individual, which guides moral and ethical decisions. This principle underpinned Whittier's commitment to Peace as a core value.

John Greenleaf Whittier was a passionate abolitionist, dedicating his life to the fight against slavery. His poem "The Slave Ships" poignantly captures the horrors of the transatlantic slave trade and calls for an end to the institution. He worked tirelessly to advance the cause of emancipation and racial equality, believing that the abolition of slavery was a fundamental step toward achieving Peace and justice.

Whittier's commitment to social justice extended to other causes as well. He advocated for women's rights, Native American rights, and temperance. His broad-ranging advocacy exemplified his belief that Peace was intrinsically connected to a just and equitable society.

John Greenleaf Whittier used his talent as a poet to articulate his vision of Peace and justice. His poems, often characterized by their moral clarity and evocative language, served as a powerful means of conveying his beliefs to a broad audience. "Dear Lord and Father of Mankind," for instance, is a poem that calls for a return to simplicity, humility, and a rejection of the material world. The poem expresses a longing for inner Peace and a closer connection to the Divine.

Whittier's poem "The Peace of Europe" captures his desire for a lasting global Peace. It reflects his concern for the widespread conflicts and violence in the world and calls for nations to seek reconciliation, understanding, and peaceful solutions to disputes.

John Greenleaf Whittier's influence on the understanding of Peace and social justice is enduring. His poetry and advocacy helped shape public opinion and contributed to the anti-slavery movement's success. His commitment to the principles of non-violence, equality, and humanitarianism continues to inspire individuals and movements dedicated to Peace and social reform.

In conclusion, John Greenleaf Whittier's understanding of Peace was rooted in his Quaker faith, his dedication to abolitionism and social justice, and his belief in the power of poetry to convey moral and ethical principles. His work stands as a testament to the enduring relevance of Peace as a guiding value in the quest for justice and equality. Whittier's legacy reminds us of the enduring power of words and actions in advancing the cause of Peace and social reform.

34   Ken Jebsen: Accountability and Transparency against Propaganda

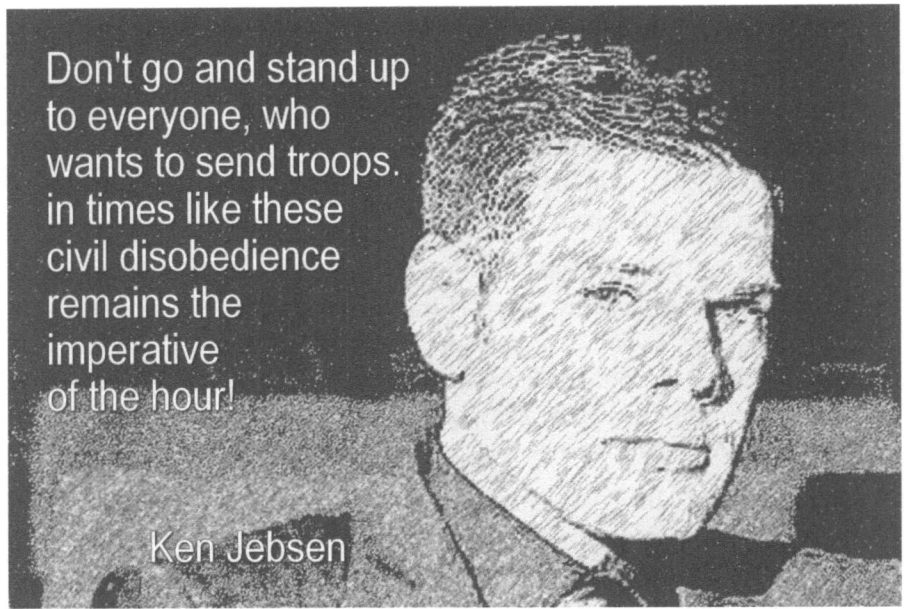

Don't go and stand up to everyone, who wants to send troops. in times like these civil disobedience remains the imperative of the hour!

Ken Jebsen

Ken Jebsen is a German journalist, political activist, and public figure who has made a name for himself through his YouTube channel and podcast, KenFM. While his views and understanding of Peace may vary from individual to individual, as of my last knowledge update in September 2021, Jebsen has expressed opinions and beliefs that can be used to explore his understanding of Peace. It's important to note that Ken Jebsen's perspectives are controversial and may not represent the mainstream or widely accepted views on Peace.

Ken Jebsen's understanding of Peace is rooted in his broader views on politics, media, and the global order. He is known for his criticism of the mainstream media and the political establishment, often accusing them of perpetuating conflicts, wars, and divisive narratives. In this context, Jebsen's understanding of Peace can be framed as a call for critical thinking, political transparency, and an end to what he sees as destructive narratives.

One of the central pillars of Jebsen's understanding of Peace is his vocal opposition to war and imperialism. He has been an outspoken critic of Western military interventions in the Middle East and other regions, arguing that such actions lead to instability, suffering, and a cycle of violence. Jebsen believes that Peace can only be achieved when nations and powerful entities refrain from aggressive and militaristic actions.

Ken Jebsen is known for his critique of mainstream media, which he often accuses of spreading propaganda and misinformation. From his perspective, a peaceful world can only emerge when the media provides accurate, unbiased information to the public, enabling people to make informed decisions and hold governments accountable. His emphasis on media transparency and responsible journalism aligns with his vision of achieving Peace through a better-informed citizenry.

Jebsen's vision of Peace also revolves around the idea of political accountability and transparency. He believes that Peace can be achieved when governments and institutions are held responsible for their actions and when political decision-making processes are open and inclusive. In his view, an engaged and informed citizenry can play a crucial role in fostering a more peaceful society.

Jebsen often delves into discussions about power structures and their impact on global conflicts. He argues that Peace can only be attained when individuals and societies critically analyse and challenge the power dynamics that underlie many international disputes. This includes questioning the roles of governments, corporations, and influential interest groups in shaping global events.

Ken Jebsen's understanding of Peace is deeply intertwined with his views on war, media, political accountability, and power structures. While his perspectives may be considered controversial or even radical by some, they reflect a call for greater transparency, accountability, and critical thinking in the pursuit of Peace. Ultimately, Jebsen's vision of Peace underscores the importance of addressing the root causes of conflict and working toward a more informed, just, and equitable global order. However, it is crucial to note that his views represent one perspective among many, and discussions about Peace can vary significantly based on individual beliefs and contexts.

35 Kofi Annan: Global Cooperation and Multilateralism

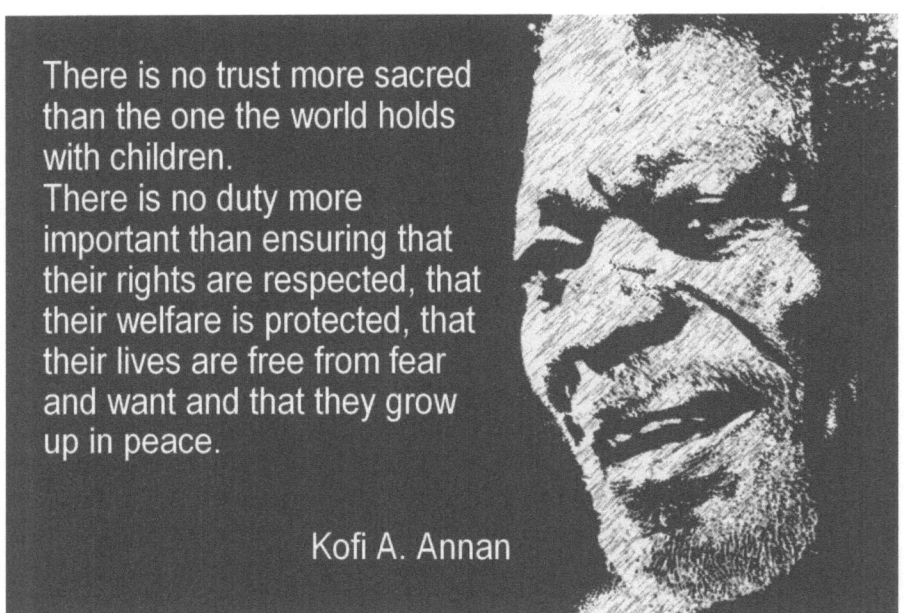

There is no trust more sacred than the one the world holds with children.
There is no duty more important than ensuring that their rights are respected, that their welfare is protected, that their lives are free from fear and want and that they grow up in peace.

Kofi A. Annan

Kofi Annan, the Ghanaian diplomat and former Secretary-General of the United Nations, had a profound and multifaceted understanding of Peace. Throughout his distinguished career, Annan tirelessly worked to promote global Peace, security, and development. His perspective on Peace was deeply rooted in the principles of diplomacy, cooperation, human rights, and the idea that Peace is not merely the absence of war but the presence of justice, equity, and well-being. To appreciate Kofi Annan's perspective on Peace, it is essential to explore the key elements of his philosophy, his life experiences, and the enduring impact of his work on the pursuit of Peace and international relations.

Kofi Annan's understanding of Peace was profoundly shaped by his diplomatic career. He believed that dialogue, negotiation, and diplomacy were essential tools for resolving conflicts and preventing violence. As the head of the United Nations, he facilitated Peace talks and negotiations in various regions of the world, from Kosovo to East Timor. His commitment to finding peaceful solutions to complex conflicts reflected his belief in the power of dialogue to prevent and resolve disputes.

Annan was a staunch advocate for multilateralism, emphasizing the importance of global cooperation and the United Nations as a forum for addressing international issues. He recognized that the challenges facing the world, including poverty, disease, and climate change, could not be effectively tackled by individual nations in isolation. His understanding of Peace encompassed the idea that a collaborative, united world was more likely to achieve lasting Peace and prosperity.

Kofi Annan's perspective on Peace extended to his deep commitment to human rights and justice. He believed that Peace could only be achieved when fundamental human rights were respected and upheld. Annan was a strong proponent of the Responsibility to Protect (R2P) doctrine, which called on the international community to intervene when governments failed to protect their own citizens from mass atrocities. His understanding of Peace thus included the notion that Peace required a commitment to justice and the protection of vulnerable populations.

Annan also recognized that Peace was closely intertwined with development and economic prosperity. He was a leading voice for the Millennium Development Goals (MDGs), which sought to reduce poverty and improve the well-being of people around the world. He understood that Peace could not be achieved in societies marked by extreme poverty, inequality, and social injustice.

One of Annan's key contributions to Peace was his focus on conflict prevention and early warning mechanisms. He believed that anticipating and addressing potential conflicts before they escalated was essential in maintaining Peace. His efforts in this regard led to the establishment of the UN Department of Political Affairs and the development of early warning systems to identify potential crises.

Kofi Annan's impact on the understanding of Peace and international relations is profound. His leadership and dedication to global Peace earned him the Nobel Peace Prize in 2001. Annan's legacy continues to inspire diplomats, policymakers, and individuals around the world to work towards a more peaceful, just, and equitable world.

In conclusion, Kofi Annan's understanding of Peace was characterized by a commitment to diplomacy, multilateralism, human rights, development, and conflict prevention. His work at the United Nations and his advocacy for Peace, justice, and cooperation serve as a testament to the enduring potential of international collaboration in advancing the cause of Peace and global well-being. Kofi Annan's legacy stands as a reminder of the vital role of leaders and institutions in shaping a more peaceful and harmonious world.

36   Kurt Tucholsky: Soldiers are Murderers

In Germany,
the person who points out
the dirt is considered much
more dangerous than the
person who makes the dirt.

Kurt Tucholsky

Kurt Tucholsky, a prominent German writer and intellectual, emerged as a fervent pacifist during a time marked by political turmoil and the ominous clouds of war. This essay seeks to delve into the nuances of Tucholsky's pacifism, exploring the philosophical underpinnings, the contextual influences, and the enduring relevance of his commitment to non-violence. The quote "soldiers are murderers" comes from an article that Tucholsky published in 1931.

Tucholsky's concept of Peace emerges from a deep-seated critique of war and militarism. In works such as "*Der Mensch*" ("Man') and "*Soldaten sind Mörder*" ("Soldiers Are Murderers"), he vehemently condemned the destructive nature of armed conflict. Tucholsky believed that war not only led to physical devastation but also eroded the moral fabric of society.

As a satirist, Tucholsky employed humour as a potent weapon against the glorification of war. His satirical pieces ridiculed the absurdity of militaristic propaganda, unmasking the contradictions inherent in jingoistic ideologies. Tucholsky believed that satire had the power to awaken critical thinking and expose the dangers of unchecked militarism. Through humour and wit, he exposed the absurdity of nationalist fervour and the jingoistic ideologies that propelled nations into conflict. Tucholsky's satirical approach aimed to provoke thought and challenge the prevailing attitudes that glorified war.

> *At which a diplomat from France replies: "The war? I can't find it too terrible! The death of one man: that is a catastrophe. One hundred thousand deaths: that is a statistic!"*

Tucholsky's pacifism was deeply rooted in intellectual discourse. His engagement with the works of thinkers such as Bertha von Suttner, Leo Tolstoy, and Erich Maria Remarque shaped his understanding of the futility of war and the moral imperative of pursuing peaceful alternatives. Tucholsky's essays, such as "*Militarismus*" ("Militarism") and "*Friedensmoral*" ("Peace Ethics"), reflect his intellectual grappling with the ethical dimensions of conflict.

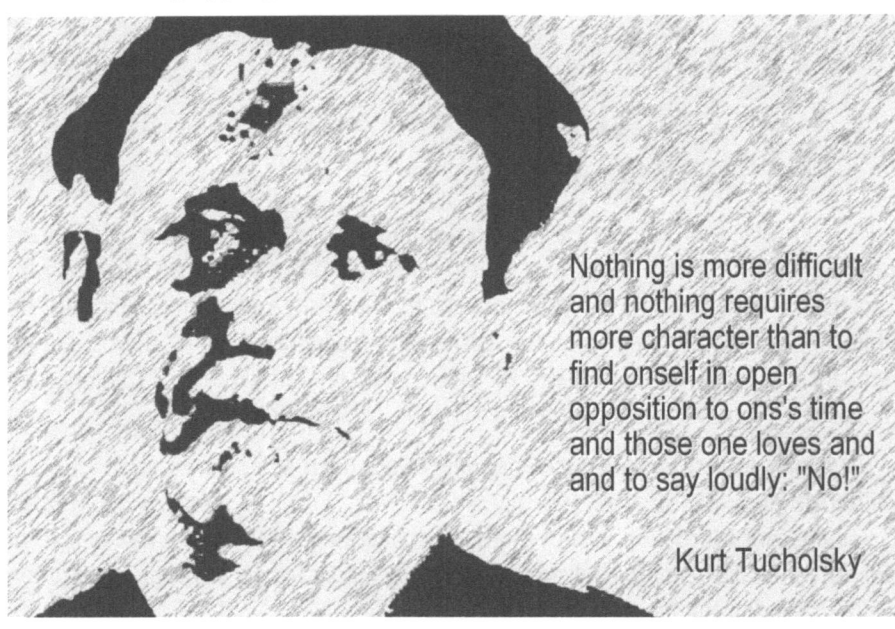

Nothing is more difficult and nothing requires more character than to find onself in open opposition to ons's time and those one loves and and to say loudly: "No!"

Kurt Tucholsky

Tucholsky's vision of Peace was inherently internationalist. He advocated for a world where nations transcended narrow interests and collaborated for the common good. In his essay "*Politik ist keine exakte Wissenschaft*" ("Politics is not an Exact Science"), Tucholsky expressed the need for a humanistic approach to global affairs, emphasizing the shared humanity that binds people across borders. Central to Tucholsky's pacifist vision was the idea of international cooperation and collective security. He envisioned a world where nations would prioritize diplomacy, dialogue, and cooperation over aggression. Tucholsky's advocacy for disarmament and a unified global effort to prevent war reflected a pragmatic understanding of the interconnectedness of nations.

Tucholsky believed in the power of culture and intellect to foster lasting Peace. He recognized the role of education and the arts in shaping a society that valued reason and compassion over aggression. Tucholsky's writings, spanning essays, poems, and political commentary, aimed to stimulate intellectual engagement and cultivate a culture that rejected the allure of militarism.

Tucholsky's vision of Peace was not utopian; it was grounded in a pragmatic understanding of the consequences of war. Through his writings, he sought to warn society about the inevitable horrors and human costs associated with armed conflict. Tucholsky's insights were prescient, foreshadowing the devastation that would unfold during the subsequent decades of the 20th century.

Tucholsky's pacifist writings, though rooted in the specific historical context of his time, carry a timeless message. In an era grappling with contemporary conflicts, his insights into the corrosive nature of militarism and the imperative of Peace remain relevant. Tucholsky's legacy endures as a reminder of the intellectual and moral responsibility to resist the allure of war and champion the cause of Peace. Tucholsky's pacifism evolved against the backdrop of the interwar period in Germany, a time marred by the aftermath of World War I and the rise of militaristic ideologies. Having witnessed the devastating consequences of war, Tucholsky became a vocal critic of militarism, nationalism, and the political forces that, in his view, propelled nations towards armed conflict.

Kurt Tucholsky's concept of Peace was a multifaceted and dynamic vision that drew from his experiences in a turbulent era. Through his sharp critiques, satirical prowess, and advocacy for internationalism, humanism, and cultural contributions, Tucholsky left an indelible mark on the discourse surrounding Peace. In a world still grappling with the challenges of conflict and division, Tucholsky's insights remain relevant, urging us to reflect on the enduring importance of Peace and the collective responsibility to strive for a more harmonious and just world.

37   Leo Tolstoy: Non-Violence and Rejection of State Violence

The meaning of life is the multiplication of love on earth.

Leo Tolstoi

Leo Tolstoy, the renowned Russian writer, philosopher, and social reformer, possessed a profound and influential understanding of Peace. His perspective on Peace was deeply rooted in his personal journey, spiritual awakening, and his commitment to advocating for non-violence, Love, and social justice. To appreciate Tolstoy's perspective on Peace, it is essential to explore the key elements of his philosophy, his life experiences, and the enduring impact of his work on the pursuit of a more peaceful and just world.

Leo Tolstoy's understanding of Peace was profoundly shaped by his own struggles and spiritual journey. Despite his literary success and affluence, he grappled with profound existential questions and a sense of emptiness. His quest for meaning and inner Peace ultimately led him to a deep spiritual awakening.

Tolstoy underwent a transformation that led him to embrace the teachings of Jesus Christ, particularly the principles of non-violence, Love for one's fellow human beings, and the rejection of materialism. He began to live a life of simplicity, humility, and devotion to ethical and moral principles. These spiritual revelations had a profound impact on his understanding of Peace.

Tolstoy's philosophy of Peace was fundamentally rooted in non-violence and the rejection of state-sanctioned violence. He vehemently opposed war, militarism, and state oppression. His views were articulated in works like "War and Peace" and "The Kingdom of God Is Within You." Tolstoy argued that true Peace could only be achieved when nations and individuals rejected violence as a means of achieving their goals.

Tolstoy's belief in non-resistance to evil and the power of Love to transform conflicts significantly influenced the thinking of figures like Mahatma Gandhi and Martin Luther King Jr., who would later use non-violent resistance as a powerful tool in their own struggles for justice and Peace.

Leo Tolstoy's understanding of Peace extended to a broader commitment to social justice. He wrote extensively about the injustices of his time, including the exploitation of peasants, poverty, and inequality. His advocacy for social reform was deeply rooted in his belief in the interconnectedness of Peace and justice. He saw true Peace as an outcome of a just and equitable society.

Leo Tolstoy's influence on the understanding of Peace and non-violence is profound and enduring. His work continues to inspire individuals and movements dedicated to the pursuit of Peace and social justice. His writings on non-violence and Love as agents of change have left a lasting legacy, and his ethical and philosophical principles continue to shape conversations about Peace and social reform.

In conclusion, Leo Tolstoy's understanding of Peace was deeply rooted in his spiritual awakening, commitment to non-violence, and advocacy for social justice. His work serves as a powerful reminder of the interconnectedness of these principles and their enduring relevance in the quest for a more peaceful, just, and harmonious world. Tolstoy's legacy stands as a testament to the transformative power of personal conviction and ethical principles in the pursuit of Peace and social change.

38   Leonard Bernstein: Peace Through Music - The Universal Language

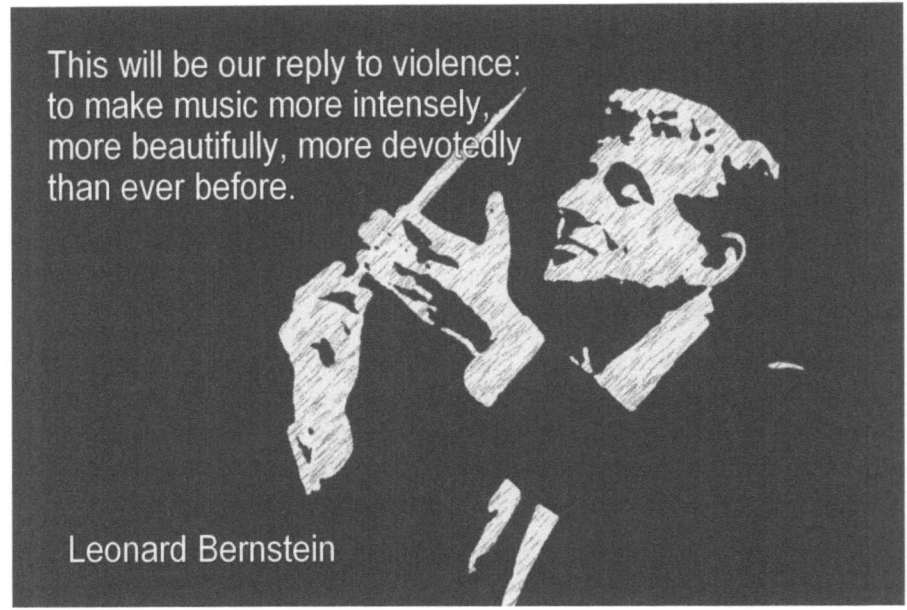

This will be our reply to violence: to make music more intensely, more beautifully, more devotedly than ever before.

Leonard Bernstein

Leonard Bernstein, the iconic American composer, conductor, and music educator, had a deep and multifaceted understanding of Peace that transcended the boundaries of music. His views on Peace were not confined to the absence of war, but rather extended to a vision of Peace as a complex and interwoven tapestry of harmony, cultural exchange, and education.

Leonard Bernstein was a firm believer in the unifying power of music. He viewed music as a universal language that transcended barriers of language, culture, and nationality. For Bernstein, music had the remarkable ability to bring people from diverse backgrounds together, fostering understanding and harmony. His famous quote, "This will be our reply to violence: to make music more intensely, more beautifully, more devotedly than ever before," epitomized his belief in the transformative potential of music as a means to counteract violence and promote Peace.

One of Bernstein's most memorable expressions of his commitment to Peace and unity was his performance of Beethoven's Ninth Symphony in Berlin on Christmas Day in 1989, just weeks after the fall of the Berlin Wall. In this iconic concert, Bernstein replaced the word "*Freude*" (joy) with "*Freiheit*" (freedom) in Friedrich Schiller's poem, "Ode to Joy," to celebrate the newfound freedom of the German people. The event symbolized Bernstein's belief that music could be a catalyst for political and social change, ushering in an era of Peace and cooperation. Bernstein was a passionate advocate for music education. He believed that teaching music to young people was a powerful way to promote Peace and harmony. Through education, he aimed to impart the values of discipline, cooperation, and appreciation for the arts, instilling in students a sense of empathy and cultural understanding. He famously said, "The best way to 'know' a thing is in the context of another discipline."

In 1989, Bernstein created a television program called "Bernstein's 'Beethoven," which explored the life and music of Ludwig van Beethoven. The series was not only a celebration of Beethoven's genius but also a commentary on the human condition, war, and Peace. In these dialogues, Bernstein demonstrated that music could be a vehicle for meaningful discussions about the human experience and the pursuit of Peace.

Bernstein was not just an advocate for Peace on the global stage; he was deeply committed to Peace and justice at home. He was a vocal supporter of civil rights, lending his talents and influence to the struggle for racial equality. His work in this realm was an extension of his broader commitment to a more just and equitable society as an essential aspect of achieving Peace.

Leonard Bernstein's understanding of Peace was multifaceted, encompassing the transformative power of music, the importance of education, and social activism. He saw Peace as a dynamic and active force, not merely the absence of conflict, but a state that required engagement, dialogue, and the celebration of human creativity. Bernstein's legacy reminds us that Peace can be achieved through art, education, and the coming together of cultures, and it serves as a testament to the enduring power of music to promote harmony and understanding in a world marked by divisions and strife. Through his work, he continues to inspire individuals to make music more intensely and strive for a more peaceful world.

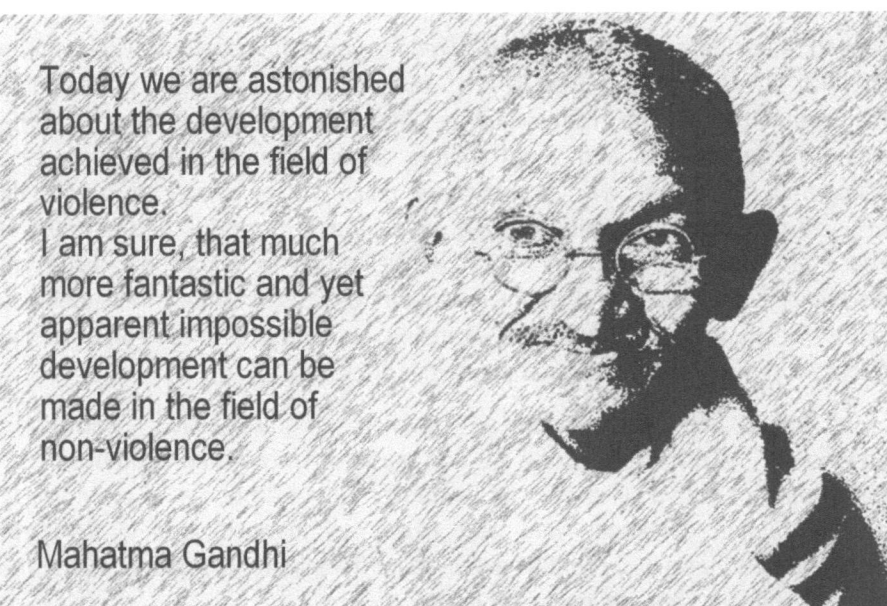

Today we are astonished about the development achieved in the field of violence.
I am sure, that much more fantastic and yet apparent impossible development can be made in the field of non-violence.

Mahatma Gandhi

Mahatma Gandhi, one of the most influential figures in the history of the world, is renowned not only for his role in India's struggle for independence but also for his profound understanding of Peace. His philosophy of non-violence, or "*Ahimsa*," remains a cornerstone of his legacy and continues to inspire people worldwide. To truly comprehend Gandhi's understanding of Peace, it is essential to explore the key elements of his philosophy, his life experiences, and the lasting impact of his teachings.

Gandhi's concept of Peace was deeply rooted in his spiritual and moral beliefs. *Ahimsa*, often translated as "non-violence" or "non-injury," was at the core of his understanding of Peace. For Gandhi, Peace was not merely the absence of physical violence; it encompassed every facet of human existence. He believed that true Peace could only be achieved when individuals sought to live harmoniously with each other, nature, and themselves.

Central to Gandhi's philosophy of Peace was the idea that violence begets violence. He argued that responding to hatred and aggression with more of the same would only perpetuate a cycle of conflict and suffering. Gandhi saw violence as a manifestation of fear, ignorance, and anger, and he believed that the path to lasting Peace lay in addressing the root causes of these negative emotions. Through Ahimsa, he encouraged individuals to confront their adversaries with Love and understanding, rather than retaliation.

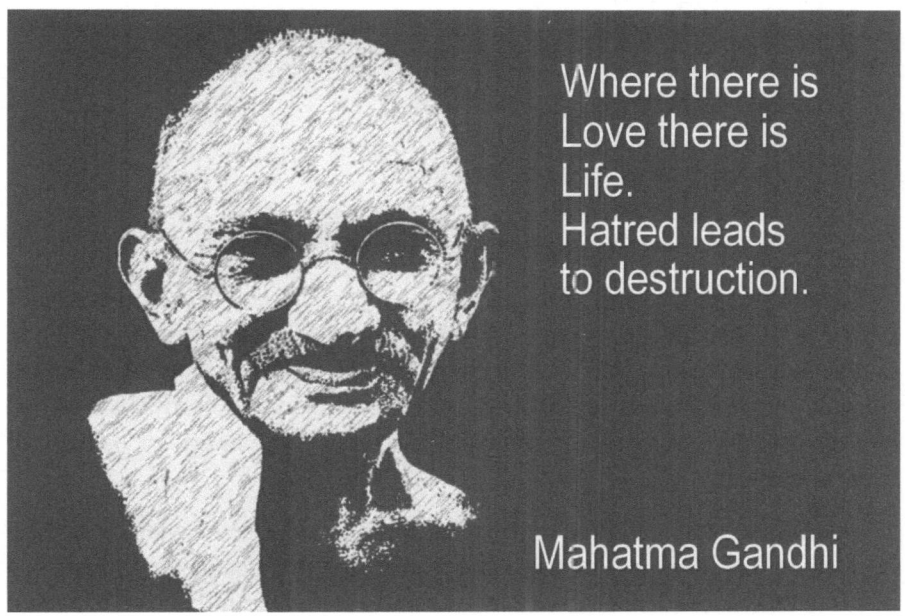

Where there is Love there is Life. Hatred leads to destruction.

Mahatma Gandhi

Gandhi's understanding of Peace was not limited to political or international contexts. He believed that Peace must start within each individual. He famously said, "You must be the change you wish to see in the world." This statement emphasized the importance of personal transformation and self-discipline as a means to bring about broader societal change. To Gandhi, Peace was a way of life, and it required individuals to cultivate inner Peace through self-control, self-reflection, and ethical conduct.

Furthermore, Gandhi's commitment to the idea of "Satyagraha" (truth force) was a vital aspect of his approach to Peace. Satyagraha involved the use of non-violent resistance as a means of asserting one's beliefs and rights, while also seeking to convert opponents through the moral strength of one's actions. Through Satyagraha, Gandhi demonstrated that peaceful means could be powerful tools for social and political change, even against formidable adversaries. His methods were influential in various civil rights movements and have served as an inspiration for leaders like Martin Luther King Jr. and Nelson Mandela.

> *I offer you Peace.*
> *I offer you Love.*
> *I offer you friendship.*
> *I see your beauty.*
> *I hear your need.*
> *I feel your feelings.*
> *My wisdom flows from the highest source.*
> *I salute that source in you.*
> *Let us work together. For unity and Peace.*

Gandhi's understanding of Peace was not merely theoretical; it was deeply rooted in his own life experiences. He led by example, personally participating in non-violent campaigns and civil disobedience to challenge oppressive British colonial rule in India. His commitment to truth, non-violence, and Peace earned him the reverence of millions of people who saw in him a living embodiment of these principles.

Gandhi's legacy in the realm of Peace and non-violence extends far beyond his lifetime. His ideas and methods have continued to influence individuals and movements worldwide, demonstrating the enduring power of his understanding of Peace. His teachings have found resonance in the realms of civil rights, social justice, and conflict resolution, and continue to inspire people to seek peaceful solutions to even the most challenging problems.

In conclusion, Mahatma Gandhi's understanding of Peace was grounded in the profound principles of *Ahimsa, Satyagraha*, and inner transformation. His philosophy emphasized that Peace is not merely the absence of physical violence but a comprehensive way of living, encompassing personal, social, and political dimensions. Gandhi's life and teachings serve as a testament to the enduring power of non-violence and the potential for transformative change when individuals commit themselves to the pursuit of Peace. His legacy continues to inspire and guide those who seek a more just and peaceful world.

Peace is what every
human being is
craving for,
and it can be brought
about humanity
through the child.

Maria Montessori

Maria Montessori, an Italian physician and educator, was a pioneer in the field of early childhood education. Her educational philosophy emphasizes the development of the whole child, encompassing physical, social, emotional, and cognitive aspects. Within the Montessori approach, the concept of Peace holds a central and profound role. Montessori's vision of Peace extends beyond the absence of war and conflict; it involves the cultivation of inner harmony, social justice, and a deep respect for humanity and the environment.

Avoiding *war is the work of politics, establishing Peace is the work of education.*

In 1946, after WWII, Montessori wrote that men "have earnestly tried to create a world where Peace could reign. And they have not succeeded... 'Love one another' has been preached for centuries, and yet Peace has not come."

In Montessori's view, the right approach to education is the way to achieve Peace, first within the individual, then within society, and finally between nations. Her lectures on this topic have been collected in the book "Education and Peace," but she makes this point in almost all of her books.

> *Everyone* talks about Peace, but no one educates for Peace. In this world, they educate for competition, and competition is the beginning of any war. When educating to cooperate and owe each other solidarity, that day we will be educating for Peace.

One fundamental aspect of Montessori's concept of Peace is rooted in the idea of creating a prepared environment that fosters the child's natural inclination toward order and harmony. In a Montessori classroom, careful attention is given to the arrangement of materials, the organization of space, and the establishment of routines. This order is not imposed externally but is a result of the child's own exploration and engagement with the environment. Through such an environment, Montessori believed that children develop a sense of security and inner Peace, laying the foundation for their overall well-being and more Peace in the world.

> *It* is therefore useless to try to achieve unity amongst men by inviting them to work for each other, since this has been happening for centuries. Instead, the question is to bring about a radical change in the way we view human relations, endeavouring to influence men's consciousness by giving them new ideals, fighting indifference and incomprehension; to awaken in man's spirit a sense of gratitude towards other men. This can also be done with children.

Montessori also emphasized the importance of nurturing the child's independence and self-discipline. By allowing children to make choices and take responsibility for their actions, educators empower them to become confident and capable individuals. This sense of autonomy contributes to a peaceful classroom atmosphere where children learn to cooperate, collaborate, and resolve conflicts through communication rather than confrontation.

Furthermore, Montessori education places a strong emphasis on the development of empathy and social consciousness. Children are encouraged to understand and appreciate differences, fostering a sense of unity among diverse individuals. Montessori classrooms often include activities that promote cultural awareness and global understanding, instilling in children a sense of interconnectedness with the broader human family.

Montessori's concept of Peace extends beyond the individual and the immediate social environment to encompass a broader perspective of global citizenship. She envisioned education as a means to create a more just and peaceful world. Montessori believed that the foundations of Peace lay in the education of the child, and she advocated for an education that promotes the values of cooperation, compassion, and environmental stewardship.

In conclusion, Maria Montessori's concept of Peace is a holistic and multifaceted approach that goes beyond the absence of conflict. It involves creating environments that support the child's natural development, fostering independence and self-discipline, promoting empathy and cultural understanding, and ultimately contributing to the cultivation of responsible global citizens. Montessori's vision of Peace remains a timeless and relevant contribution to the field of education, emphasizing the transformative power of fostering inner Peace and harmony in individuals as a foundation for a more peaceful world.

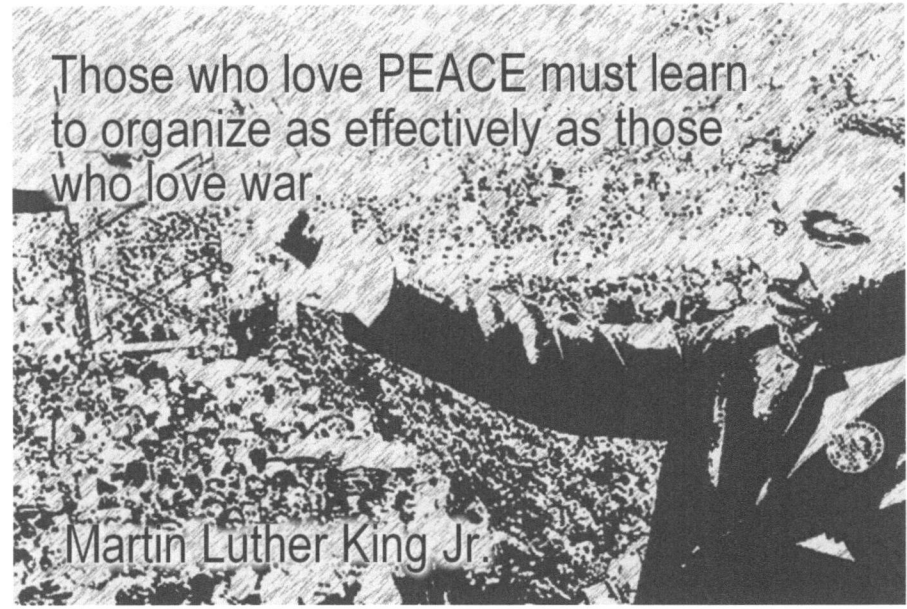

Those who love PEACE must learn to organize as effectively as those who love war

Martin Luther King Jr.

Martin Luther King Jr., an iconic figure in the American civil rights movement, possessed a profound understanding of Peace that was intricately connected to his philosophy of non-violence and his unwavering commitment to justice and equality. Dr. King's approach to Peace went beyond the mere absence of conflict; it encompassed a vision of a just and inclusive society. To truly grasp his understanding of Peace, it is essential to explore the core elements of his philosophy, his life experiences, and the enduring impact of his teachings.

Dr. King's concept of Peace was rooted in the principle of non-violence, a philosophy he often referred to as "soul force" or "Agape Love." He believed that non-violence was not only a tactical choice but a way of life. Non-violence, for King, meant seeking justice without resorting to physical force or hatred. He viewed non-violence as a powerful tool for social change and the means to break the cycle of hatred and violence.

Central to King's understanding of Peace was the idea that hatred and violence could never eradicate the root causes of social injustice. Instead, he argued that only Love and non-violent resistance could create lasting change. His famous quote, "Darkness cannot drive out darkness; only light can do that. Hate cannot drive out hate; only Love can do that," encapsulates this core belief. Dr. King's commitment to non-violence was evident in the Montgomery Bus Boycott, the Birmingham Campaign, and the March on Washington, where he advocated for civil rights and equality through peaceful means.

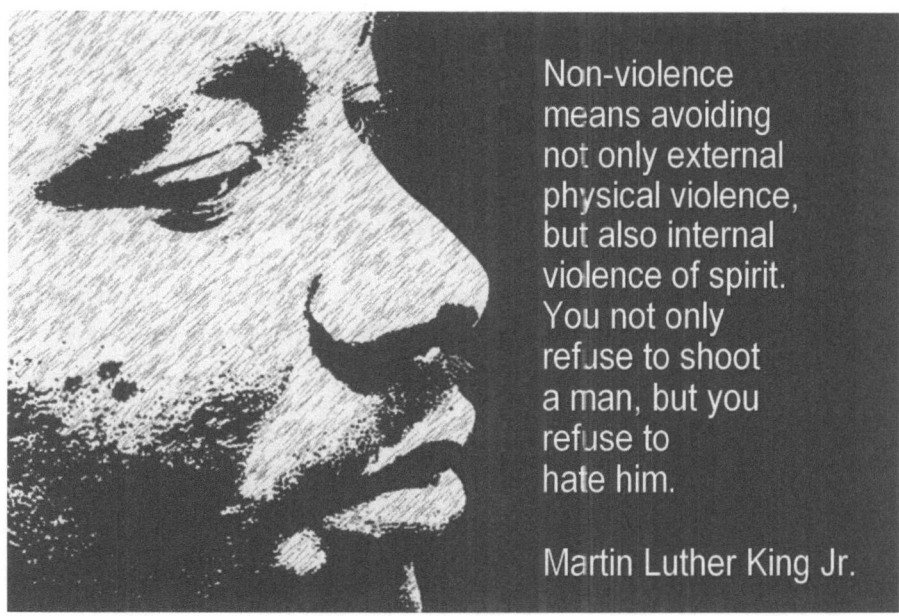

Non-violence means avoiding not only external physical violence, but also internal violence of spirit. You not only refuse to shoot a man, but you refuse to hate him.

Martin Luther King Jr.

Moreover, King's vision of Peace extended beyond the absence of physical violence to address the deep-seated systemic inequalities that plagued American society. He believed that true Peace could only be achieved by rectifying the injustices faced by marginalized communities, particularly African Americans. He argued that "justice" and "Peace" were inseparable, and that without justice, Peace would remain elusive. This perspective underscored his commitment to dismantling institutional racism and promoting economic and social equality.

Dr. King's understanding of Peace also emphasized the importance of civil disobedience as a means to confront injustice. He advocated for non-violent resistance to unjust laws and policies, asserting that individuals had a moral obligation to challenge such injustices. This approach, known as "passive resistance," sought to provoke the conscience of the oppressor while emphasizing the moral strength of the oppressed.

King's personal experiences profoundly influenced his understanding of Peace. Raised in a segregated society, he witnessed the pervasive discrimination and violence endured by African Americans. His leadership in the civil rights movement, coupled with his commitment to non-violence, demonstrated that individuals could overcome oppression and achieve transformative change through peaceful means.

The impact of Martin Luther King Jr.'s understanding of Peace is immeasurable. His leadership in the civil rights movement inspired millions of people to peacefully confront injustice and seek equality. His vision of Peace, rooted in non-violence and Love, resonated with individuals and movements worldwide, influencing struggles for justice and civil rights globally. Dr. King's legacy endures not only in the celebration of Martin Luther King Jr. Day but in the ongoing pursuit of his dream for a more equitable, just, and peaceful society.

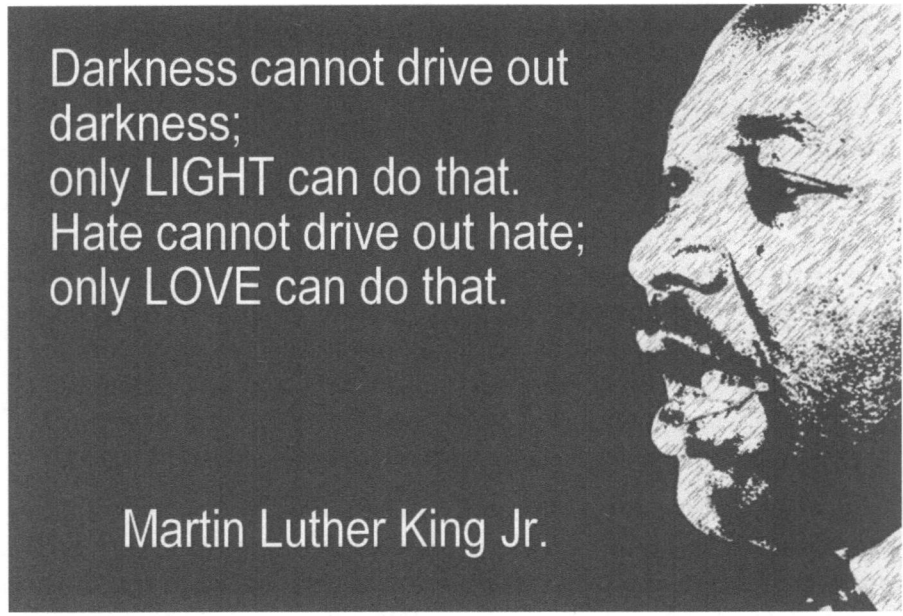

Darkness cannot drive out darkness;
only LIGHT can do that.
Hate cannot drive out hate;
only LOVE can do that.

Martin Luther King Jr.

42 Michael Jackson: The Power of Music as a Message of Peace

Peace.
That's what I want
all around the world.
Everywhere I go,
I always do the peace
sign with my fingers.

Michael Jackson

Michael Jackson, the King of Pop, was not only a legendary entertainer but also a cultural icon whose understanding of Peace left an indelible mark on the world. Through his music, philanthropic efforts, and advocacy, Jackson conveyed a powerful message of Peace, Love, and unity. To fully grasp his perspective on Peace, it is essential to explore the key elements of his philosophy, his life experiences, and the enduring impact of his work on the pursuit of a more harmonious and just world.

Michael Jackson's music was a vehicle for promoting Peace and unity. His hit songs like "Heal the World," "Man in the Mirror," and "We Are the World" conveyed messages of social change, compassion, and global harmony. "Heal the World," in particular, called for environmental responsibility and empathy, emphasizing the need to protect the planet for future generations. These songs served as anthems for Peace and humanitarianism, inspiring listeners to become agents of positive change.

We have to heal our wounded world. The chaos, despair, and senseless destruction we see today are a result of the alienation that people feel from each other and their environment.

Jackson was passionate about breaking down barriers of race and culture. His own experiences as an African American artist in a predominantly white industry gave him a unique perspective on the importance of promoting diversity and unity. In his music video for "Black or White," Jackson's transformation into various races and ethnicities highlighted the idea that humanity is interconnected and that diversity should be celebrated. His commitment to transcending racial, cultural, and religious boundaries made him a symbol of global unity.

Michael Jackson's understanding of Peace extended beyond music. He was a dedicated humanitarian who used his fame and fortune to make a positive impact on the world. His philanthropic efforts included substantial contributions to children's hospitals, HIV/AIDS research, disaster relief, and education. Notably, he established the Heal the World Foundation, a non-profit organization dedicated to promoting children's rights and creating a safer, healthier world for young people.

If you want to make the world a better place, take a look at yourself, and make a change.

Through songs like "Man in the Mirror," Jackson advocated for personal responsibility and self-improvement as essential components of social change. He believed that true Peace could only be achieved when individuals took steps to better themselves and contribute positively to society. This message encouraged people to examine their own actions and attitudes, emphasizing that Peace begins at the individual level.

As a wise man once said, 'If not us, then who; if not now, then when?'

While Michael Jackson's message of Peace and Love was widely celebrated, his life was marked by personal challenges and controversies. His own struggles with fame, media scrutiny, and legal issues serve as a reminder of the complex nature of the pursuit of Peace, both on a personal and societal level. His experiences underscore the need for compassion and understanding in dealing with the complexities of human existence.

Michael Jackson's impact on the understanding of Peace goes beyond his music and humanitarian work. He was a symbol of hope and unity during times of global strife, including the end of the Cold War and humanitarian crises. His music and message continue to inspire individuals and movements dedicated to Peace, Love, and global harmony.

Be *humble, believe in yourself, and have the love of the world in your heart.*

In conclusion, Michael Jackson's understanding of Peace was shaped by his commitment to using his music and platform for social change, his dedication to humanitarian causes, and his belief in the power of Love, unity, and personal transformation. His legacy serves as a reminder that, in a world often marked by conflict and division, individuals and artists can use their talents and influence to inspire positive change and promote a more peaceful and just world.

In *a world filled with hate, we must still dare to hope. In a world filled with anger, we must still dare to comfort. In a world filled with despair, we must still dare to dream. And in a world filled with distrust, we must still dare to believe.*

We need Peace.
We need Giving.
We need Love.
We need Unity

43 Mohammed Ali: The strong Conscientious Objector

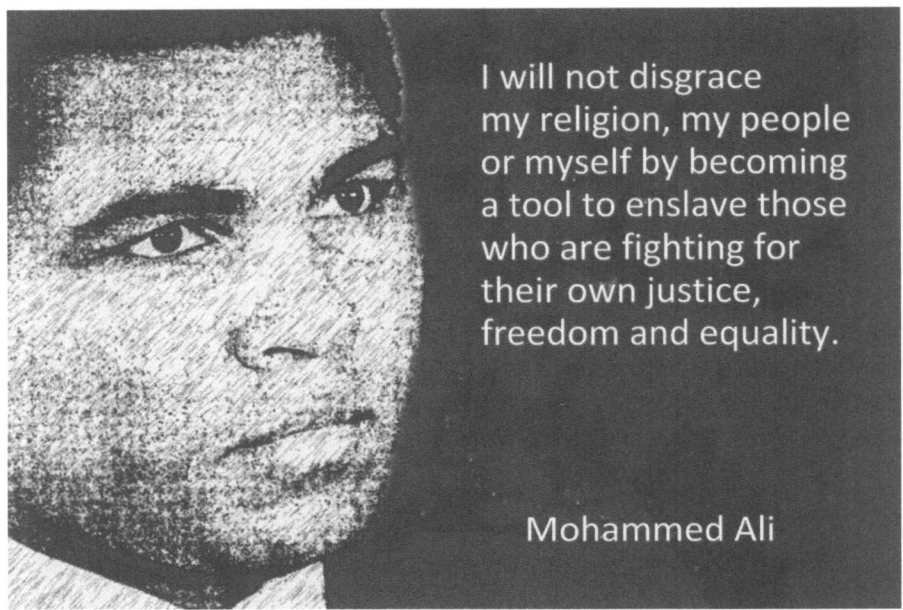

I will not disgrace my religion, my people or myself by becoming a tool to enslave those who are fighting for their own justice, freedom and equality.

Mohammed Ali

Muhammad Ali, the world-famous boxer, was not a strict pacifist, but he refused military service during the Vietnam War Ali was a converted Muslim and a member of the Nation of Islam. His decision to refuse the draft was based on his religious beliefs and the conviction that war contradicted his Islamic principles. Ali publicly stated that he had "no quarrel with the Vietcong" and refused to fight against people who had not oppressed him. This decision led to his being charged with draft evasion. Ali had his title stripped in 1967, and he spent several years in legal battles before the Supreme Court of the United States overturned the conviction in 1971. He became a symbol of resistance against the Vietnam War and an advocate for the rights of conscientious objectors.

Why should they ask me to put on a uniform and go 10,000 miles from home and drop bombs and bullets on Brown people in Vietnam while so-called Negro people in Louisville are treated like dogs and denied simple human rights?

44   Mother Teresa: The Pursuit of Peace through Love and Action

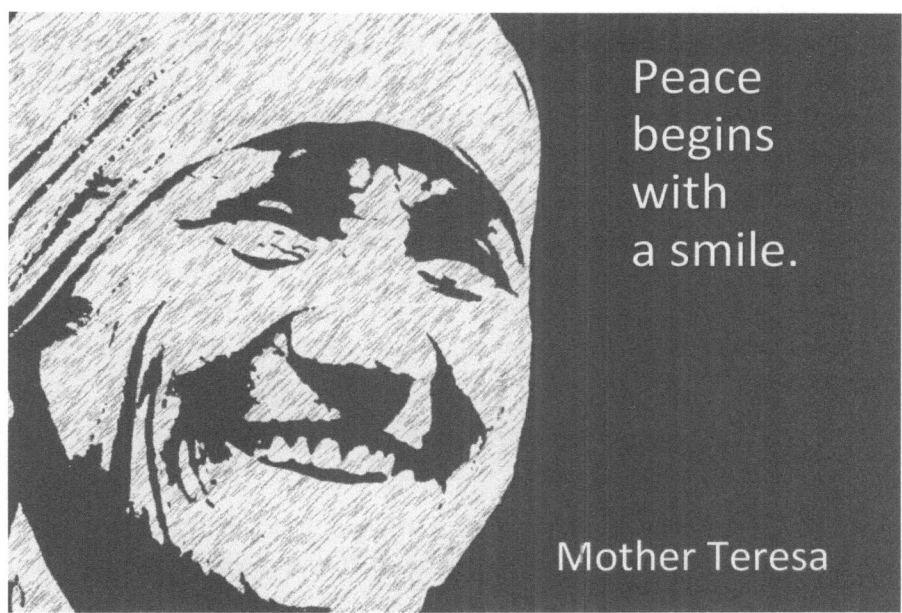

Peace begins with a smile.

Mother Teresa

Mother Teresa, the iconic Albanian-Indian Catholic nun and humanitarian, possessed a profound and unwavering understanding of Peace. Her perspective on Peace was deeply rooted in her faith, her life of service to the poorest of the poor, and her unyielding commitment to compassion, Love, and selfless devotion to humanity. To appreciate Mother Teresa's perspective on Peace, it is essential to explore the key elements of her philosophy, her life experiences, and the enduring impact of her work on the pursuit of Peace and humanitarianism.

For Mother Teresa, the essence of Peace lay in the virtues of compassion and Love. She believed that true Peace could only be achieved when individuals and societies embraced the suffering of others with open hearts and selfless Love. Her life's work was a testament to this belief, as she dedicated herself to serving the most destitute and marginalized individuals in the slums of Calcutta and beyond.

Mother Teresa's understanding of Peace was inextricably linked to the recognition of the inherent dignity of every human being. She saw the divine spark in the most impoverished and neglected individuals and believed that acknowledging this inherent worth was a crucial step toward Peace and justice. Her mission was to provide dignity and respect to those society had marginalized.

Mother Teresa was not merely a proponent of Peace in words; she believed in the pursuit of Peace through action. Her Missionaries of Charity were actively engaged in providing care, Love, and support to the sick, the hungry, and the dying. She once said, "Prayer in action is Love, Love in action is service." Her work exemplified her belief that Peace was a tangible outcome of selfless service.

Mother Teresa's work transcended religious boundaries. While she was a Catholic nun, she extended her Love and care to people of all faiths and backgrounds. She believed that true Peace required interfaith understanding, tolerance, and the recognition of a shared humanity. Her actions were a testament to her belief that Love could unite people of diverse beliefs and backgrounds.

If we have no Peace, it is because we have forgotten that we belong to each other.

Mother Teresa's impact on the understanding of Peace and humanitarianism is immeasurable. Her unwavering commitment to the service of the poor and marginalized, her belief in the power of Love and compassion, and her dedication to the recognition of human dignity continue to inspire individuals and organizations worldwide. She was awarded the Nobel Peace Prize in 1979 for her work, and her legacy endures through the ongoing efforts of the Missionaries of Charity.

In conclusion, Mother Teresa's understanding of Peace was profoundly rooted in Love, compassion, service, and the recognition of the inherent dignity of every human being. Her life and work serve as a powerful reminder of the potential for individuals to bring about Peace and positive change through selfless service and unwavering devotion to the welfare of humanity. Mother Teresa's legacy stands as a testament to the enduring power of Love, compassion, and selfless action in the pursuit of Peace and humanitarianism.

45 Nelson Mandela: Reconciliation and Forgiveness

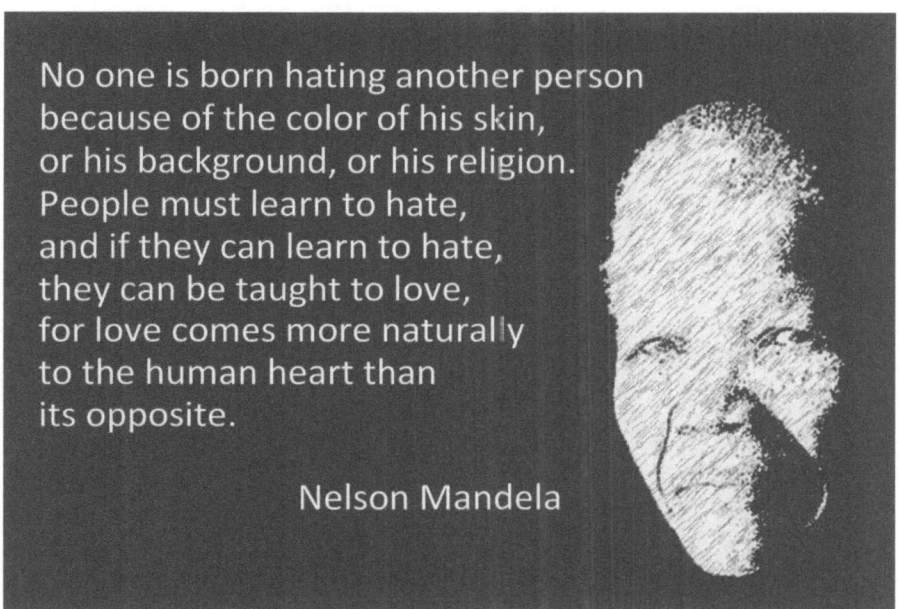

No one is born hating another person because of the color of his skin, or his background, or his religion. People must learn to hate, and if they can learn to hate, they can be taught to love, for love comes more naturally to the human heart than its opposite.

Nelson Mandela

Nelson Mandela, the revered South African anti-apartheid revolutionary and statesman, possessed a profound and multifaceted understanding of Peace. His perspective on Peace was deeply rooted in his lifelong struggle for justice, reconciliation, and the dismantling of apartheid. To appreciate Nelson Mandela's perspective on Peace, it is essential to explore the key elements of his philosophy, his life experiences, and the enduring impact of his work on the pursuit of Peace and social justice.

At the core of Nelson Mandela's understanding of Peace was the concept of reconciliation and forgiveness. Following his release from prison in 1990 after 27 years of incarceration, Mandela chose the path of reconciliation over revenge. His ability to forgive those who had oppressed him and his people was a defining moment in South Africa's history. Mandela's belief in the power of forgiveness and the need for all South Africans to work together toward a common future became a guiding principle in the quest for Peace.

Mandela's vision of Peace was closely aligned with his commitment to justice and equality. He recognized that true Peace could only be achieved in a society where all individuals, regardless of their race or background, enjoyed equal rights and opportunities. His fight against apartheid was fundamentally a fight for justice, and his advocacy for a democratic South Africa was rooted in the belief that Peace required the elimination of institutionalized racism and discrimination.

Courageous people do not fear forgiving for the sake of peace.

Nelson Mandela

While Nelson Mandela's early activism included acts of civil disobedience and support for armed struggle, he later embraced non-violence and political negotiation as means to bring about change. His involvement in the peaceful transition to majority rule in South Africa, characterized by negotiations and dialogue, exemplified his understanding of Peace as a product of diplomacy and political compromise.

Mandela's understanding of Peace extended beyond South Africa's borders. He recognized that the struggle for Peace and justice was not limited to one nation but was a global endeavour. He believed in the importance of international solidarity and cooperation in addressing global issues and promoting Peace.

Nelson Mandela's impact on the understanding of Peace and social justice is immeasurable. His leadership and commitment to reconciliation and forgiveness earned him international recognition and the Nobel Peace Prize in 1993. His legacy continues to inspire leaders, activists, and individuals around the world to work toward a more just, equitable, and peaceful society.

In conclusion, Nelson Mandela's understanding of Peace was characterized by a commitment to reconciliation, forgiveness, justice, and equality. His life and work serve as a testament to the enduring potential of individuals to bring about Peace and social change through unwavering dedication to the principles of justice and reconciliation. Nelson Mandela's legacy stands as a reminder of the transformative power of forgiveness, diplomacy, and the pursuit of a more peaceful and just world.

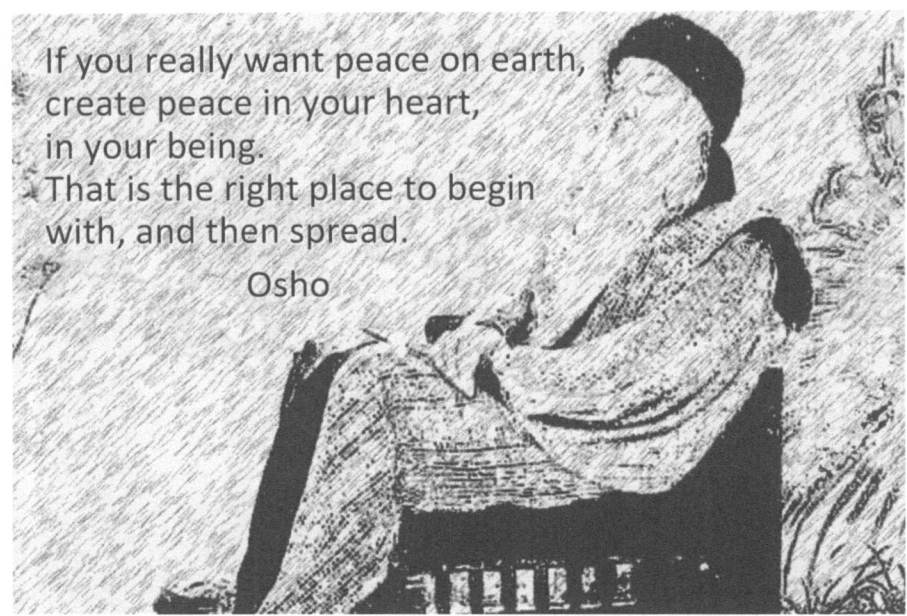

If you really want peace on earth,
create peace in your heart,
in your being.
That is the right place to begin
with, and then spread.

Osho

Osho, the Indian mystic, philosopher, and spiritual teacher, had a unique and profound understanding of Peace that transcended traditional boundaries of religion and philosophy. His perspective on Peace was deeply rooted in his teachings on meditation, consciousness, and the human experience. Osho's approach to Peace emphasized inner transformation, mindfulness, and the realization that true Peace can only be found within oneself. To appreciate Osho's perspective on Peace, it is essential to explore the key elements of his philosophy, his contributions to spirituality, and the enduring impact of his teachings on the pursuit of inner and outer Peace.

Osho placed great emphasis on meditation as a means to achieve inner Peace. He believed that the mind is the source of restlessness and turmoil, and that through meditation, one could silence the mind's incessant chatter and discover a profound sense of calm and inner tranquillity. In his view, inner Peace was the foundation upon which external Peace could be built.

One of Osho's core teachings was centred on mindfulness and the practice of living in the present moment. He argued that much of our inner turmoil stems from dwelling on the past or worrying about the future. By being fully present in the here and now, individuals could experience a profound sense of Peace and freedom.

Osho advocated for the acceptance of life as it is, rather than resisting or trying to control it. He believed that true Peace could only be found by letting go of attachments, desires, and expectations. By embracing life's impermanence and unpredictability, individuals could find a sense of serenity.

Man has lived under the calamity of war too long. We have to destroy all gods of war; instead we have to create a temple of love. We should kill all gods of war, because only through their death — the god of war dead, all gods of war dead — will the god of love be born.

War exists. Not because there are warring groups outside in the world; fundamentally war exists because man is in conflict. The root of war is within; on the outside you only see the branches and the foliage of it. After each ten years, humanity needs a great world war. In ten years time, man accumulates so much rage, madness, insanity, inside him that it has to erupt.

Unless we transform the very script of man, unless we give him a totally new programme of living and being, we can go on talking about Peace but we will go on preparing for war. That's what we have been doing for thousands of years: talking of Peace and creating war. The absurdity is that even in the name of Peace we have been fighting: the greatest wars have been fought in the name of Peace. This has been a sheerly destructive past. With the same energy, man could have created paradise on earth; and all that we have done is to create a hell instead. But it is not a question of changing the political ideologies of the world, it is not a question of teaching people to be brotherly, because these things have been done and they have all failed. (Osho: Won't You Join The Dance, Ch 4)

47 Richard von Weizäcker: Emphasis on Democracy and Human Rights

The plea to the young people is:
Do not let yourselves ber driven
into enmity and hatred against
other people, against Russians or
Americans, against Jews or Turks,
against alternative or conservative,
against black or white.
Learn to live together,
instead of against each other.

Richard von Weizäcker

Richard von Weizsäcker, the distinguished German statesman and former President of Germany, possessed a profound understanding of Peace that was deeply rooted in his experiences, his role in shaping post-World War II Germany, and his commitment to reconciliation, diplomacy, and a unified Europe. Weizsäcker's perspective on Peace emphasized the importance of historical responsibility, diplomacy, and international cooperation as means to prevent conflicts and promote reconciliation. To appreciate Richard von Weizsäcker's perspective on Peace, it is essential to explore the key elements of his philosophy, his life experiences, and the enduring impact of his work on the pursuit of Peace, particularly in the context of post-Cold War Europe.

Weizsäcker's understanding of Peace was deeply influenced by the historical context of his time. As a post-World War II figure, he recognized Germany's historical responsibility for the atrocities of the Holocaust and the devastation of the war. He believed that facing this historical responsibility and seeking reconciliation with neighboring countries, especially France and Poland, were essential steps in securing lasting Peace. Weizsäcker was a strong advocate for European integration, particularly through the European Union. He believed that a united Europe was a cornerstone of Peace on the continent. He viewed the European Union as a project that could help prevent the recurrence of the devastating conflicts that had plagued Europe in the past. Weizsäcker was a vocal proponent of nuclear disarmament and arms control. He recognized the existential threat posed by nuclear weapons and the importance of international diplomacy in reducing the risk of nuclear conflict. He believed that peaceful dialogue and negotiation were essential for global security and Peace.

Weizsäcker's perspective on Peace included a strong emphasis on democracy and human rights. He believed that upholding these values was crucial for maintaining Peace, not only within nations but also on the international stage. He viewed the protection of human rights and the promotion of democratic governance as integral to preventing conflicts. He played a significant role during the tumultuous period of German reunification. His leadership and commitment to peaceful reunification, alongside figures like Chancellor Helmut Kohl, were instrumental in shaping a post-Cold War Europe. The peaceful reunification of Germany in 1990 marked a historic moment of Peace and diplomacy.

Richard von Weizsäcker's impact on the understanding of Peace and international relations is substantial. His commitment to historical responsibility, European integration, nuclear disarmament, and the promotion of democracy and human rights has left an enduring mark on post-Cold War Europe. His leadership and dedication to peaceful reunification continue to inspire leaders and diplomats working towards Peace, unity, and stability in Europe and beyond.

In conclusion, Richard von Weizsäcker's understanding of Peace was characterized by a recognition of historical responsibility, a commitment to European integration, diplomacy, nuclear disarmament, and the promotion of democracy and human rights. His life and work serve as a testament to the transformative power of individuals and nations to learn from history, embrace reconciliation, and work together to prevent conflicts and build a more peaceful and united world. Weizsäcker's legacy stands as a reminder of the potential for responsible leadership and diplomacy to shape a more peaceful and harmonious global landscape.

48 Romain Rolland: Art and Culture as Forces of Life

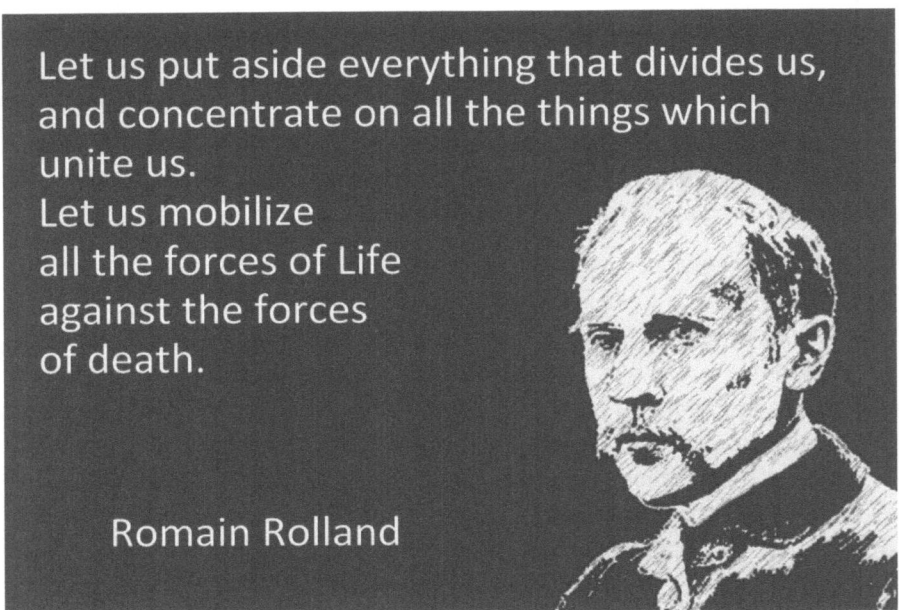

Let us put aside everything that divides us, and concentrate on all the things which unite us.
Let us mobilize
all the forces of Life
against the forces
of death.

Romain Rolland

Romain Rolland, the celebrated French writer, essayist, and Nobel laureate, possessed a profound understanding of Peace that was deeply rooted in his intellectual pursuits, artistic contributions, and his commitment to fostering harmony and unity among individuals and nations. Rolland's perspective on Peace was marked by his belief in the transformative power of art, culture, and the human spirit in the pursuit of global reconciliation and the prevention of conflict. To appreciate Romain Rolland's perspective on Peace, it is essential to explore the key elements of his philosophy, his literary works, and the enduring impact of his ideas on the promotion of Peace and international understanding.

Romain Rolland believed that art and culture held the key to achieving Peace and understanding among nations. He saw art as a bridge that could transcend national borders, linguistic barriers, and political differences. His own literary works, such as "Jean-Christophe," exemplify this perspective, as they aimed to create a universal sense of fraternity and solidarity among people of various backgrounds. Rolland was a staunch intellectual idealist and pacifist. He abhorred the senseless violence and destruction brought about by World War I and passionately advocated for a peaceful and just world order. He believed that reason, dialogue, and intellectual exchange should be the primary means of resolving international disputes, rather than armed conflict.

Romain Rolland embraced cosmopolitanism and internationalism, advocating for a world where individuals would transcend narrow nationalistic loyalties in favour of a shared humanity. He believed that a sense of international fraternity and unity would be instrumental in preventing future conflicts and establishing a lasting Peace. Humanitarianism was a cornerstone of Rolland's understanding of Peace. He recognized the significance of empathy, compassion, and solidarity in addressing the suffering and needs of individuals, particularly in times of war and crisis. His dedication to humanitarian causes underscored his belief in the importance of alleviating human suffering and fostering Peace.

Romain Rolland was critical of nationalism and militarism, which he believed were at the root of conflicts and wars. He saw these ideologies as divisive forces that fuelled animosity and competition between nations. His critique of these ideologies was a call for a shift toward international cooperation and the pursuit of peaceful coexistence.

Romain Rolland's impact on the understanding of Peace and international relations is enduring. His activism, writings, and intellectual contributions inspired subsequent generations of thinkers, writers, and activists to advocate for Peace, cultural exchange, and the rejection of militarism and nationalism. His steadfast commitment to the idea that art, culture, and intellectual exchange can promote Peace serves as a powerful reminder of the potential for the human spirit to transcend conflicts and strive for a more peaceful and harmonious world.

In conclusion, Romain Rolland's understanding of Peace was characterized by a belief in the unifying power of art and culture, intellectual idealism, internationalism, humanitarian values, and a critique of divisive ideologies. His life and work serve as a testament to the enduring potential of individuals to contribute to the promotion of Peace, unity, and international understanding through their intellectual and artistic endeavours. Rolland's legacy stands as a reminder of the transformative power of ideas and culture in the pursuit of global reconciliation and harmony.

49   Sophie Scholl & Hans Scholl: A Testament to Resistance and Humanity

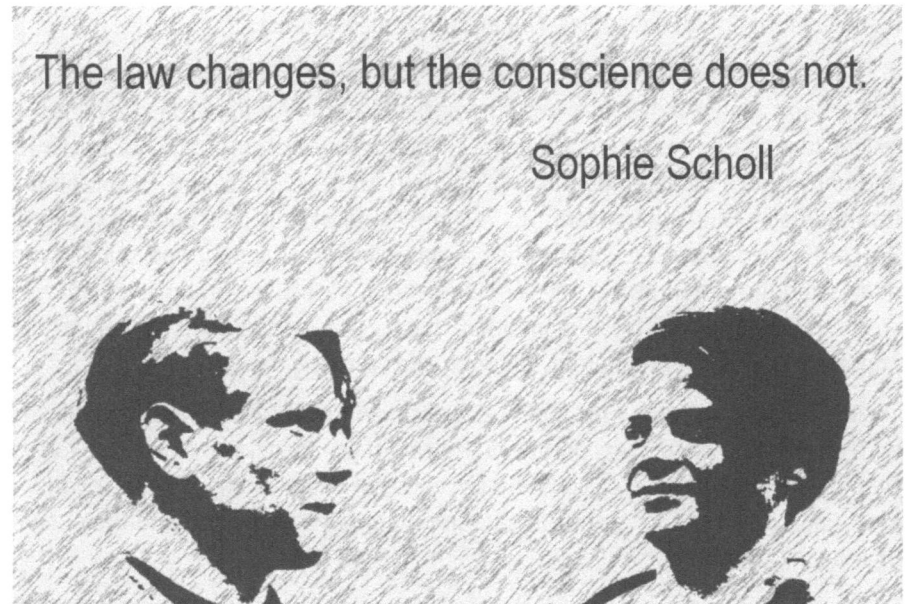

The law changes, but the conscience does not.

Sophie Scholl

Hans and Sophie Scholl, two courageous siblings at the heart of the White Rose resistance group in Nazi Germany, exemplified a profound commitment to Peace in the face of tyranny. Born in 1918 and 1921, respectively, Hans and Sophie Scholl, along with their fellow members of the White Rose, left an indelible mark on history through their resistance to the oppressive Nazi regime. This essay explores the Scholl siblings' concept of Peace, examining how their ideas were shaped by the tumultuous historical context in which they lived.

The rise of Adolf Hitler and the Nazi Party in Germany during the 1930s marked a dark period in history characterized by totalitarianism, militarism, and the suppression of dissent. In this oppressive atmosphere, the Scholl siblings, inspired by their moral convictions and driven by a profound sense of justice, emerged as key figures in the resistance against the Nazis. The White Rose, founded by Hans and his friends, including Sophie, sought to promote non-violent resistance against the atrocities committed by the regime.

The key Elements of the Scholl Siblings' concept of Peace are:

1. Intellectual Resistance: Central to the Scholl siblings' vision of Peace was their commitment to intellectual resistance. They believed in the power of ideas and words to counteract the propaganda and misinformation propagated by the Nazi regime. Through the distribution of leaflets calling for resistance and critical thinking, the White Rose aimed to awaken the conscience of the German people and inspire them to reject the atrocities committed in their name.

2. Non-violence and Human Dignity: The Scholls' concept of Peace was grounded in non-violence and a deep respect for human dignity. They rejected the militarism and aggression promoted by the Nazis, advocating instead for a peaceful and just society where individuals were treated with respect and compassion. The White Rose's emphasis on the inherent value of every human being was a direct challenge to the dehumanizing ideology of the Nazi regime.

3. Ethical Responsibility: Hans and Sophie Scholl believed in the ethical responsibility of individuals to resist injustice. They understood that true Peace could only be achieved through the collective efforts of those willing to stand up against tyranny. The White Rose's call to action was an appeal to the moral conscience of Germans, urging them to recognize their responsibility in the face of widespread atrocities.

4. Courage in the Face of Tyranny: The Scholl siblings' concept of Peace was inseparable from their extraordinary courage in the face of tyranny. Despite the severe consequences they faced, including the risk of imprisonment and execution, Hans and Sophie Scholl remained steadfast in their commitment to resistance. Their courage became a beacon of hope for those who believed in the possibility of a more just and peaceful future.

The legacy of Hans and Sophie Scholl is one of unwavering commitment to Peace, justice, and human dignity. Their sacrifice, along with that of their fellow White Rose members, serves as a powerful reminder of the importance of standing up against oppression and injustice. The Scholl siblings' concept of Peace continues to inspire individuals and movements worldwide, emphasizing the enduring significance of intellectual and moral resistance in the pursuit of a more just and peaceful world.

Hans and Sophie Scholl's concept of Peace, forged in the crucible of Nazi Germany, transcends its historical context to speak to universal values of justice, human dignity, and moral responsibility. Their legacy challenges us to reflect on the role of intellectual and non-violent resistance in the face of oppression, inspiring future generations to strive for a world where Peace is not merely the absence of conflict but a reflection of our shared commitment to justice and humanity.

50 Wendell Berry: Harmony with Nature and Community

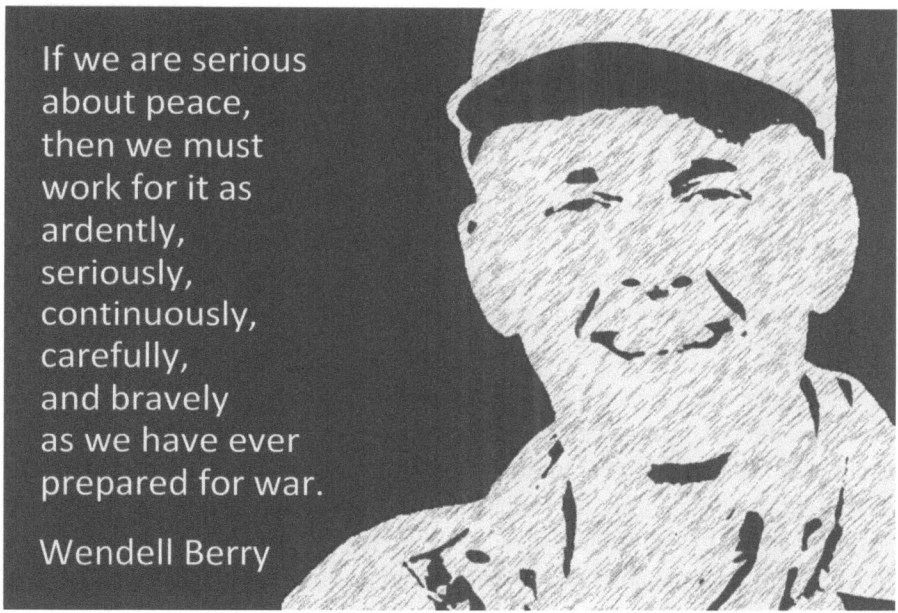

If we are serious about peace, then we must work for it as ardently, seriously, continuously, carefully, and bravely as we have ever prepared for war.

Wendell Berry

Wendell Berry, a prolific American writer, poet, and environmental activist, has long been an advocate for a more peaceful and sustainable world. His understanding of Peace is deeply rooted in a profound connection with nature, a sense of community, and a commitment to responsible stewardship of the Earth.

Wendell Berry's understanding of Peace begins with a reverence for the natural world. He views Peace as the result of living in harmony with the Earth, rather than exploiting or dominating it. Berry's writings emphasize the importance of sustainable agriculture, responsible land use, and the preservation of biodiversity. In his vision, Peace is inextricably linked with our ability to live in ecological balance.

One of Berry's most famous essays, "The Unsettling of America," critiques the negative impacts of modern industrial agriculture on the environment and calls for a return to a more harmonious relationship with the land. He argues that this reconnection with the Earth is essential for achieving a state of Peace and well-being.

Wendell Berry places great importance on the idea of localism and a strong sense of community. He believes that true Peace can only be achieved by fostering healthy relationships with the people in one's immediate surroundings. Berry's advocacy for local economies, agrarian values, and small-scale farming is grounded in the belief that strong, close-knit communities are essential for both social and ecological harmony.

Berry's writings often lament the erosion of rural communities and the displacement of small farmers by industrial agriculture. He argues that a return to localized, community-oriented ways of living is crucial for achieving Peace, as these systems inherently promote a sense of interconnectedness and cooperation.

In Wendell Berry's view, Peace is closely linked to leading simple, sustainable lives. He emphasizes the need to embrace moderation, reduce consumerism, and avoid the excesses that can lead to ecological destruction and personal discontent. This emphasis on simplicity not only contributes to environmental sustainability but also allows individuals to find Peace within themselves by freeing them from the pressures of materialism and overconsumption.

A fundamental aspect of Wendell Berry's vision of Peace is the idea of stewardship and responsibility. He advocates for a profound sense of responsibility toward the environment, which involves taking care of the land and the resources it provides. Berry contends that true Peace is impossible without this ethical duty to protect and preserve the Earth for future generations.

Wendell Berry's understanding of Peace is a holistic and interconnected concept that encompasses harmony with nature, community, and oneself. He calls for a return to localism, sustainable agriculture, and agrarian values as a means to achieve Peace and well-being. By promoting ecological stewardship, local community connections, and a commitment to simplicity, Berry's vision of Peace is not only an antidote to the ecological and social challenges of our time but also a source of inspiration for those seeking a more harmonious and peaceful world. In his writings, Berry's vision of Peace serves as a reminder of the importance of living in balance with nature and fostering meaningful connections with others to create a more peaceful and sustainable future.

51 Wolfgang Borchert: Self-Responsibility - Say NO

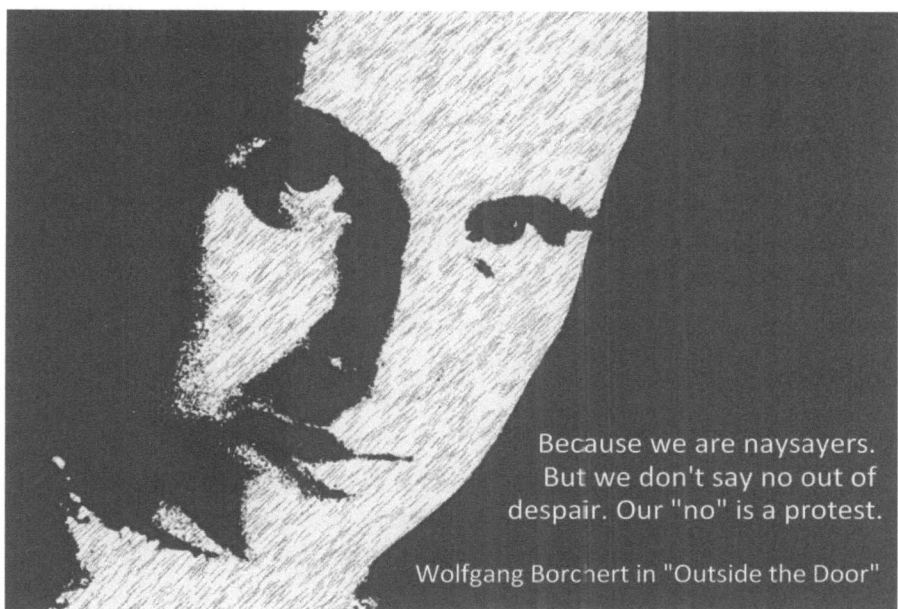

Because we are naysayers. But we don't say no out of despair. Our "no" is a protest.

Wolfgang Borchert in "Outside the Door"

Wolfgang Borchert (1921-1947) was a renowned German writer, playwright, and poet who lived during a tumultuous period in European history. His literary works, notably his short stories and plays, were deeply influenced by his experiences during World War II and its aftermath. Borchert's writings grapple with the profound consequences of war and the yearning for Peace in a world scarred by conflict. In this essay, we will explore the concept of Peace as envisioned by Wolfgang Borchert, examining how his works vividly illustrate the enduring human desire for tranquillity and the devastating effects of war.

Borchert's own experiences as a soldier during World War II deeply informed his literary output. After being wounded on the Eastern Front and later captured as a prisoner of war, he witnessed the horrors of battle and the physical and emotional toll it exacted on individuals. His writings frequently centre on the profound trauma experienced by soldiers and civilians during and after the war.

The concept of Peace, in his works, often emerges as a counterpoint to the brutality and suffering he witnessed.

One of Borchert's most famous works, the play "*Draußen vor der Tür*" (The Man Outside), features the character Beckmann, a returning soldier who struggles to find his place in a post-war world. The play captures the isolation, despair, and alienation felt by many war veterans. Beckmann's longing for Peace and acceptance is a central theme, reflecting the universal desire for solace and reconciliation in the aftermath of conflict.

For Borchert self-responsibility is a very important way to oppose violence. People have to say no, to demands and events they do not want to happen. They should resist taking part in any way.

Testimony to this state of mind is his expressive poem "say no":

> ### Say No
>
> *Then there's only one thing!*
>
> *You. Man at the machine and man in the workshop. If they order you tomorrow, you shall no longer make water pipes and cooking pots - but steel helmets and machine guns, then there's only one thing: Say NO!*
>
> *You. Girl behind the counter and girl in the office. If they order you tomorrow to fill grenades and assemble scopes for sniper rifles, then there's only one thing: Say NO!*
>
> *You. Factory owner. If they order you tomorrow to sell gunpowder instead of powder and cocoa, then there's only one thing: Say NO!*
>
> *You. Researcher in the laboratory. If they order you tomorrow to invent a new death against old life, then there's only one thing: Say NO!*
>
> *You. Poet in your study. If they order you tomorrow not to sing love songs, but to sing hate songs, then there's only one thing: Say NO!*

You. Doctor at the sickbed. If they order you tomorrow to classify men as fit for war, then there's only one thing: Say NO!

You. Priest on the pulpit. If they order you tomorrow to bless murder and sanctify war, then there's only one thing: Say NO!

You. Captain on the steamer. If they order you tomorrow to carry no more wheat but cannons and tanks, then there's only one thing: Say NO!

You. Pilot on the airfield. If they order you tomorrow to drop bombs and phosphorus over the cities, then there's only one thing: Say NO!

You. Tailor on your cutting table. If they order you tomorrow to cut uniforms, then there's only one thing: Say NO!

You. Judge in your robes. If they order you tomorrow to go to a war tribunal, then there's only one thing: Say NO!

You. Man at the station. If they order you tomorrow to signal the departure for the munitions train and the troop transport, then there's only one thing: Say NO!

You. Man in the village and man in the city. If they come tomorrow and bring you the conscription order, then there's only one thing: Say NO!

You. Mother in Normandy and mother in Ukraine, you, mother in Frisco and London, you, on the Hoangho and the Mississippi, you, mother in Naples and Hamburg and Cairo and Oslo - mothers on all continents, mothers in the world, if they order you tomorrow to bear children, nurses for war hospitals, and new soldiers for new battles, mothers in the world, then there's only one thing: Say NO! Mothers, say NO!

Because if you do not say NO, if YOU do not say no, mothers, then: then: In the noisy, steamy port cities, the large ships will groan to a silent halt and sway like titanic mammoth corpses, waterlogged and sluggish, against the dead and deserted quays, covered with algae, seaweed, and mussels. They will be peacefully smelling of fish, fragile, sick, dead -

The trams will lie there like senseless, tarnished, glass-eyed cages, dented and peeled, beside the confused steel skeletons of the wires and tracks. Behind rotting, hole-riddled sheds, in lost, crater-torn streets -

A mud-gray, thick, pasty, leaden silence will roll in, devouring, growing, will grow into the schools and universities and theatres, on sports and children's playgrounds, gruesome and greedy, unstoppable -

The sunny, juicy wine will rot on the overgrown slopes, the rice will dry up in the withered soil, the potatoes will freeze on the barren fields, and the cows will stretch their stiff legs like overturned milking stools toward the sky -

In the institutes, the ingenious inventions of the great doctors will sour, rot, and turn mouldy with fungi -

In the kitchens, pantries, and cellars, in the cold storage rooms and storerooms, the last sacks of flour, the last jars of strawberries, pumpkins, and cherry juice will spoil -

The bread under the overturned tables and on shattered plates will turn green, and the spilled butter will stink like lye soap. The grain on the fields will sink into the ground like a beaten army beside rusty ploughs, and the smoking brick chimneys, the kitchens, and the factory chimneys will crumble, covered by eternal grass -

Then the last man, with shredded intestines and poisoned lungs, will wander about, answer-less and alone, under the poisonous, glowing sun and among the swaying stars, among the cold, giant idols of the deserted, concrete, lifeless cities, the last man, emaciated, insane, blasphemous, lamenting -

And his terrible lament: WHY? will go unheard in the steppe, rustle through the cracked ruins, sink in the rubble of churches,

150

> *clap against high bunkers, fall into blood puddles, unheard,*
> *answer-less, last animal's cry of the last human animal - all this*
> *will come to pass, tomorrow, perhaps, perhaps tonight already,*
> *perhaps tonight, if - -*
>
> *if - -*
>
> *if you do not say NO.*

Borchert's works underscore the importance of compassion and empathy in achieving Peace. His characters often grapple with their own moral and ethical dilemmas, questioning the senselessness of war and its destructive consequences. Borchert's call for understanding and empathy resonates as a plea for a more peaceful world, where the suffering of war is never forgotten.

Wolfgang Borchert's writings had a lasting impact on post-war German literature and the broader discourse on Peace and reconciliation. His emphasis on the human cost of war, the search for Peace, and the importance of empathy influenced subsequent generations of writers, artists, and intellectuals. Borchert's works continue to serve as a reminder of the enduring importance of Peace in a world marked by conflict and division.

Wolfgang Borchert's concept of Peace, as reflected in his literary works, transcends the mere absence of war. It is a profound yearning for solace, reconciliation, and understanding in the aftermath of conflict. Borchert's own experiences as a soldier, his empathy for those who suffered, and his powerful writings serve as a poignant reminder of the human capacity to seek Peace even in the darkest of times. His legacy endures as a testament to the enduring quest for Peace, healing, and hope in a world marked by the scars of war.

III. Exploring the Philosophy of Pacifism: A Path to Peace

52 Introduction to Pacifism

Pacifism, derived from the Latin word "*pax*" meaning Peace, is a philosophical and political stance that advocates for non-violence and the peaceful resolution of conflicts. Rooted in the belief that war and violence are inherently wrong, pacifism is a multifaceted point of view that has deep historical roots and continues to influence social, political, and ethical discourse today. In this chapter, we will explore the origins, key principles, and various forms of pacifism, as well as its contemporary relevance in an ever-changing world.

Origins of Pacifism

Pacifism is a philosophy that has ancient origins and has been espoused by various cultures and religions throughout history. Some of the earliest recorded instances of pacifist thought can be traced to ancient India, particularly in Jainism and Buddhism. These traditions emphasize non-violence, compassion, and the avoidance of harm to all living beings. Jainism, for instance, promotes the idea of "*Ahimsa*" (non-violence) as a foundational principle of Life.

Similarly, the teachings of Confucius in ancient China emphasized the importance of cultivating inner Peace and harmony as a means to achieve social and political stability without resorting to violence. In the West, figures like Socrates, who famously drank poison rather than escape from prison, and Jesus Christ, who preached Love, forgiveness, and turning the other cheek, have also contributed to the development of pacifist thought.

Key Principles of Pacifism

Pacifism is not a monolithic philosophy; rather, it encompasses a range of beliefs and principles. However, there are some common themes that unite pacifists:

1. Non-Violence: The central tenet of pacifism is the rejection of violence and the belief that it is never morally justifiable to harm or kill others, regardless of the circumstances.

2. Non-Aggression: Pacifists advocate for the avoidance of aggressive actions, whether they be personal, national, or international. This includes the renunciation of offensive wars and pre-emptive strikes.

3. Conflict Resolution: Pacifists emphasize the importance of peaceful means for resolving conflicts, such as diplomacy, negotiation, and non-violent resistance.

4. Human Dignity: A strong belief in the intrinsic value and dignity of all human beings underlies pacifism. This leads pacifists to reject any actions that harm or dehumanize individuals.

5. International Cooperation: Many pacifists support international organizations and treaties that promote cooperation and collective security, such as the United Nations, as alternatives to military conflicts.

Forms of Pacifism

There are various forms and degrees of pacifism, each with distinct nuances and interpretations. Some common forms of pacifism include:

1. Absolute Pacifism: This form of pacifism maintains an unwavering commitment to non-violence, rejecting violence under all circumstances. Absolute pacifists may be willing to endure personal suffering or harm rather than resort to violence.

2. Conditional Pacifism: Conditional pacifists are open to the idea of using force as a last resort, such as in cases of self-defence or protecting innocent lives. However, they maintain a strong preference for non-violent alternatives.

3. Pragmatic Pacifism: Pragmatic pacifists acknowledge that violence may be necessary in certain situations, such as in defence against aggression or to prevent grave injustices. However, they argue for the minimization of violence and the exhaustion of non-violent options before resorting to force.

4. Pacifist Activism: This form of pacifism involves actively working for Peace and non-violence, often through means like civil disobedience,

protests, and advocacy. Prominent figures like Mahatma Gandhi and Martin Luther King Jr. embodied pacifist activism.

Historical Context

Pacifism has a rich historical background that encompasses various religious, philosophical, and social movements. Some of the key moments and influences in the development of pacifist thought include:

1. Religious Influences: Many religions, including Christianity, Buddhism, and Jainism, have elements of pacifism in their teachings. For example, Jesus' Sermon on the Mount in the Christian tradition emphasizes turning the other cheek and loving one's enemies.

2. Tolstoy and Gandhi: Leo Tolstoy and Mahatma Gandhi were influential figures in the modern pacifist movement. Tolstoy's writings, such as "The Kingdom of God Is Within You," and Gandhi's philosophy of *Satyagraha* (truth-force) helped shape contemporary pacifist thought and practice.

3. Anti-War Movements: The 20th century witnessed significant pacifist movements, particularly during the two World Wars. Activists and conscientious objectors, driven by pacifist principles, refused military service and played a role in raising awareness about the devastating consequences of war.

Contemporary Relevance

Pacifism's relevance in the contemporary world cannot be overstated. In a global context marked by armed conflicts, terrorism, and military tensions, pacifist ideals continue to shape public discourse, social movements, and international relations.

1. Conflict Resolution: Pacifist principles are instrumental in mediating and resolving conflicts through diplomacy and dialogue. International organizations, such as the United Nations, often prioritize peaceful resolutions to disputes.

2. Human Rights and Social Justice: The pacifist tradition intersects with broader movements for human rights, social justice, and equality. It

underpins the non-violent protests and civil disobedience seen in the Civil Rights Movement, anti-war demonstrations, and various other social justice causes.

3. Anti-Nuclear and Disarmament Movements: The threat of nuclear warfare has led to the emergence of anti-nuclear and disarmament movements. These movements advocate for the elimination of nuclear weapons and are deeply influenced by pacifist ideals.

4. Environmental Concerns: Many environmental activists adopt pacifist principles in their advocacy, promoting non-violent means to address environmental protection problems.

5. Promoting Compassion and Empathy: Pacifism encourages individuals and societies to cultivate compassion, empathy, and non-violent communication, which can contribute to a more peaceful and harmonious world.

Challenges to Pacifism in the Modern World

While pacifism remains a powerful and compelling philosophy, it faces various challenges in today's complex and often conflict-ridden world:

1. Realpolitik and Geopolitical Conflicts: In the face of international conflicts and realpolitik considerations, pacifism can be criticized as idealistic and impractical. National security concerns sometimes override pacifist principles.

2. Terrorism and Non-State Actors: Dealing with terrorism and non-state actors who use violence poses a unique challenge to pacifism. Finding non-violent means to counter such threats can be difficult.

3. Ethical Dilemmas: In situations of moral ambiguity, individuals and governments may struggle to balance the ethical demands of pacifism with the imperative to protect innocent lives or prevent genocide.

4. Effectiveness: Critics argue that pacifist methods may not always be as effective as military force in achieving certain outcomes, such as stopping aggressive regimes.

Pacifism cannot be politically or pragmatically justified, and it cannot be morally mandated. Instead, it is the outcome of a religiously humanitarian conviction. " (Eugen Drewermann)

Conclusion

Pacifism is a multifaceted and evolving philosophy rooted in non-violence, compassion, and the pursuit of Peace. Its historical origins and contemporary relevance make it a powerful force for promoting human rights, resolving conflicts, and advancing social justice. While pacifism may face criticism and challenges in a world marked by violence and military conflicts, its principles continue to inspire individuals and movements dedicated to the pursuit of a more peaceful and just world. Whether in the realm of personal ethics or international diplomacy, pacifism serves as a valuable and enduring guide towards a more peaceful and harmonious world.

53   Jesus, the Pacifist

The words of Jesus, as recorded in the New Testament of the Christian Bible, have played a significant role in the establishment and promotion of pacifist principles. While not all interpretations of Jesus' teachings lead to pacifism, many argue that his words and actions advocate for non-violence and peaceful conflict resolution. The extent to which Jesus' words establish pacifism can vary based on one's interpretation and understanding of his teachings. Here are some key aspects of Jesus' words that have contributed to pacifist beliefs:

1. The Sermon on the Mount: In the Sermon on the Mount (found in the Gospel of Matthew, chapters 5-7), Jesus delivered some of his most famous teachings, including the Beatitudes and the commandment to "turn the other cheek" when someone strikes you. He also encouraged his followers to love their enemies, bless those who curse them, and pray for those who persecute them. These teachings are often seen as advocating non-resistance and a commitment to non-violence.

2. "Love Your Neighbour as Yourself": Jesus emphasized the importance of Love and compassion, teaching his followers to love their neighbours as themselves. This broad Love and compassion can be interpreted as extending to all people, even one's enemies, which supports the pacifist ideal of refusing to harm others.

3. "Those Who Live by the Sword, Die by the Sword": Jesus famously said, "All who draw the sword will die by the sword" (Matthew 26:52). This statement is often cited by pacifists as a condemnation of violence and a warning about the consequences of using force.

4. The Prince of Peace: In the book of Isaiah, there is a prophecy about a "Prince of Peace." Many Christians believe this prophecy is fulfilled in Jesus, and they see him as a symbol of Peace and reconciliation.

5. Early Christian Practices: In the early centuries of Christianity, many followers of Jesus were known for their commitment to pacifism. Early Christian writings, such as the "Didache" (Teaching of the Twelve Apostles), emphasized the rejection of violence and warfare.

In conclusion, the words and teachings of Jesus have strongly influenced the development of pacifism. Jesus' emphasis on Love, forgiveness, and non-violence continues to be a source of inspiration for those who advocate for peaceful conflict resolution and non-violent resistance to oppression.

Blessed are the people who know about their poverty and stand by it.

Blessed are those who weep, for their hearts will be pure.

Blessed are the defenceless, for only they will be able to make Peace.

Blessed are those who suffer persecution for the sake of right living before God.

Blessed are those who hunger and thirst for the right life.

54 Mahatma Gandhi about Jesus and His Teachings

Allow me to say that Jesus did not preach a new religion, but a new life.

Mahatma Gandhi often admired Jesus Christ for his message of non-violence and peace, particularly as portrayed in the Sermon on the Mount. Gandhi saw a deep alignment between Jesus' teachings and his own principles of non-violence (*Ahimsa*) and passive resistance (*Satyagraha*). He regarded Jesus as one of the greatest examples of non-violence to have ever lived and frequently drew parallels between Jesus' teachings and the ethical foundations of Hinduism concerning non-violence and compassion.

A famous quote from Gandhi about Jesus is: *"I like your Christ, I do not like your Christians. Your Christians are so unlike your Christ."* While this quote is often cited to illustrate Gandhi's view of Christianity and Christians, it highlights his admiration for Jesus and his teachings while simultaneously critiquing those who, in his opinion, do not live out Jesus' principles in their daily Lives.

Gandhi was critical of any form of religion, including Christianity, that preached or justified violence. He emphasized that true faith and true spirituality should manifest in the practice of non-violence and Love toward all living beings. For Gandhi, following Jesus was not defined by ritual practices or affiliation with a specific religion but by embodying the principles of Love, forgiveness, and non-violence in everyday Life.

Gandhi's relationship with Christianity was therefore complex. He deeply valued Jesus and his teachings but was critical of institutional churches and Christian missionaries, particularly when he felt their practices did not align with the message of love and non-violence that Jesus taught. Gandhi's engagement with Christianity was part of his broader commitment to interfaith dialogue and his belief that all religions contain truths that can contribute to the realization of Peace and non-violence.

55   The Essene Gospel of Peace

The Essene Gospel of Peace is a collection of ancient texts attributed to the Essene community, an ascetic Jewish sect that existed around the same time as the Second Temple period in Jerusalem. The texts describe their beliefs, practices, and a profound understanding of the concept of Peace. The Essene Gospel of Peace places a strong emphasis on inner Peace, harmony with nature, and the interconnectedness of all living beings.

In the midst of chaos, seek the calm within. Peace is not found in the external world but within your heart and soul. Embrace inner stillness and let it be your guide to harmony with all of creation.

One of the central themes in the Essene Gospel of Peace is the idea that true Peace begins within the individual. According to the Essenes, Peace is not merely the absence of conflict but a state of inner tranquillity and balance. They believed that physical health and spiritual well-being were closely linked, and that by maintaining a healthy body and mind, one could achieve a deeper sense of Peace. The Essene Gospel of Peace describes various dietary and lifestyle practices aimed at achieving and maintaining this inner Peace, including fasting, vegetarianism, and natural healing methods.

The Essenes also emphasize the importance of living in harmony with nature. They believed that the natural world held the key to spiritual enlightenment and inner Peace. The Essene Gospel of Peace encourages a deep connection with the natural world, including a reverence for the Earth, its elements, and the cycles of life. This connection to nature is seen as a pathway to Peace, as it helps individuals to better understand their place in the grand tapestry of existence.

Furthermore, the Essene Gospel of Peace promotes the idea of the interconnectedness of all living beings. This concept aligns with the broader theme of Peace as it underscores the importance of compassion, empathy, and non-violence toward all creatures. The Essenes advocated a vegetarian lifestyle, believing that the killing of animals for food disrupted the harmony of nature and was incompatible with their vision of Peace. They also preached the principle of "do unto others as you would have them do unto you," emphasizing the need to treat all living beings with kindness and respect.

The Essene Gospel of Peace also includes teachings on forgiveness and reconciliation. It underscores the idea that harbouring anger, resentment, or hatred disrupts an individual's inner Peace and creates external conflicts. To achieve true Peace, one must learn to forgive, let go of grudges, and seek reconciliation with others.

The Angel of Peace

The "Angel of Peace" is a concept frequently mentioned in the Essene Gospel of Peace, The Angel of Peace represents a spiritual guide or presence associated with inner Peace, healing, and harmony. The text contains teachings and practices for attaining physical and spiritual well-being, often with a focus on natural remedies and a holistic approach to health. While the concept of the Angel of Peace is central to the text, it doesn't refer to a specific individual but rather symbolizes a state of inner tranquillity and balance or a cosmic holy power to which one can connect through prayer or meditation to find inner and out Peace.

Seek *the Angel of Peace in everything that lives, in everything you do, in every word you speak. For Peace is the key to all knowledge, to every secret, to all life. Where there is no Peace, darkness prevails. And the sons of darkness desire most to steal the Peace of the children of light. Therefore, go in this night to the golden stream of light that is the garment of the Angel of Peace. And bring back in the morning the Peace of God, which surpasses understanding, is higher than all human reason, so that you may comfort the hearts of the sons of men.*

In summary, the Essene Gospel of Peace is a set of ancient texts that offers a unique perspective on the concept of Peace. It places a strong emphasis on inner Peace, harmony with nature, and the interconnectedness of all living beings. The Essenes believed that true Peace could only be achieved by first attaining a sense of inner tranquillity, and then extending that Peace to the external world through compassionate living. Their teachings continue to inspire those who seek a deeper understanding of Peace, both within themselves and in the broader context of human and environmental relations.

The hard-cover edition has illustrations in colour and a textile ribbon bookmark.
(ISBN 978-3739241692)

The budget paperback edition has illustrations in black and white only.
(ISBN 978-3741285820)

56 The Ethical Underpinnings of Pacifism in the Bhagavad Gita

The Bhagavad Gita, a sacred text within the Indian epic Mahabharata, is a profound philosophical and spiritual work that explores complex moral dilemmas, human nature, and the path to enlightenment. One of the most striking themes within the Bhagavad Gita is the concept of pacifism. Despite being set on the battlefield of Kurukshetra, where the great war is about to commence, the Gita delves deeply into the principles of non-violence, shedding light on the nuances of pacifism in a context fraught with conflict. This essay aims to elucidate the ethical underpinnings of pacifism in the Bhagavad Gita, emphasizing its significance as a guide to peaceful living.

Pacifism in the Bhagavad Gita

1. Arjuna's Moral Dilemma: At the outset of the Bhagavad Gita, Arjuna, the great warrior, is plagued by moral conflict. He is torn between his duty as a warrior (Kshatriya) and his revulsion at the prospect of killing his kinsmen, teachers, and friends. Arjuna's internal struggle reflects the human dilemma when facing violence and the ethical quandaries that emerge during times of war.

2. Dharma and Non-Violence: The concept of '*dharma*' (duty) is central to the Gita's discourse. Lord Krishna, Arjuna's charioteer and guide, urges him to perform his duty as a warrior, but not without addressing the imperative of non-violence (*Ahimsa*). This sets the stage for a nuanced exploration of pacifism in the context of fulfilling one's duty.

3. The Yoga of Self-Realization: Throughout the Gita, Krishna expounds on different paths (yogas) toward self-realization and spiritual awakening. The path of knowledge (*jnana yoga*), the path of devotion (bhakti yoga), and the path of meditation (*dhyana yoga*) are discussed. Each of these paths emphasizes inner Peace and the realization of the divine, fostering an atmosphere of non-violence.

4. Steadfastness in Devotion: Krishna encourages Arjuna to perform his duties with unwavering devotion to the divine. By emphasizing single-minded devotion, Krishna guides Arjuna toward a state of inner calm, which is essential for practising pacifism in the midst of conflict.

5. Transcending the Material World: The Bhagavad Gita teaches that transcending attachment to the material world is vital for achieving true inner Peace. This detachment, coupled with devotion to a higher power, is seen as the key to practising pacifism and responding to external events with equanimity.

Ethical Implications of Pacifism in the Bhagavad Gita

1. The Primacy of Non-Violence: The Bhagavad Gita underscores the importance of non-violence in human life. It encourages adherents to seek peaceful means of conflict resolution and to cultivate a mindset of compassion and understanding.

2. Conflict Resolution: The Gita guides individuals in resolving conflicts through dialogue, empathy, and non-violent means. The principles of non-violence can be extended beyond the battlefield to everyday life, encouraging peaceful coexistence.

3. Self-Realization and Peace: By promoting self-realization and spiritual growth, the Gita provides a framework for inner Peace. This inner Peace,

it suggests, is the foundation for external Peace and harmonious relationships with others.

4. Detachment and Equanimity: The practice of non-attachment and equanimity in the face of external circumstances is central to pacifism in the Bhagavad Gita. This allows individuals to respond to situations with calmness and without reactive violence.

The Bhagavad Gita, despite its setting on a battlefield, serves as a profound source of ethical guidance on pacifism. It presents a complex and nuanced perspective on the principles of non-violence, emphasizing the importance of duty, inner Peace, and devotion. While it recognizes that external conflicts may be unavoidable, it encourages individuals to navigate these challenges with a steadfast commitment to non-violence, empathy, and spiritual growth. In this way, the Bhagavad Gita offers a timeless and universal message about the ethical underpinnings of pacifism that extend far beyond the context of warfare, making it a valuable guide for leading a peaceful and harmonious life.

57   *Ahimsa –* The concept of Non-Violence in Hinduism

One who practices ahimsa shows respect and kindness to all living beings and practices non-violence in thought and deed.

Hinduism, one of the world's oldest religions, encompasses a rich tapestry of philosophical, cultural, and spiritual traditions. At its core lies the profound concept of *Ahimsa*, or non-violence. This philosophy, deeply rooted in Hindu scriptures and teachings, has played a pivotal role in shaping the ethical and moral framework of Hindu thought. This essay explores the philosophy of non-violence in Hinduism, tracing its origins, understanding its significance, and examining its impact on both personal conduct and societal harmony.

The roots of *Ahimsa* can be traced back to ancient Hindu scriptures, particularly the Vedas and Upanishads. The Rigveda, for instance, contains hymns that extol the virtues of non-violence and advocate harmony with all living beings. The concept gains further prominence in later texts such as the Mahabharata and the Bhagavad Gita, where it is intricately woven into the moral fabric of the epics.

At its essence, *Ahimsa* extends beyond mere physical non-violence; it encompasses a comprehensive commitment to harmlessness in thought, word, and deed. Adherents of *Ahimsa* strive to cultivate compassion and empathy, recognizing the interconnectedness of all life. The philosophy encourages individuals to approach conflicts with a mindset of dialogue, seeking resolutions that promote understanding rather than resorting to aggression.

While *Ahimsa* has ancient roots, its modern interpretation owes much to the teachings and practices of Mahatma Gandhi. Drawing inspiration from Hindu scriptures, particularly the Bhagavad Gita, Gandhi integrated the philosophy of non-violence into the Indian independence movement. His approach emphasized the power of truth and non-violence as potent instruments for social and political change.

Gandhi emphasized that *Ahimsa* relies on two essential pillars: truth (*Satyagraha*) and compassion. Without either of these components, *Ahimsa* cannot be realized in our lives. The presence of coercion, ego gratification, or a sense of separateness diminishes the essence of *Ahimsa*. Therefore, the true strength of *Ahimsa* emerges through profound self-awareness, the expression of active compassion, and the courage to acknowledge and learn from mistakes. Gandhi conveyed that, while achieving complete adherence to *Ahimsa* may be challenging, we should strive to comprehend its spirit and earnestly work towards making it a reality in our lives.

The philosophy of non-violence has transcended the boundaries of Hinduism and found resonance on the global stage. Scholars, activists, and leaders worldwide have embraced *Ahimsa* as a guiding principle for social justice, environmental sustainability, and conflict resolution. Its universal appeal lies in its recognition of the fundamental dignity of all living beings and the acknowledgment that violence begets more violence.

While *Ahimsa* represents a noble ideal, its practical application faces challenges in a world marked by crime, conflict and strife. Critics argue that absolute non-violence may not always be feasible in situations where self-defence or defence of others (e.g. by the police) is imperative. Additionally, interpretations of *Ahimsa* may vary, leading to debates about its practicality and relevance in certain contexts.

The philosophy of non-violence, deeply embedded in the tapestry of Hinduism, transcends religious and cultural boundaries. *Ahimsa*, with its emphasis on compassion, interconnectedness, and the pursuit of truth, continues to inspire individuals and movements worldwide. As humanity grapples with the complexities of the modern world, the enduring relevance of Ahimsa serves as a timeless reminder of the transformative power inherent in choosing non-violence as a way of life.

PEACE

It does not mean to be in a place where there is no noise, trouble or hard work.
It means to be in the midst of those things and still be calm in your heart, be
filled with peace and radiate peace and love to everything and everybody.

J<3

58 *Namasté*: An Ancient Greeting with Profound Relevance for Peace

"*Namasté*" is a widely recognized greeting and salutation in many South Asian countries, particularly in India and Nepal. The term, derived from Sanskrit, carries deep cultural and spiritual significance, and its understanding and practice have implications that extend beyond mere cultural exchange. *Namasté* is not just a word or gesture; it embodies a philosophy that is relevant to the pursuit of Peace in our interconnected world. To truly appreciate the concept of *Namasté* and its relevance for Peace, it is essential to explore its core elements, its cultural and spiritual origins, and its broader implications for human relationships and global harmony.

In fact, in its original cultural settings, Namasté is rather a gesture than a spoken word.

At its core, *Namasté* is a greeting that conveys deep respect, reverence, and humility. It is often translated as "I bow to you" or "The divine in me bows to the divine in you." The word is derived from two Sanskrit words: *namah*, which means "bow" or "obeisance," and *te*, which means "to you." *Namasté* is both a spoken word and a physical gesture in which one brings their palms together at chest level and bows their head slightly. The gesture is accompanied by the spoken word, which is used as a greeting, farewell, or sign of respect.

The practice of Namasté finds its roots in Hinduism, but it has transcended religious boundaries to become a widely accepted custom across many South Asian cultures. It reflects the fundamental Hindu belief that there is a divine spark or *atman* within every individual. When one says *Namasté* to another person, they are recognizing and honouring the divine essence within that person, irrespective of their background or beliefs. It signifies a profound acknowledgment of the interconnectedness of all beings.

The concept of *Namasté* holds significant relevance for Peace on various levels:

1. Respect for the Individual: *Namasté* encourages a fundamental respect for every human being. It promotes the idea that we are all interconnected and that each person deserves recognition and respect. This philosophy counters prejudice, discrimination, and dehumanization, which are often at the root of conflicts and violence.

2. Cultural Understanding: By recognizing and practising *Namasté*, individuals can deepen their understanding and appreciation of diverse cultures and beliefs. It serves as a bridge for cultural exchange and promotes tolerance and peaceful coexistence.

3. Inner Peace: *Namasté* underscores the importance of inner Peace and self-awareness. When individuals recognize the divine within themselves, they are more likely to cultivate a sense of personal harmony and equanimity. In this way, inner Peace can contribute to outer Peace.

4. Interconnectedness: The greeting reminds us of our interconnectedness with others and with the world around us. This recognition of shared humanity can foster empathy, compassion, and a sense of responsibility toward global issues, such as Peace, environmental protection problems, and social justice.

5. Conflict Resolution: *Namasté* emphasizes mutual respect and humility, which are crucial components of effective conflict resolution. When people come together with respect and open hearts, they are more likely to find peaceful solutions to their disputes.

In a world marked by division, conflict, and intolerance, the concept of *Namasté* serves as a powerful reminder of our shared humanity and interconnectedness. It offers a path toward Peace by promoting respect, understanding, and the acknowledgment of the divine spark within every individual. As individuals and societies embrace the principles embodied in *Namasté,* they contribute to the broader pursuit of Peace, not only in the context of interpersonal relationships but also in the global quest for harmony and unity.

The 1960s counterculture movement, often associated with the term "hippies," was a transformative cultural and social phenomenon that emerged as a response to the tumultuous events of the era, including the Vietnam War, civil rights struggles, and widespread societal upheaval. Central to the hippie culture was a profound understanding of Peace that rejected the prevailing norms of violence, consumerism, and conformity. The concept of Peace within the hippie movement was more than the mere absence of war; it represented a holistic vision of social, personal, and spiritual harmony.

At the heart of the hippie culture's understanding of Peace was a rejection of militarism and a desire for global disarmament. The movement emerged against the backdrop of the Vietnam War, which was deeply unpopular and resulted in widespread protests. Hippies were vocal advocates for Peace and non-violence, organizing anti-war rallies, demonstrations, and acts of civil disobedience. They believed that Peace could only be achieved when the destructive machinery of war and militarism was dismantled.

Hippies sought to create a society founded on Love, tolerance, and compassion. Their vision of Peace was deeply humanistic, emphasizing personal relationships and community building. They believed that by promoting Love and understanding among individuals, a broader culture of Peace and acceptance could be established. Many hippies adopted the phrase "Make Love, not war" as a mantra, underscoring their belief in the power of Love to overcome conflict.

The counterculture of the 1960s was characterized by a rejection of the materialism and consumerism that dominated American society. Hippies embraced a simple, communal lifestyle that eschewed the pursuit of wealth and status. Their understanding of Peace extended to a desire for economic and ecological sustainability. They advocated for a return to nature, emphasizing environmental conservation, sustainable living, and a rejection of the "rat race" that had come to symbolize modern society.

Spirituality and the search for higher consciousness were central to the hippie culture's understanding of Peace. Many embraced Eastern philosophies, meditation, and the use of mind-altering substances to expand their consciousness. They believed that achieving inner Peace and self-awareness was integral to creating a more peaceful world. This spiritual dimension of the Peace movement was exemplified by the famous Woodstock Festival of 1969, which celebrated music, Love, and unity in the context of peaceful protest.

The impact of the hippie culture's understanding of Peace was profound and continues to resonate in contemporary discussions about Peace, activism, and alternative lifestyles. Although the counterculture of the 1960s has been romanticized and criticized in equal measure, it played a significant role in influencing social and political change. The Peace movement of the era contributed to the withdrawal of U.S. forces from Vietnam and the development of a more critical and engaged citizenry.

In conclusion, the hippie culture of the 1960s offered a distinctive and holistic understanding of Peace that emphasized non-violence, Love, communal living, spirituality, and a rejection of consumerism. While it may have been viewed as a countercultural phenomenon in its time, the hippie vision of Peace continues to inspire those who seek a more compassionate, environmentally sustainable, and harmonious world. Their legacy reminds us of the power of idealism and the enduring relevance of the pursuit of Peace and Love.

60   The Peace Movement 1970s to 1980s

The Peace movements in the United States and Europe during the 1970s and 1980s were significant social and political phenomena that emerged in response to various global issues, with the overarching goal of promoting Peace and challenging the militarization of their respective societies. These movements were informed by distinct concepts of Peace and life, reflecting the specific historical, political, and social contexts of each region. To understand these Peace movements, it is essential to explore their key characteristics, goals, and underlying philosophies.

The Peace Movements in the United States

The Peace movement in the United States during the 1970s and 1980s was primarily a response to the Vietnam War and the escalating arms race of the Cold War. The concept of Peace in this context was deeply rooted in anti-war sentiments and opposition to the draft. It aimed to end American military involvement in Vietnam, prevent further military interventions, and curtail the nuclear arms race.

One of the most significant Peace movements during this era was the anti-Vietnam War movement. Activists, often young people, protested against the U.S. government's involvement in the war, citing its moral and political illegitimacy. These activists sought to bring American troops home, end the destruction in Southeast Asia, and promote diplomacy and negotiation over military action.

Additionally, the U.S. Peace movement of this period emphasized civil liberties, freedom of expression, and the right to protest. It was closely connected to broader social justice and civil rights movements, advocating for equality and justice for all citizens. Peace activists called for a redirection of resources from the military-industrial complex toward social programs and initiatives that would enhance the quality of life for all Americans.

The Peace Movements in Europe

In Europe, the Peace movements of the 1970s and 1980s had a slightly different focus. They were shaped by Cold War tensions, the presence of NATO and Warsaw Pact forces, and the deployment of nuclear weapons on European soil. The concept of Peace in Europe was closely associated with disarmament and the prevention of a nuclear conflict.

One of the most notable European Peace movements was the "Nuclear Freeze" movement. It called for a halt to the deployment of new nuclear weapons in Europe and sought to reduce the risk of a nuclear confrontation between the superpowers. Peace activists in Europe argued that a nuclear conflict would be catastrophic for the continent and its inhabitants.

These European Peace movements often had a transnational character, with activists and organizations from various countries collaborating to promote disarmament and peaceful coexistence. Demonstrations, rallies, and protests were common tactics used to raise awareness and demand policy changes. The Peace movements also emphasized the importance of dialogue and cooperation between East and West as a means to build trust and reduce tensions.

In Germany, the "*Friedensbewegung*", a loose interest group of many different initiatives, could gather up to one million people in a famous protest in Bonn against weapon upgrading by the Americans in Germany.

During the first American intervention in Iraq, protests in Germany were intense and included activities of civil disobedience. Germany did finally not join the American/NATO forces in that war.

Concepts of Peace and Life

In both the United States and Europe during the 1970s and 1980s, the concepts of Peace and life were rooted in opposition to the threat of nuclear war, the desire to prevent further military conflicts, and the quest for a better quality of life for citizens. Peace was seen as the absence of armed conflict and the presence of social justice, equal rights, and a commitment to diplomacy over military solutions.

Both movements emphasized the importance of individuals actively participating in political and social processes. They believed that ordinary citizens could influence government policies and bring about meaningful change. The Peace movements fostered a sense of empowerment and the idea that collective action could shape a more peaceful and just world.

In conclusion, the Peace movements in the United States and Europe during the 1970s and 1980s were characterized by their opposition to war, nuclear weapons, and militarization, as well as their dedication to social justice and civil rights. These movements reflect the power of citizen activism in shaping the political and social landscape and continue to serve as a reminder of the importance of working towards a more peaceful and just world.

61   Native American Vision of Peace

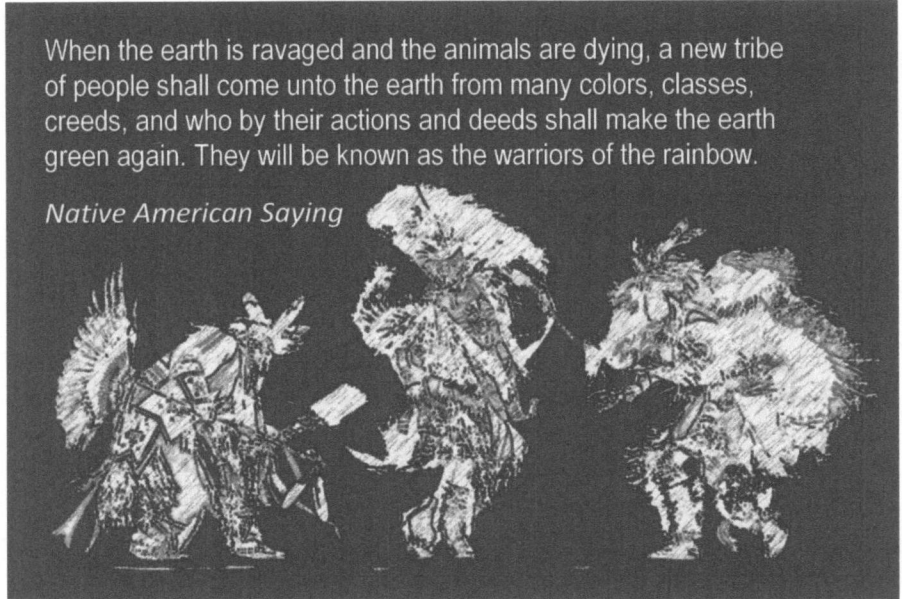

When the earth is ravaged and the animals are dying, a new tribe of people shall come unto the earth from many colors, classes, creeds, and who by their actions and deeds shall make the earth green again. They will be known as the warriors of the rainbow.

Native American Saying

Native American wisdom, often rooted in centuries-old traditions and deeply connected to the natural world, offers a unique and profound understanding of Peace. Native American cultures across the continent share common themes in their perspectives on Peace, emphasizing harmony, balance, interconnectedness, and respect for all living beings. To appreciate Native American wisdom's perspective on Peace, it is essential to explore the key elements of their philosophy, their rich cultural heritage, and the enduring impact of their teachings on the pursuit of Peace and environmental stewardship.

At the heart of Native American wisdom's understanding of Peace is the recognition of the interconnectedness between humans and the natural world. Many indigenous cultures view the Earth as a living being, and they believe that all living creatures, including humans, are part of a sacred and harmonious web of life. This recognition of interconnectedness underscores the importance of living in balance with nature, preserving ecosystems, and respecting the Earth as a source of Peace and sustenance.

The concept of the "circle of life" is a fundamental element of Native American wisdom. It symbolizes the cyclical nature of existence, where birth and death are interconnected parts of the same continuum. Understanding the circle of life informs the Native American perspective on Peace, as it underscores the need to live in harmony, showing respect for all life forms and maintaining balance within the circle.

Native American cultures place great value on ancestral knowledge and traditions. Elders are revered for their wisdom and teachings. This respect for the wisdom of past generations and the passing down of cultural heritage contribute to a sense of continuity and Peace within their communities.

Spirituality plays a central role in the understanding of Peace within Native American traditions. Ceremonial practices, which often involve prayer, song, and dance, are conducted to maintain spiritual and physical balance, seek guidance, and express gratitude. These ceremonies foster a sense of inner Peace, community unity, and a deep connection to the spiritual world.

Native American wisdom emphasizes the importance of equilibrium and harmony in all aspects of life. This includes relationships with others, the environment, and the self. The pursuit of Peace is seen as an ongoing journey of maintaining balance, resolving conflicts, and promoting harmony both within and beyond the community.

Native American cultures have a deep respect for the Earth and its resources. They understand that ecological harmony is integral to achieving Peace. Environmental stewardship, sustainable practices, and respect for the land and its inhabitants are essential elements of their philosophy.

Native American wisdom has had a lasting impact on individuals and movements dedicated to environmental conservation and the pursuit of Peace. Their reverence for nature and emphasis on interconnectedness continue to inspire a holistic approach to addressing local and global challenges.

62　The Concept of Peace in Buddhism

Peace is a fundamental and enduring aspiration of humanity, sought after throughout history in various forms and contexts. In Buddhism, a profound and ancient spiritual tradition, the concept of Peace holds a central place. Buddhism's approach to Peace is not merely the absence of conflict or war but encompasses a holistic, inner and outer Peace that resonates with individuals and extends to society and the world. This essay explores the profound concept of Peace in Buddhism, including its philosophical foundations, practices, and societal implications.

Buddhism, founded by Siddhartha Gautama, known as the Buddha, teaches that the path to Peace begins within the individual. The Four Noble Truths and the Noble Eightfold Path, central tenets of Buddhism, provide a framework for understanding and attaining Peace.

1. The Four Noble Truths

    • The First Noble Truth acknowledges that suffering (dukkha) is an inherent part of life.

- The Second Noble Truth identifies the origin of suffering in attachment and craving.

- The Third Noble Truth proclaims the possibility of ending suffering by achieving enlightenment.

- The Fourth Noble Truth prescribes the path to liberation from suffering.

2. The Noble Eightfold Path

- Right understanding, intention, speech, action, livelihood, effort, mindfulness, and concentration are the eight components of the path.

- These components guide individuals towards ethical conduct, mental development, and wisdom.

The foundation of Peace in Buddhism lies in recognizing the nature of suffering and the path to its cessation. Peace is, thus, not just the absence of conflict but the attainment of inner tranquillity and enlightenment.

Buddhism offers a multitude of practices designed to help individuals attain Peace:

1. Meditation: Meditation is a cornerstone of Buddhist practice. Through mindfulness and concentration, individuals cultivate inner Peace, clarity, and self-awareness. Vipassana and Zen meditation are examples of methods aimed at fostering inner tranquillity.

2. Compassion and Loving-Kindness: Buddhism encourages the development of compassion and loving-kindness towards all beings. The Metta Sutta, for instance, is a recitation that cultivates Love and goodwill for oneself and others.

3. Ethical Conduct: The practice of moral precepts (sila) fosters Peace by encouraging virtuous behaviour and reducing harm to others. The Five Precepts, which include refraining from killing, stealing, and lying, are central to this practice.

4. Non-Attachment: Buddhism teaches that attachment to desires and material possessions leads to suffering. By practising non-attachment, individuals can attain a state of Peace unburdened by cravings.

Buddhism's concept of Peace extends beyond individual attainment and influences societal dynamics. The principles of Buddhism promote social harmony, justice, and non-violence.

1. *Ahimsa* (Non-Harming): The principle of non-violence and non-harming, borrowed from Jainism, has influenced Buddhism significantly. It advocates non-violence in thought, word, and deed, emphasizing the avoidance of harm to all sentient beings.

2. Compassionate Action: Buddhism encourages individuals to engage in compassionate actions, not only for personal growth but also for the welfare of society. Engaging in acts of generosity, kindness, and social responsibility contributes to peaceful coexistence.

3. Conflict Resolution: Buddhist principles have influenced conflict resolution and reconciliation efforts in various societies. The Dalai Lama's advocacy for peaceful negotiations and reconciliation in Tibet exemplifies this aspect.

The concept of Peace in Buddhism goes far beyond a mere absence of conflict. It is rooted in a profound understanding of human suffering, the path to its cessation, and a commitment to ethical and compassionate living. Buddhism's emphasis on inner Peace, ethical conduct, and loving-kindness has far-reaching implications for the individual, society, and the world at large. By adopting these principles, individuals can find inner tranquillity, and societies can aspire to greater harmony and peaceful coexistence. Buddhism offers a timeless message that remains relevant and essential in the quest for lasting Peace.

63   The Philosophy of Non-Violence in Buddhism

Buddhism, founded by Siddhartha Gautama in the 6th century BCE, is a spiritual tradition that has profoundly influenced the philosophical and ethical landscape of Asia and beyond. Central to Buddhist teachings is the principle of *Ahimsa*, or non-violence, which forms a cornerstone of the religion's ethical framework and was adopted from the original religion of Hinduism. This essay explores the philosophy of non-violence in Buddhism, tracing its origins, understanding its significance, and examining its practical applications in personal and societal contexts.

The concept of *Ahimsa* in Buddhism finds its roots in the fundamental teachings of Siddhartha Gautama, commonly known as the Buddha. The first of the Five Precepts, ethical guidelines for Buddhist lay followers, is a commitment to abstain from harming living beings. The Buddha's emphasis on compassion, empathy, and the interconnectedness of all life laid the groundwork for the development of Ahimsa as a guiding ethical principle.

Buddhism extends the philosophy of non-violence through the concept of the Bodhisattva, an enlightened being who vows to attain Buddhahood for the benefit of all sentient beings. The Bodhisattva's path emphasizes the cultivation of compassion, altruism, and the rejection of harmful actions, embodying the spirit of non-violence in both thought and deed.

In Buddhism, *Ahimsa* extends beyond physical non-violence to encompass mental and verbal non-violence as well. Practitioners are encouraged to cultivate mindfulness, awareness, and right intention to avoid causing harm through their thoughts, speech, and actions. This holistic approach to Ahimsa reflects Buddhism's commitment to a compassionate and ethical way of life.

Buddhism recognizes the inevitability of conflict in human existence but advocates for non-violent resolutions. The practice of non-violence encourages individuals to address conflicts with understanding, dialogue, and reconciliation rather than resorting to aggression. This approach has implications for broader societal issues, promoting social justice, and the alleviation of suffering.

The philosophy of non-violence in Buddhism, encapsulated by the principle of Ahimsa, remains a vital and enduring aspect of the religion's ethical teachings. As individuals and societies grapple with the complexities of the modern world, Buddhism's emphasis on compassion, mindfulness, and the rejection of harm provides a timeless guide for fostering Peace, understanding, and well-being. Ahimsa stands as a testament to Buddhism's profound impact on shaping ethical consciousness and contributing to the quest for a more compassionate and harmonious world.

64   The Quaker Concept of Peace and Pacifism

The Quaker concept of Peace and pacifism is deeply rooted in the religious tradition of the Religious Society of Friends, commonly known as Quakers. Quakerism, which emerged in 17th-century England, is characterized by a commitment to non-violence, social justice, and a profound belief in the inner light of God within each individual. This essay explores the Quaker understanding of Peace and pacifism, tracing its historical development, its theological foundations, and its practical applications in the modern world.

The Quaker commitment to Peace and pacifism can be traced back to the founding figures of the movement, including George Fox and Margaret Fell. Early Quakers were deeply influenced by the turmoil and violence of their time, particularly the English Civil War, and they sought an alternative to the prevailing religious and political conflicts. The testimonies of non-violence and Peace emerged as a central aspect of Quaker faith.

The theological foundations of the Quaker tradition of non-violence are:

1. The Inner Light: Quakerism's core theological concept is the belief in the "Inner Light," an understanding that every individual possesses a direct connection to God. This concept underpins Quaker pacifism because it affirms the sanctity of life and the inherent worth of every person. Quakers believe that violence against another human being is a violation of the divine presence within them.

2. Testimonies: Quaker Peace and pacifism are part of a set of "testimonies" that guide Quaker life. These testimonies also include simplicity, equality, and truth. The Peace testimony asserts the rejection

of all forms of violence and a commitment to non-violent conflict resolution.

3. Advices and Queries: Quakers use Advices and Queries, a collection of spiritual guidelines and questions, to reflect on their actions. These texts often emphasize Peace and the avoidance of harm to others.

The practical applications are:

1. Conscientious Objection: Throughout history, Quakers have been known for their conscientious objection to military service. Quaker belief in non-violence has led many to refuse participation in wars, even in the face of persecution and imprisonment. Their unwavering commitment to Peace is a testament to their faith.

2. Peace Advocacy: Quakers have a long history of engaging in Peace advocacy and conflict resolution. Organizations like the American Friends Service Committee and Quaker Peace and Social Witness in the United Kingdom work to address issues such as disarmament, human rights, and social justice on a global scale.

3. Peaceful Activism: Quakers are actively involved in various social justice movements, such as the civil rights movement, the anti-war movement, and environmental activism. They use non-violent methods of protest and civil disobedience to advocate for change.

4. Mediation and Reconciliation: Quaker meetings often serve as spaces for mediation and reconciliation in conflicts, both within their community and in broader society. Their emphasis on listening, open dialogue, and the peaceful resolution of disputes aligns with their pacifist principles.

The Quaker concept of Peace and pacifism is a profound and enduring aspect of their faith. Rooted in the belief in the Inner Light, Quakers are guided by a commitment to non-violence, social justice, and the pursuit of Peace in a world often marked by conflict. Their historical legacy of conscientious objection and their contemporary efforts in Peace advocacy and activism continue to make a significant impact on the world, demonstrating the enduring relevance of their commitment to Peace and pacifism. Quakerism offers an inspiring example of how faith can guide individuals and communities towards a more peaceful and just world.

65 The Concept of Non-Violence in the Eyes of Psychology

The concept of non-violence, as viewed through the lens of psychology, delves into the intricacies of human behaviour, cognition, and emotional regulation. Psychology offers valuable insights into the factors influencing aggressive tendencies, the mechanisms behind conflict resolution, and the psychological underpinnings of non-violent approaches to conflict. This essay explores the psychological perspective on non-violence, examining its roots in human nature, its manifestations in behaviour, and its implications for individual and societal well-being.

Psychology acknowledges that aggression is a natural aspect of human behaviour, shaped by biological, environmental, and social factors. Evolutionary psychology suggests that aggression may have been adaptive in certain ancestral environments. However, the modern world calls for a nuanced understanding of aggression, recognizing that not all aggression is inherently harmful or maladaptive. On the other hand, we see a deep longing for Peace and non-violence as universal human thinking. Mythology and religion explain aggression as something that has arisen, caused by wrong, forbidden or malicious behaviour.

Non-violence, as a psychological concept, involves the cultivation of cognitive and emotional processes that inhibit aggressive impulses. Cognitive-behavioural theories posit that individuals interpret and appraise situations, and their interpretations influence emotional responses and subsequent behaviour. Non-violence requires individuals to develop cognitive strategies that promote empathy, perspective-taking, and the ability to find peaceful resolutions to conflicts.

Emotional regulation is central to the practice of non-violence. The ability to manage and express emotions constructively reduces the likelihood of resorting to aggressive behaviours. Psychologists emphasize the importance of teaching emotional intelligence skills, including self-awareness and social awareness, as integral components of non-violent behaviour.

Albert Bandura's social learning theory highlights the role of observational learning in the acquisition of behaviour. Individuals learn from observing others, and this includes learning both aggressive and non-violent responses to conflict. Psychologically, the promotion of non-violence involves modelling peaceful behaviours, providing positive reinforcement for non-aggressive actions, and fostering a social environment that encourages empathy and cooperation.

Psychological theories of conflict resolution emphasize the importance of communication, negotiation, and problem-solving skills in resolving interpersonal and societal conflicts. Non-violent conflict resolution involves teaching individuals to express their needs and concerns assertively, actively listen to others, and collaborate on mutually beneficial solutions. This approach aligns with the principles of non-violence by seeking peaceful resolutions without resorting to aggression.

Psychology recognizes the profound impact of trauma on an individual's propensity for violence. Individuals who have experienced trauma may struggle with emotional regulation and exhibit aggressive behaviours as a coping mechanism. The promotion of non-violence in psychological contexts involves addressing and healing trauma, providing mental health support, and teaching alternative coping mechanisms that do not involve aggression.

The application of non-violence at the societal level involves the implementation of psychological principles in education, conflict resolution programs, and social policies. Creating environments that nurture emotional intelligence, empathy, and non-violent communication contributes to the development of peaceful communities.

The psychological perspective on non-violence underscores the complex interplay of cognitive, emotional, and social factors in shaping human behaviour. By understanding the psychological mechanisms that influence aggression and conflict resolution, psychologists can contribute to the development of interventions and strategies that promote non-violent alternatives. Ultimately, the concept of non-violence in psychology aligns with the broader goal of fostering individual and societal well-being through the cultivation of empathy, emotional regulation, and constructive conflict resolution skills.

66   The Concept of Non-Violence in Jainism

Jainism, an ancient Indian religious tradition, is renowned for its profound commitment to the principle of non-violence, known as "*Ahimsa*," as in Hinduism and Buddhism. It can be said that Jainism seeks to perfect and realise *Ahimsa* to the extreme. Rooted in the teachings of revered spiritual leaders like Mahavira, Jainism emphasizes the cultivation of compassion and harmlessness towards all living beings.

Ahimsa, in Jain philosophy, extends beyond physical violence to encompass thoughts, words, and actions. Jains believe in the interconnectedness of all life and strive to minimize harm in every aspect of their existence. This principle has far-reaching implications, shaping not only individual conduct but also influencing social, economic, and political perspectives.

At its core, Jain non-violence advocates for the avoidance of intentional harm and the promotion of a peaceful coexistence with all sentient beings. This commitment to *Ahimsa* is reflected in the dietary choices of Jains, who often adopt vegetarian or vegan lifestyles to minimize their impact on other living entities. This dietary discipline is an outward manifestation of their inner commitment to non-violence.

Jain ascetics, known for their strict adherence to Ahimsa, take extraordinary measures to avoid causing harm. They may wear masks to prevent accidentally inhaling tiny organisms and sweep the ground before walking to avoid stepping on insects. These practices symbolize a deep respect for life in all its forms and serve as a powerful reminder of the importance of mindful living.

The ethical principle of *Ahimsa* extends to the realm of interpersonal relationships. Jains emphasize the importance of kind and truthful communication, promoting harmony and understanding. By practising non-violence in speech and conduct, individuals contribute to a more compassionate and cooperative society.

Jain teachings also emphasize the concept of "Anekantavada" or the doctrine of non-absolutism. This philosophy recognizes the complexity of truth and encourages individuals to consider multiple perspectives before forming judgments. By embracing the idea that truth is multifaceted and often beyond complete human comprehension, Jains foster tolerance and understanding, further reinforcing the spirit of non-violence.

The impact of Jain non-violence extends beyond personal and social spheres. It has influenced movements advocating for Peace and justice, inspiring individuals to seek non-violent solutions to conflicts. Mahatma Gandhi, a prominent figure in the Indian independence movement, drew inspiration from Jain principles of *Ahimsa* in his philosophy of non-violent resistance.

In conclusion, Jainism's concept of non-violence, *Ahimsa*, represents a profound and holistic approach to ethical living. From individual choices in diet and lifestyle to interpersonal relationships and societal structures, the principles of *Ahimsa* guide Jains in creating a world that values compassion, understanding, and harmony. Through its enduring influence, Jain non-violence continues to inspire individuals and movements dedicated to building a more peaceful and interconnected world.

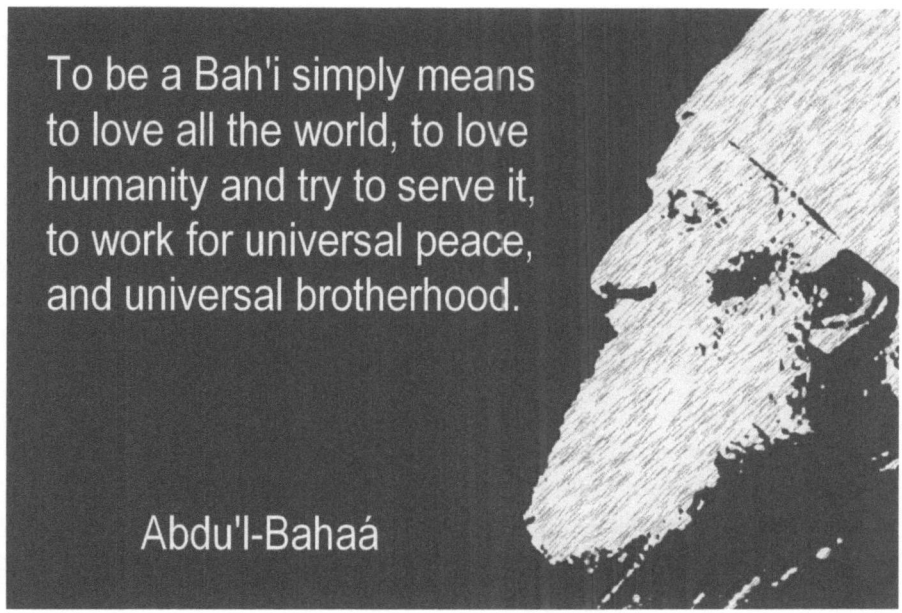

To be a Bah'i simply means to love all the world, to love humanity and try to serve it, to work for universal peace, and universal brotherhood.

Abdu'l-Bahaá

The Bahá'í Faith, a relatively modern but rapidly growing world religion, places a significant emphasis on the principle of non-violence as a fundamental tenet of its teachings. Rooted in the visionary insights of Bahá'u'lláh, the founder of the Bahá'í Faith, the concept of non-violence within this religious framework is intricately connected to the broader notions of unity, justice, and the oneness of humanity.

At the heart of Bahá'í teachings is the principle of the oneness of humanity. This foundational belief underscores the interconnectedness of all people, transcending differences of race, nationality, and creed. Non-violence, in the Bahá'í context, is seen as a natural outgrowth of recognizing this profound unity. Bahá'ís are encouraged to promote Peace and harmony, both in their personal lives and within the larger society.

Bahá'í scriptures explicitly advocate for the elimination of prejudice and the establishment of justice as essential components of building a peaceful world. The commitment to non-violence is not merely the absence of physical force but extends to the eradication of social, economic, and systemic injustices that can breed conflict and strife.

One key aspect of Bahá'í teachings on non-violence is the concept of "consultation." Bahá'u'lláh emphasized the importance of individuals coming together in a spirit of unity and mutual respect to consult and collaborate on matters affecting their community. This process of consultation seeks to transcend divisive power struggles and promote collective decision-making based on justice and the common good.

The Bahá'í Faith also places a strong emphasis on education as a means to promote understanding and eliminate ignorance, which are often precursors to conflict. By fostering knowledge and enlightenment, Bahá'ís believe that individuals can overcome prejudices and work towards the betterment of humanity.

Bahá'u'lláh's teachings advocate for the establishment of a world federal system to ensure lasting Peace. This global perspective on non-violence envisions a world where nations collaborate in the pursuit of common goals, and disputes are resolved through peaceful means rather than through the use of force. The Bahá'í community, although not involved in partisan politics, actively supports initiatives that align with the principles of justice, equality, and Peace.

In practice, Bahá'ís around the world strive to embody the principle of non-violence in their daily lives. Whether facing personal challenges or engaging in community-building activities, adherents of the Bahá'í Faith seek to promote understanding, foster unity, and contribute to the betterment of society.

The *well-being of mankind, its Peace and security, are unattainable unless and until its unity is firmly established. (Bahá'u'lláh)*

In conclusion, the concept of non-violence within the Bahá'í Faith is deeply intertwined with its core principles of the oneness of humanity, justice, and unity. By advocating for the elimination of prejudice, the establishment of justice, and the promotion of global collaboration, the Bahá'í Faith offers a vision of a world where non-violence is not just an ideal but a guiding principle for individuals and societies alike.

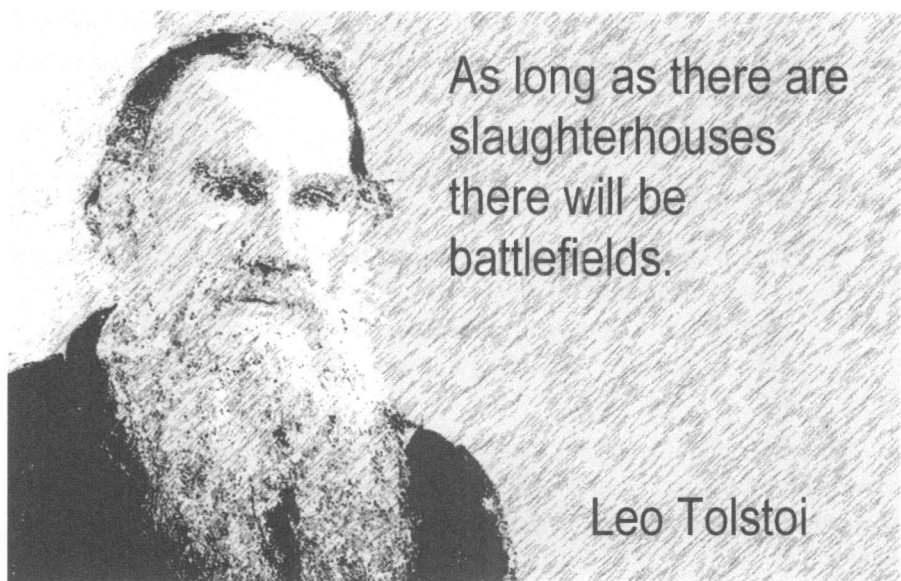

As long as there are slaughterhouses there will be battlefields.

Leo Tolstoi

The relationship between vegetarianism and war has been explored by various philosophers and authors from different perspectives. One notable connection is often drawn between the consumption of animal products and the ethical considerations surrounding violence, war, and human behaviour. Some key points include:

1. Non-Violence and Compassion: Philosophers like Mahatma Gandhi emphasized non-violence (*Ahimsa*) and compassion towards all living beings. Vegetarianism, for Gandhi, was a way to extend this principle to one's diet and lifestyle.

2. Ethics and Morality: Some philosophers argue that the choice to avoid meat is linked to broader ethical considerations. They posit that a society that values life and avoids unnecessary harm to animals might be more inclined to promote peaceful resolutions to conflicts.

3. Spiritual and Moral Development: Certain philosophical and religious traditions associate vegetarianism with spiritual and moral development.

The idea is that a diet free from violence (in the form of killing animals for food) can contribute to a more peaceful and harmonious society.

4. Resource Allocation and Global Conflict: Authors and environmentalists have explored the link between meat consumption, resource allocation, and global conflict. The argument suggests that the resources used in meat production, such as land and water, could be redirected to address issues like hunger and poverty, potentially reducing the root causes of some conflicts.

5. Cultural and Societal Reflections: Some authors examine the cultural and societal implications of dietary choices. They argue that a shift towards vegetarianism could signify a broader shift in human consciousness and values, potentially influencing the way societies approach conflicts and war.

Different cultural, religious, and ethical frameworks contribute to diverse viewpoints on this issue. Additionally, while some argue for a direct link between diet and behaviour, others may view the relationship as more complex and indirect.

Here are a few notable figures, who have explored the link between meat consumption and war:

> *Out* of one hundred educated and sensitive people, ninety would probably never eat meat again if they had to kill or stab the animal they were eating. (Bertha von Suttner)

Leo Tolstoy

Leo Tolstoy believed killing and eating animals is against the human heart. He was a proponent of vegetarianism and believed that abstaining from meat consumption was linked to non-violence. He argued that violence against animals in the form of meat consumption contributed to a culture of violence that extended to human conflict. Tolstoy was a devote Christian and believed that all living sentient beings had spirits, souls, felt emotions and suffered, and that because of these humans did not have the right to kill or harm animal beings. He said, eating flesh is "simply immoral as it involves the performance of an act which is contrary to any moral feeling – killing; and is called forth only by greed and the desire for tasty food."

> *A* *man can live and be healthy without killing animals for food therefore, if he eats meat, he participates in taking animal life merely for the sake of his appetite. (Leo Tolstoy)*

George Bernard Shaw

George Bernard Shaw, the Irish playwright and critic, was a vegetarian and advocate for the ethical treatment of animals. He connected meat consumption with societal violence and expressed his views on vegetarianism in various writings.

Shaw approached the dietary choice not merely as a matter of personal preference but as an ethical imperative rooted in compassion. He argued that the act of consuming meat involved the unnecessary infliction of pain and suffering upon animals, emphasizing the moral responsibility of individuals to consider the consequences of their dietary choices. Shaw believed that a vegetarian lifestyle reflected a commitment to non-violence and the recognition of the interconnectedness of all living beings.

> *We* *are the living graves of murdered beasts, slaughtered to satisfy our appetites. We never pause to wonder at our fests, if animals, like men, can possibly have rights. We pray on Sundays that we may have light, to guide our footsteps on the path we tread. We're sick of war, we do not want to fight – the thought of it now fills our hearts with dread, and yet – we gorge ourselves upon the deal.*

Shaw drew a conceptual link between vegetarianism and the broader issue of war. He contended that a society's ethical framework, as manifested in its treatment of animals, had implications for its approach to human conflict. According to Shaw, a culture that sanctioned the violence inherent in the slaughter of animals for food might be predisposed to accept or engage in broader acts of violence, including war.

In Shaw's eyes, the violence associated with meat consumption contributed to a desensitization to suffering, fostering a mindset that could extend beyond the treatment of animals to human interactions. By adopting a vegetarian lifestyle, individuals could align themselves with a philosophy of compassion and non-aggression, potentially contributing to a societal ethos that valued peaceful coexistence.

Shaw's exploration of vegetarianism extended beyond his personal choices into his literary works. In plays like "Man and Superman" and "Pygmalion," he embedded characters and dialogues that reflected his vegetarian ideals. Through his characters, Shaw conveyed the ethical dilemmas surrounding meat consumption and portrayed vegetarianism as a conscious choice aligned with moral principles.

John Robbins

John Robbins, an American author and environmentalist, has been a prominent voice in advocating for vegetarianism, not only for personal health reasons but also for the profound ethical and environmental implications it carries. Central to Robbins' perspective is the belief that adopting a vegetarian lifestyle is not only a matter of individual choice but a collective responsibility with far-reaching consequences for societal well-being and global harmony.

Robbins' journey into vegetarianism was inspired by ethical considerations. His seminal work, "Diet for a New America," delves into the ethical and moral implications of food choices, particularly the impact of meat consumption on animal welfare. Robbins argues that the industrialized production of meat involves immense cruelty to animals, contributing to a culture of desensitization to violence. For Robbins, choosing a vegetarian lifestyle is a conscious decision to align personal choices with compassion, reflecting an ethical stance that extends beyond the individual to the broader society.

Beyond ethics, Robbins emphasizes the environmental toll of meat production as a key motivation for embracing vegetarianism. He highlights the inefficiency of the meat industry in terms of resource allocation, pointing to the vast amounts of land, water, and energy required to sustain livestock compared to plant-based agriculture. Robbins contends that a shift towards plant-based diets could alleviate the strain on global resources, potentially reducing the root causes of conflict related to resource scarcity.

In addition to animal welfare and environmental concerns, Robbins underscores the impact of dietary choices on global health and social justice. He argues that a diet centred on plant-based foods can contribute to better health outcomes, reducing the burden on healthcare systems and fostering a more equitable distribution of resources. Robbins suggests that a healthier, more equitable society is less prone to internal strife, addressing some of the socioeconomic factors that can lead to conflict and war.

Robbins sees vegetarianism as a means to cultivate a culture of compassion and interconnectedness. By choosing foods that are not linked to the suffering of animals, individuals can contribute to a broader societal shift in values. Robbins contends that a society grounded in compassion is more likely to prioritize diplomatic solutions to conflicts, viewing violence as a last resort rather than a default option.

Erich Fromm

Fromm's humanistic philosophy emphasized the importance of cultivating positive human qualities and fostering a deep sense of interconnectedness. While not explicitly a vegetarian himself, Fromm expressed concern about the ethical implications of meat consumption. He argued that the act of killing animals for food, when unnecessary for survival, could desensitize individuals to the value of life and contribute to a culture that tolerates violence.

Fromm believed that embracing a vegetarian lifestyle was rooted in an ethical commitment to non-violence and compassion. By choosing a diet that abstains from the unnecessary killing of animals, individuals could align themselves with a broader philosophy of respect for life, creating a foundation for societal values that prioritize Peace over violence.

Fromm's exploration of the psychological dimensions of human behaviour led him to consider how dietary choices might influence individual and collective psyches. He suggested that the violence inherent in meat consumption could contribute to a mindset that accepts aggression as a normal part of life. By contrast, a vegetarian diet, according to Fromm, could encourage a more empathetic and compassionate world-view, fostering qualities conducive to peaceful coexistence.

Beyond personal ethics, Fromm's humanistic vision extended to considerations of global harmony and social responsibility. He argued that a shift toward vegetarianism could have positive effects on the world at large by addressing issues such as resource allocation, environmental sustainability, and the alleviation of world hunger. Fromm believed that a society committed to ethical dietary choices would be more likely to prioritize social justice and global cooperation, mitigating the conditions that could lead to conflict and war.

Fromm's perspective on vegetarianism was not merely about individual dietary habits but also about cultural transformation. He envisioned a society in which ethical considerations permeate all aspects of life, including food choices. By consciously choosing a diet that reflects values of compassion and non-violence, individuals contribute to a cultural shift that prioritizes the well-being of all living beings, laying the groundwork for a more harmonious and Peace-oriented world.

Mahatma Gandhi

Gandhi saw a clear link between the violence inflicted on animals for food and the potential for violence in human conflicts. Gandhi himself adopted a vegetarian lifestyle as part of his commitment to non-violence.

These are just a few authors and thinkers who recognized a connection of meat eating and a tendency to aggressive behaviour. More thoughts should be given on this subject, and more research needs to be done.

69 Desertion and Whistleblowing: The Power to Disobey

Imagine there is a war and nobody goes to fight.

PEACE

War, with its profound impact on individuals and societies, has often been met with resistance from those who question its morality, legality, and human cost. Among the dissenters are deserters and whistleblowers, individuals who, for various reasons, choose to defy the established norms and speak out against the machinery of war.

Chelsea Manning

Former U.S. Army intelligence analyst Chelsea Manning gained international attention in 2010 when she leaked classified documents to WikiLeaks. Manning's revelations exposed government secrets, including the collateral murder video, diplomatic cables, and military logs from the Iraq and Afghanistan wars. Manning's actions were driven by a desire to bring transparency to the consequences of war and shed light on potential war crimes.

Daniel Ellsberg

Renowned for his role in the Pentagon Papers case during the Vietnam War, Daniel Ellsberg was a military analyst who leaked a top-secret Department of Defense study revealing the U.S. government's misleading public statements about the war. Ellsberg's courageous act challenged the narrative of the war and played a pivotal role in shaping public opinion.

Hugh Thompson Jr.

During the My Lai Massacre in Vietnam, helicopter pilot Hugh Thompson Jr. intervened to save civilians from being killed by U.S. soldiers. Thompson's courageous actions went against the orders of his superiors and showcased the moral dilemmas faced by individuals caught in the midst of war atrocities.

Ehren Watada

U.S. Army officer Ehren Watada became a prominent war resistor during the Iraq War by refusing to deploy to Iraq, citing moral and legal objections to the conflict. Watada's stand against the war underscored the internal conflicts faced by military personnel when asked to participate in actions they find ethically questionable.

Thomas Young

A paralysed Iraq War veteran, Thomas Young became a vocal anti-war activist, speaking out against the Iraq War's legitimacy and the human toll it exacted. Young's journey from a soldier in the war to a passionate advocate for Peace highlighted the personal transformations that war can catalyse.

Ron Ridenhour

After learning about the My Lai Massacre, Ron Ridenhour, a former soldier who had served in Vietnam, played a crucial role in exposing the atrocity. Ridenhour's decision to speak out against the massacre contributed to the public's understanding of the harsh realities of war and the importance of accountability.

Camilo Mejia

An infantryman in the Iraq War, Camilo Mejia became one of the first U.S. soldiers to publicly denounce the war. Mejia's decision to go AWOL and speak out against the war stemmed from his experiences witnessing human rights abuses and the impact of war on both Iraqis and American soldiers.

Joshua Key

U.S. Army Conscientious Objector Joshua Key refused to participate in the Iraq War and sought asylum in Canada. Key's story reflects the struggles faced by those whose moral convictions clash with their military obligations, emphasizing the human cost of war on the individuals who serve.

Refuseniks in Israel

The term "*refuseniks*" refers to Israeli military personnel who have refused to serve in the occupied territories or engage in actions they deem morally objectionable. These individuals challenge the prevailing narrative and raise questions about the ethical implications of military actions, contributing to internal debates within Israeli society.

Julian Assange

Julian Assange, the founder of WikiLeaks, is a prominent figure in the realm of whistleblowers and activists against government secrecy and war. While Assange himself did not serve in the military, his contributions to exposing classified information have had a significant impact on public awareness and discussions surrounding war, diplomacy, and government actions.

Assange gained international attention through the publication of classified documents provided by whistleblowers, most notably Chelsea Manning. The releases included the "Collateral Murder" video, which depicted a U.S. Apache helicopter attack in Baghdad that resulted in the deaths of civilians, including two Reuters journalists. The WikiLeaks publications also included the Iraq and Afghanistan war logs and U.S. diplomatic cables, providing unprecedented insights into the conduct of wars and international relations.

If wars can be started by lies,
they can be stopped by truth.

Julian Assange

Assange's motivations are rooted in a belief in transparency, accountability, and the right of the public to be informed about government actions. He sees WikiLeaks as a platform for whistleblowers to reveal information that challenges official narratives and holds governments and powerful entities accountable for their actions.

Without conviction or the right of defence, Julian Assange was tortured by the American secret service in the UK and ultimately illegally imprisoned.

Desmond Doss

A conscientious objector during World War II, Doss served as a combat medic and became the first conscientious objector to receive the Medal of Honour for his heroism on the battlefield. Doss, a Seventh-day Adventist, refused to carry a weapon but insisted on serving as a medic to save lives.

Florian Pfaff

As a major in the German army, he refused to obey orders in the Iraq war, which violated international law.

Felix Hall

An African American soldier in the U.S. Army during World War I, Hall was executed for mutiny in 1918. His case highlighted racial tensions within the military and the challenges faced by African American soldiers during the war.

Percy Toplis

A British soldier during World War I, Toplis became known for his involvement in mutinies and desertion. He resisted military discipline and was eventually shot by a military police officer in 1920 during an attempt to apprehend him.

Sometimes you have to pay a heavy price to live in a free society.
(Chelsea Manning)

Conclusion

Deserters and whistleblowers against war play a crucial role in challenging the status quo and prompting reflection on the morality and consequences of armed conflicts. These individuals, driven by a sense of duty, morality, or a desire for truth, have left an indelible mark on history by forcing societies to confront the harsh realities of war. As their stories unfold, it becomes evident that the voices of dissent are essential in fostering accountability, promoting transparency, and ultimately contributing to a more just and peaceful world.

There are probably countless deserters in every war who refuse to fight because of their religious convictions or their conscience, and accept harsh punishments or even death for doing so. They are the true heroes of all wars.

In many countries, people are still forced to do military service. Those who refuse to serve out of conviction or conscience must expect harsh punishments and consequences. This approach is contrary to human rights and must finally stop.

In most cases, however, desertion is a taboo subject, the mere mention of which is considered and punished as draft evasion.

IV Jay B Joyful:
Speeches, Lectures, Scripts

70   About Peace

Dr. Jörg Berchem, alias Jay B Joyful in: " *Meditationen der Kinder des Lichts*"

ISBN 978-3741285745

Peace is a universal principle. Universal Peace is an expression of cosmic harmony. Harmony in cosmic laws calls for Peace. The universally intuitive desire for Peace is an expression of cosmic laws. Peace develops from within to the outside. One of the great recurring mistakes of humans is wanting to develop Peace from the outside in. By imposing Peace externally, one believes to create Peace internally. External Peace becomes a precondition. However, Peace is unconditional, like Love. When we find Peace within ourselves, and only there can we find it, then Peace externally becomes a necessary consequence. Peace with oneself and the entire universe is the only Peace that the One Law recognizes. Love and Peace are the highest achievements of which humans are capable. They are the greatest treasures of humanity. They are feelings, but where else can humans find feelings if not within themselves? Without recognizing the meaning of Peace and developing it in their consciousness, filling their entire being with it, expressing it in their thoughts, actions, and feelings, humans are not capable of spiritual evolution. Without Peace, human life is meaningless. The creative work of Peace begins in each individual. It is the great duty of humans to create Peace within themselves and in their surroundings. Through communion with the Angel of Peace, we let Peace happen and act, sending this feeling and its energy into all our relationships, our environment, to all fellow creatures, the past, present, and future, and into the entire universe. The expression of this manifestation is the deep wish and blessing in the greeting, "Peace be with you."

71   Tolerance Is an Ugly Word

‖ *Tolerance*   *is an ugly word (Osho)*

These words from Osho, like many of his thoughts, carry deep wisdom and truth. Most people today believe that tolerance is an important and good value in a modern democratic society. They think it is therefore necessary to create rules and laws to enforce and establish tolerance.

A look at the etymology of the word already hints that tolerance is not as great as it is often portrayed. The Latin word *"tolerare"* means "to endure," "to bear," "to tolerate," and this already sounds far less positive and pleasant – much less like the idea of a "colourful, multicultural, and gender-flexible society where everyone is happy together and with each other."

Osho said that the one who tolerates merely humbles the one being tolerated through their tolerance. By tolerating, they imply that they are higher, holier, more understanding than the one being tolerated. The tolerant person graciously endures the tolerated person in their otherness, thereby manifesting that person's dependency on the goodwill of others, while their otherness is made visible and fixed for all to see.

It is important that people meet each other on an equal level, and this requires not tolerance, but acceptance. Every person has a natural right to be themselves. This right does not stem from tolerance; it is inherent and proven simply by the mere existence of every individual. The fact that someone is born as they are and exists as they are is evidence of the natural right to acceptance: The universe, God, the natural order have already accepted every person as they are, from the very first moment. Tolerance, however, tries to place those being tolerated under a supposed protection that they do not need if their natural right to acceptance were respected.

Tolerance labels, categorizes, and separates. Acceptance, on the other hand, requires no labels and makes no distinctions. Acceptance unites, and its guiding principle is "We are one, but we are not the same" (loosely paraphrased from the band U2). Acceptance knows no "BIPOC" ("Black," "Indigenous," and "People of Colour") and no "White" (Are "Asians" considered "White," or are they simply ignored by the tolerant woke?). Acceptance knows only people.

Acceptance does not need "cancel culture" (the culture of silencing and suppressing the unpopular) or ministries of truth. Acceptance does not ban political parties or dismiss people based on their nationality or ideology. Acceptance makes no distinctions between "woke" (supposedly meaning "awakened") and "anti-woke."

Acceptance simply accepts. You are who you are, and you are allowed to be. And I am who I am, and I am allowed to be. And because I accept you as you are, and you accept me as I am, we can communicate with each other. This also includes questioning and criticizing each other, sometimes arguing and reconciling. Acceptance enables discourse, openness, and dialogue. Always and with everyone.

Tolerance, in the end, is a form of devaluation and ignorance: One endures what the other does or is. But one can only endure something that is inherently considered wrong, harmful, and undesirable – as "different," "deviant," or, at best, "special." The natural right to acceptance is ignored and replaced by a right to tolerance granted by the grace of the "normal" and the "noble tolerant."

Acceptance requires no quotas, special rules, or prescribed language policies. Acceptance does not need safe spaces, and certainly not distinctions based on skin colour or origin. Tolerance reveals itself in the present as neo-racism, where special rules, closed groups, and exclusive time slots in museums are created for people with different skin tones or gender identities. The being of these people is presented as a disability or special vulnerability, rather than as a strength or "normality." Whoever favours or gives special treatment to people because of their being – e.g., granting them a job or a seat in parliament on this basis alone – is acting in a highly racist or discriminatory way. Whoever seeks to protect people from criticism or allows them to stand out or blend into the crowd solely because of their skin colour acts in a racist way. Whoever protects people from criticism simply because they belong to a particular religion acts in an exclusionary and condescending manner. Whoever protects people from criticism or social equality because they express a particular gender identity or practice certain forms of eros and sexuality acts in the highest degree discriminatory.

Marginalized groups have not fought for equality for centuries or decades only to now be segregated, given special treatment, and labelled again by people who call themselves "awakened" (woke). Equality also means not being handled with kid gloves but facing criticism, discussion, and responsibility. A biological man who identifies as a woman must also face the discussion of why he thinks in "woman vs. man" categories while denying their existence and reducing women to makeup and so-called feminine clothing. Those who think gendering makes the world a better place must also be open to the argument that there is a difference between grammatical categories and natural genders. Those who fail to recognize the distinction between biological sex and gender identity, and conflate this with sexual orientation, must face scientific arguments against it and questions about their reasoning. Those who believe "white people" should not "steal culture" and must forgo alleged cultural assets of "coloured cultures" must also face accusations of racism and the question of why "people of colour" should not likewise forgo "white cultural assets" (like cars, electricity, suits, etc.). Assigning blame to today's "white old men" for negative developments and episodes in world history also requires recognizing their positive contributions and the excellent achievements of numerous "white old men" in the past and present, while also acknowledging negative episodes involving "people of colour," such as Arab and African slave trade, African child soldiers, religiously motivated mutilations, and more. It is evident that this path leads to a mentality of mutual blame and devaluation; therefore, it is fundamentally wrong. And in its one-sidedness, it must be rejected, as it could be used to justify racism, discrimination, oppression, and genocide, as has repeatedly occurred in the past.

It is perhaps telling that the German and English languages have an adjective for "tolerant," but none for "acceptant." We have to rely on the participle "accepting," which describes an ongoing action but not a character trait. Thus, there are tolerant people, but no "acceptant" people. This is a dilemma.

Acceptance is nourished by the knowledge that all people are as they are, that they face the same opportunities and challenges, and may grow or fail as a result. Acceptance is nourished by the certainty that all people, truly all, are equal in their rights, dignity, and freedom, and are only responsible for what they, as individuals, have caused.

A society that conveys acceptance rather than tolerance as a value does not label, categorize, or place people into boxes. It does not think in terms of guilt, shame, ideology, and dogma. An "accepting society" is one carried by compassion, Love, and Peace.

72   Resilience, where do we get it from?

Speech given by Dr. Jörg Berchem, alias Jay B Joyful, during protests against the restrictions of fundamental rights and state violence during the so-called „Corona Pandemic" in August 2020

The Japanese poet Rionusuki Akutagawa, in his "Tales Under the Rain Moon," has a monk say, "Worse than a conflagration, an earthquake, or war is when one person can no longer believe another."

What he means is that when lying becomes the "new normal," violence rules. In Schopenhauer's sense, violence is any act of injustice.

The best solution to conflicts is not to feel attacked. That is so important; I must repeat it: The best solution to conflicts is not to feel attacked.

But how can we achieve that?

A very powerful is re-framing. This is not neglecting or looking away. It is rather finding another name to better understand, to look behind the image we have.

Let us make an exercise: Spontaneous Differentiation [...]

The Defamation is in reality nothing else than ignorance and primitive thinking. [...]

The Attacks of the Unmasked are reality nothing else than attack of one's own doubts. [...]

So once again: The best solution to conflicts is not to feel attacked. Even if I am attacked, I don't have to feel attacked.

Protection from Transfer: The fear of those wearing masks is supposed to be transferred to the fearless, who are supposed to ensure that the fearful do not fear. Here, things are turned upside down by completely baseless statements, such as masking protects others, not oneself. But if someone has a terrible fear of contagion, they can wear a thick activated charcoal mask, a so-called visor on top of it, constantly sanitize their hands, wear gloves, and stay at home if they want. A very sinister game is being played here, and there are no scruples about imposing it even on children and telling them they are responsible for the health of their parents and grandparents. This is child abuse; children are being emotionally harmed to achieve political goals.

Entire concepts and levels of meaning are redefined. Solidarity used to mean giving up your seat on the bus for an old lady. Now, it is suddenly considered solidarity to throw an elderly lady with impaired lung function out of the bus! Conformity is called solidarity, and genuine solidarity with the weaker ones is penalized with fines.

A world in which you are always vulnerable, an environment in which you can never be sure whether your behaviour will be rewarded or punished, is a situation of torture. It is a torture method to unsettle people in such a way and turn their world upside down so that it lacks all logic and reliability. Such a torture method is used to break the will, turn off independent thinking, and turn a person into an arbitrary recipient of orders.

But how can one survive and stay healthy in a world that offers no stability, where one can be attacked at any time, where injustice is defined as right and lies as truth?

On the physical level, it is the immune system, which we call resilience. It is actually a very unpleasant word that comes from combat medicine. There is something in the body that resists apparent external attacks. In the sense of Hildegard von Bingen, I would rather speak of *Viriditas*, the Life Force and Healing Power. We all know that there is something like that, and we have felt it in our lives, because we have all been physically ill at some point and have recovered, be it just a cold or a wound.

But what about our psyche? Is there something like wound healing and an immune system there, too? Something that helps us cope with attacks and heal or stay healthy?

We are all currently exposed to powerful attacks on our psyche: fear of illness or fear of fascism, fear of a pandemic or fear of a dangerous vaccination, fear of unemployment and fear of losing freedom, fear of change and fear of the loss of friendships and social bonds. Why does all of this affect us so much now? Think about the situation in the Congo, Yemen, Syria, Somalia... refugees... or a people in the rainforest whose livelihood is being cut down, forcibly resettled, and forcibly impoverished... The list could go on... The immune system is of little help to people in such situations. But there is something similar for the psyche, which is called "resilience." And when we compare what we are suffering from right now to the attacks on the human psyche in the countries mentioned earlier, we might be alarmed: We are making a fuss about wearing masks on the bus and because there is no "Summerjam [Festival]", or because friends no longer want to have anything to do with us because we have a different opinion about the Corona measures than they do... So I wonder, how much resilience we actually have. And this resilience is not only important for personal well-being and health, but also for our movement, for our resistance, and for urgently needed actions of civil disobedience.

Just as a child's immune system is trained through natural nutrition, exercise, fresh air, and contact with so-called pathogens and provides a foundation that can be determining for the rest of their life, so it is with resilience. Its foundation is primal trust and primal Love in early childhood development, which also give rise to self-Love and self-compassion, important resources that are constantly under attack in a competitive society.

But how do we find psychological stability and balance, beyond childhood and regardless of how much trust and Love could be experienced in early development? What can we do as adult individuals to strengthen and protect our psyche in a time when fear, insecurity, and attacks on dignity, self-determination, and basic needs have become a daily occurrence? How do we stay mentally healthy in a time when lies govern and our trust in reason, security, and the rule of law is shaken every day? Where do we find the strength, courage, and orientation when old friendships break due to the inability to communicate respectfully, when we are insulted and attacked, and we feel like we've woken up in an insane asylum or science fiction? How do we stay hopeful when we see dogmatism, totalitarianism, and fascism on the rise? How can we stay healthy and happy in a world where joy of life is being destroyed to the same extent as hopelessness, dependence, vulnerability, and fear are being fuelled (from all sides)? In short, is there something that increases resilience, the ability to cope with psychological crises and overcome them healthily?

First, we must recognize that a health crisis is the type of crisis that we, as affluent people, have been made most vulnerable to. I deliberately say "made vulnerable." We have been constantly indoctrinated, consciously and unconsciously, that health and safety are the highest goods. How many birthday wishes and New Year's greetings have you received, in which it was said, "I wish you above all good health." Here we can see how propaganda works. Advertising is nothing but propaganda; it's just a prettier word. How many insurances have the average German citizen taken out to secure themselves, because they are sold security as a good, as if security has a monetary value and price, as if it's something that can be traded like tomatoes or iron ore. And with health, it's the same: Is health really a good, even the highest good? Does any part of such a belief make sense? First of all, health is not a commodity! Health cannot be bought, purchased, and certainly not "insured." The word "health insurance" implies that health can be "secured," but it is nothing more than a social fund into which contributions are made to cover the cost of treatment. This has to do with sickness, not health. It has to do with business and money, not security. The utopia of security, eternal youth, beauty, and health, which consumer and manipulation propaganda presents to us as the highest goal of life, are nothing more than illusions. The utopia of security is always a deadly utopia. Life has to be dared, and only if we dare Life, is it Life. What we have forgotten, what we have repressed, is something simple and the only certainty we have: "Life is dangerous and always ends fatally." Those who have travelled to poor countries often tell with surprise and wonder how people there can be happy despite poverty, dirt, misery, and insecurity, often even seeming happier than the bitter, decadent affluent people in their own country. How is that possible? Those who travel through Africa, Brazil, or India are often shocked by how closely joy and suffering coexist... and often somewhat naively and enviously admire this zest for Life and the ability to feel joy even in the face of suffering.

Numerous studies in resilience research have investigated very well and scientifically why some people living in violent conflicts, such as a civil war, cope better with such situations than others, even though they live in the same society and experience the same events. The results of all these studies are always the same: the more religious and spiritual people are, the higher their resilience, meaning they cope better with all kinds of crises, trauma, fear of death, torture, insecurity, and oppression. Now one might say that this is because religious people make the world look beautiful, even make misery look beautiful, and are perhaps consoled by the thought of paradise. But that's not the case at all. Religious, spiritual people have a much greater perception of suffering and compassion, so they are by no means in denial. What makes the difference is rather self-esteem and the assessment of Life itself. Those who see security and health as the highest goods and understand science as the only explanatory model for all phenomena are neglecting essential questions of existence!

Science as a pseudo-religion does not explain the meaningfulness of nature, the value of Life, or the significance of the self. Spirituality and religion are frowned upon today as esoteric and simple-minded. Science has become the new religion, and money the new God. In the process, science is becoming just as dogmatic and manipulative as the church used to be. And today's church has become Sunday entertainment for lonely old people and a minority of believers who are hardly brave enough to publicly confess their faith. And the worst thing is, that in this "corona crisis," the churches have nothing, absolutely nothing, to offer people; they kept their doors locked and announced the state's measures for distance and face coverings, just like the state media. By closing their doors, churches, mosques, synagogues prevent people from reflecting on values, engaging with higher orders than political ones, and asking questions about being rather than survival.

Those who constantly strive for their own safety and health are not only susceptible but remain underdeveloped in psychological development and understanding. However, those who have a higher, transcendent self-assessment and view of the world through religion or spirituality have significantly higher resilience.

The most beautiful symphonies, the greatest works of literature were not written by healthy, rich, beautiful, and life-assured people. Think of Beethoven, who was ill throughout his life, and eventually went deaf but composed the most famous melody of all, which is even called "Ode to Joy." Deaf, he composed the Ninth Symphony and his Missa Solemnis, the most impressive orchestral work, and numerous visionary piano sonatas. What gives a person the strength to do this? It wasn't the doctors and quacks who poisoned Beethoven more than they helped him; it was his spirituality, his constant search for transcendence, his unshakable belief in eternal truths and values.

How can we prevent a post-traumatic and embitterment disorder in 2020 after fear and delusion, which may haunt people for the rest of their lives and could even be passed on to future generations?

Along with information from the internet - and of course, along with our vigils - religion, spirituality can help us. So, if you wonder how to get through this challenging time in the healthiest way, if you wonder how to deal best with attacks, defamation, fear, the loss of long-standing friendships, and changed legal situations, you may want to start by asking yourself:

When was the last time you walked barefoot on a dewy meadow?

When did you last surrender to the admiration of an inconspicuous flower?

When did you last watch and listen to the gurgling of a stream?

When did you last dare to ask yourself why you are on this Earth at this time?

When did you last contemplate, why there is suffering in the world and immersed yourself in the beauty of world pain?

When did you last feel truly ONE with all that is?

When did you last cry just like that?

... play exuberantly like a child?

... idly watch a butterfly,

... hug a tree,

... experience a "magic moment"?

When did you last pray, bless a person, or when was the last time you encountered the divine in yourself, in another being, or in the world?

Embark on a journey, immerse yourself in the beauty, but also the pain. Look for what connects you with Life, with being, with the universe. Religion, *re-ligere* means to reconnect, re-bind ... [...]. Search for the connection that links everything to everything else, then you will never be alone, never lonely, never lost, never vulnerable ...

Religiosity and spirituality are fundamental needs of humans. Wherever you find your religiosity within you, whether you go into the forest or to the church, the mosque, or your garden, in the harmony of a symphony or in the beauty of a work of art ... wherever that is for you, that's where you belong.

In his so-called Sermon on the Mount, Jesus gave an instruction for happiness that can guide us through all crises. In a translation by Eugen Drewermann, it reads something like this:

Happy are the people who know about their poverty and stand by it.

Happy are those who weep, for their hearts will be pure.

Happy are the powerless, for only they will be able to make Peace.

Happy are those who suffer persecution for the sake of true life before God.

Happy are those who hunger and thirst for the right life.

Please note that here it says "happy are" and not "happy will be in another world," no, "happy are here and now."

Never forget: Life is not a problem; it is a mystery that wants to be lived.

73 The Eight Pillars of Joy According to Desmond Tutu and Tenzin Gyatso (Dalai Lama)

We are fragile beings, and we can find true joy – not despite, but because of this fragility. Life is full of challenges and adversity. Fear, like pain and death, cannot be avoided. Yet, all of this compels us to focus on what truly matters. (Desmond Tutu)

1st Pillar of Joy: Generosity

Sharing and generosity are so essential for our survival that the reward centres in our brains are stimulated just as strongly when giving as when taking – often even more so. Generous social behaviour enhances human relationships in a unique way. This goes beyond material generosity. Especially in our turbulent world, time and attention are true gifts. This can be time for a conversation, time for listening, time for a leisurely walk, or more time for oneself, family, and friends in general. This time does not always have to be filled with activity; leisure is a precious source of strength.

2nd Pillar of Joy: Compassion

Connection and compassion are the foundation of lasting happiness. The need for Love and recognition is shared by all people in all cultures. Bonding and empathy are deeply ingrained in us. Compassion is the healthy mix of empathy and benevolent action for others. It thus includes an active and action-oriented component and guards against the shadows of excessive empathy or pity. Compassion is not exhausted in understanding others but is always concerned with doing something good for the other. Sometimes, a loving smile is all it takes.

3rd Pillar of Joy: Gratitude

Gratitude is one of the character strengths and virtues that contribute to psychological well-being. Those who feel grateful for things that may be taken for granted possess a powerful tool for balance and joy. Gratitude is especially effective when expressed to oneself (for example, in a diary or prayer) or to others.

4th Pillar of Joy: Forgiveness

It is said: Forgiveness is like the release of a prisoner. At the moment of release, you realize that you have been the prisoner. It is not necessary to forget what has happened to forgive. Those who do not want to forgive remain imprisoned and develop hatred that steals all joy. It is often easier to forgive when we realize that a distinction must be made between the deed and the doer. Preserving the humanity of the wrongdoer and facing the wrongdoing with clarity is a key to happiness.

5th Pillar of Joy: Acceptance

Only when we accept what is can we change it. Therefore, every positive change begins with acceptance. To succeed in this, we must consider our role in the world with humility. Only those who recognize greater contexts and the greatness of creation can experience the beauty of life, despite all its pain and their own imperfection.

6th Pillar of Joy: Humour

Humility and a pure heart help to never lose humour. Humour not only makes difficult situations more bearable and reduces the severity of tiresome processes; humour is also present when dealing with one's own mistakes and shortcomings, as well as those of others. Smiling and laughter reduce the release of stress hormones and flood us with happiness hormones. To be serious without taking everything too seriously paves many paths.

7th Pillar of Joy: Humility

This is a central pillar of joy. Only those who recognize that the world does not revolve around them (or anyone else) and can wonder at the incomprehensibility of the universe have a strong foundation for joy. Humility ensures staying grounded and is an essential prerequisite for assessing relationships and circumstances healthily.

8th Pillar of Joy: Perspective

The slice of the world we see is the world we live in, and as we see the world, so we experience it. But there are different viewpoints, perspectives, and opinions on everything. If you look at an ant through a magnifying glass, you might feel fear, but as soon as you change your perspective and broaden your view, you experience the true dimension and relation. No one knows the truth; everyone only knows fragments of it. The more fragments we get to know, the more we learn about the truth. Communication is the most important means to discover other perspectives.

I consider the following prayer by St. Francis of Assisi one of the most beautiful and profound ways to install joy in life:

> *Lord, make me an instrument of your Peace,*
> *That I may Love where there is hatred;*
> *That I may forgive where there is offence;*
> *That I may reconcile where there is strife;*
> *That I may speak the truth where there is error;*
> *That I may bring faith where there is doubt;*
> *That I may instil hope where there is despair;*
> *That I may kindle light where darkness prevails;*
> *That I may bring joy where there is sorrow.*
> *Lord, let me strive, not to be comforted, but to comfort;*
> *Not to be understood, but to understand;*
> *Not to be loved, but to Love.*
> *For in giving of oneself, one receives;*
> *In forgetting oneself, one finds;*
> *In forgiving, one is forgiven;*
> *And in dying, one awakens to eternal life.*
> *Amen.*

74   About Non-Violence

Non-violence is a principle that rejects violence, seeking to overcome it while simultaneously developing alternatives to the criticized conditions. It's important to note that words or provocations can also be forms of violence.

Non-violence operates on the assumption that violence or its threat cannot solve problems or eliminate injustice and oppression. Therefore, various methods of action have been developed to achieve non-violent conflict resolution. Mahatma Gandhi wrote:

The primary meaning of non-violence is holding onto the truth, the power of truth (Satyagraha)... In the practice of non-violence, I discovered early that it does not allow for harming the opponent. Instead, the opponent must be persuaded away from their error through patience and compassion.

In this context, the term "*Ahimsa*" is often used, originating from the Upanishads and adopted by Gandhi. Ahimsa encompasses more than just non-violent resistance or non-violent action. Ahimsa refers to a way of life and a mindset that fundamentally avoids causing harm or injury to all living beings. According to Gandhi, this includes negative thoughts, lies, hatred, and excessive haste. Through endurance, patience, and ongoing effort, individuals learn to live in Peace with themselves and others.

A common misunderstanding of non-violence is equating it with defencelessness, passivity, and inaction. However, conflicts should not be avoided but consciously, constructively, and imaginatively regulated through non-violent resistance. Therefore, non-violence requires courage, determination, and civil courage. A fundamental aspect of education for non-violence is also learning methods for peaceful conflict resolution: Non-violence can and must be learned.

On November 10, 1998, the United Nations General Assembly declared the first decade of the 21st century and the 3rd millennium, the years 2001-2010, as the International Decade for a Culture of Non-Violence and Peace for the Children of the World.

75 Speech Against the Concept of Fighting as an Adequate Means

Speech held in July 2020 by Dr. Jörg Berchem, alias Jay B Joyful, during protests against the restrictions on fundamental rights during the so-called "Corona Crisis".

So much is being talked about illness like never before. What is rarely talked about is health! For example, the constant refrain we hear now, "Stay healthy!" - isn't it more of an admonition "not to get sick"?! What is health, actually? Why is there so little talk about it? Why, when it comes to the topic of health, is there so much talk about diseases?

If you listen to advertising and the mass media, health is portrayed as something constantly in danger, something I can only achieve by swallowing something, drinking something, getting vaccinated, getting regular check-ups, participating in sports and training programs, and so on. Above all, we are led to believe that you can only achieve health by constantly fighting against illness. And to make this whole apparatus of fighting and consumption run smoothly, fear comes into play. Health is no longer presented to us as a self-evident and the highest natural goal and aspiration; instead, it is disease that is portrayed as if nature constantly seeks only disease, perpetually attacking humans, and as if creation is a single fiasco full of flawed developments that make us vulnerable and weak. No more thoughts of God's perfect creation! No more of Goethe, who said, "Nature is infallible; errors belong to man."

I can't count the number of elderly people who, after decades of life experience, tell me, "Life is a struggle." The theory of infection is nothing but a struggle, built with the vocabulary of military doctors from 150 years ago. It talks about "defence" and "killer cells". I avoid using the term "conventional medicine." I prefer to speak of "academic combat medicine." The idea that one must fight against everything and for everything permeates every topic. For decades, we've been propagating the "fight against hunger". With what result? Wouldn't it be more sensible to provide people with food instead of fighting against hunger? The "fight against poverty" is talked about. But wouldn't it be better to create a just world, enable prosperity for everyone, and share resources?

We've been fighting against cancer and cancer-related diseases for decades with billions in research funding. What's the success? In prosperous countries that fight diligently, nearly every other person deals with neoplasms, the proper term for cancer, during their lifetime. The lethality, or mortality, of those treated with radiation, chemotherapy, and surgery is incredibly high, with some types of cancer and treatments resulting in over 80% mortality after five years. What do you do when you "fight against cancer"? These are your own body cells, not foreign invaders. So, you're essentially fighting against yourself. Can't there be another solution?

We are a culture of fighting, in every sense. We are seriously told that we must fight for Peace! And so, it is accepted that our German army, euphemistically called the "*Bundeswehr*", goes out into the world and allegedly fights for "Peace," "justice," and "democracy" - incidentally, also for closing escape routes and enabling access to cheap resources. Of course, it is said that terrorism must also be fought, with all means, including bullets, drones, bombs, and sanctions, sieges, and psychological torture. Truth must also be fought, as in the cases of Julian Assange, Chelsea Manning, Edward Snowden, and countless, sometimes nameless, others. Apparently, we are told, that everything can only be achieved through a fight. Democracy through a fight, Peace through a fight, freedom from terror through a fight?! Our own "German history" is nothing but a continuous slaughter of battles. And our lives are presented as a continuous battle with the purpose of fighting.

Nowadays, Life begins with a single battle. The birth process, perceived and treated as an illness, and even before that, pregnancy. As soon as a child is born, the struggle begins. Weighed and measured, compared and standardized ... There is no time for primal trust and primal Love because the struggle of Life is announced. Against fear, this primal Love and primal trust would be so important, given from elders, who are truly there for the child in the first years of Life. Instead, there is constant doubt about the Love of parents who "must self-fulfill," that is, fight in their profession, in everyday life, in society. At the age of one, children are abruptly woken up at seven o'clock in the morning and handed over to daycares and pre-school programs, which were once facilities for orphans and the abandoned, but are now the first battlegrounds where children fight for their mental and physical well-being. "Early bonding" has become "early education"; foreign languages in kindergarten, mathematics, and preferably early computer experiences since these are so-called "key qualifications" in the fight for the seemingly "better Life." School, upon closer examination, is nothing but a continuous battle; conformity is required instead of individuality, obedience instead of critical thinking, repetition instead of creativity ... Comparative tests and grades ensure competition, which is just a fancy word for battle. Full-day school turns every day into a battle, to persevere, stay awake ... it leaves no time for playing and dreaming and prevents socialization outside of authoritarian control. Just before summer vacation, [German] teachers determine the future of ten-year-olds. For many, the dream of becoming a veterinarian, a police officer, or an architect ends at the age of ten. At the end of the fourth year, it is decided whether 10-year-olds can study medicine or be parked on the sidelines of the *Hauptschule,* before they can apply for social welfare. Education barely extends to filling out the application, while the rich are already creating the first networks for their careers in private schools and with paid special support. "You didn't get a recommendation for the *Gymnasium?* Well, you must not have tried hard enough, not been diligent enough, not fought enough ..." And so it goes on ...

Even to win a loved one, you must fight. No more courting, no romance, and no Love poems, just fight for a woman or a man for a night or a phase of Life. Capitalism is nothing but a fight, and it must be clear that every euro you earn is taken from someone else. Whether it's salaries, pensions, or social assistance, it can hardly be more unjust, unequal, and combative. Even death, the release from all fighting, must still be fought! How sick is all of this?

And now we come to the really uncomfortable part of my speech; because many are here, believing they have to fight for their rights, fight for their freedom, fight for justice, fight for health, bodily integrity, vaccine freedom, humanity, fight for a better world. And in doing so, we may not even notice that we are staying in fight mode, just like those who fight for power, money, positions and pensions, influence, and of course, for voters ... We speak of "election battle" (German "*Wahlkampf*") as a matter of course.

Why is so much research done for armament and so little for Peace? Why is so much research done to combat disease instead of promoting health? Has anyone ever heard of the term "*salutogenesis*"? This is the science of researching health! It exists; but are there research funds, advertising, and speeches by politicians or virologists for it? Most doctors haven't even heard of the term *salutogenesis*, let alone what to do with it. Have you noticed that the virus is being investigated, the tested are investigated, the sick are investigated, and the dead are investigated ... But why isn't anyone investigating the healthy, the recovered, the mildly symptomatic? *Salutogenesis* would do just that. Instead of the fight mode, fighting the virus, strengthening the defence, and making things worse through vaccinations ... the question should be, why don't people who don't get sick, don't get sick? Why don't those who only show mild symptoms have severe symptoms? Why didn't the 107-year-old, who tested positive and survived, did not die? That's the approach and perspective of *salutogenesis*. Why am I telling you this?

It's not primarily about discussing the immune system, virology, and the "pandemic", the futility of measures ... It's about recognizing that whatever is happening now - whatever it is - has to do with our thinking and behaviour. It's easy to say that those up there, the politicians, the super-rich, the lunatics, the powerful, the society ... and then point the finger, always into the distance ... But society ... that's us, too. Is what is happening now not possible, especially because people have increasingly handed over the topic of health and the responsibility for it to combat medics, health ministers, health insurance companies, hospitals, and the pharmaceutical corporations that profit from illness for decades? Isn't all this possible precisely because of what is happening now? Maybe we didn't elect the politicians who are making the decisions right now. But who gives them the power if not us, who have been allowing them for years? Maybe we try not to buy the products of influential, powerful super-rich people we reject, but who has linked money to power and has accepted this principle for a long time? Also, on a smaller scale: why does a landlord have power over his tenants to determine how much of their income they must give him just to have a roof over their heads? Only through ownership? Why is the power tied to this ownership to kick an unemployed person out, or to ban a stroller in the hallway, or to deny housing to an African family? Who replaced religion with a "religion of science" and God with money? And most importantly, who accepts all of this? Who dutifully pays the taxes from which attack fighter jets are bought during the Corona crisis? And who allows this to happen? Who flies them? Who follows all the measures and rules and believes all the nonsense that is being served to us? And why? Haven't we already accepted that power reigns, that the fight is the way to achieve a goal?

Everything in the world happens through cause and effect. This is a very simple and universal principle. Everything in the world happens through cause and effect. So, when we observe a state here, it is the effect of a cause.

We could debate the causes of all the world's woes for a long time and then fall into the delusion of wanting to fight them. But we can also consider what cause we want to set now to achieve a specific desired effect that we wish for. What cause do we want to set, yes, what cause do we want to BE, to achieve a specific desired effect? What I am concerned about now is the question of what we are actually doing here and how we want to do it.

Our society is sick, sicker than ever before!

Our political system is sick, sicker than ever before!

Our media world and education are sick, sicker than ever before!

The financial system is fatally ill ...

The question is, do we really want to march in combat mode? When that is exactly the mode that has led to all this disaster? Isn't it wiser to focus on our abilities rather than fight against something? Isn't it wiser to just live the way we want to live? The way we feel inside that is right?

For example, how about entering the supermarket or train mask-free with self-compassion, self-determination, and self-responsibility, instead of entering in fear and combat mode because we cannot wear a mask for health reasons? How about ignoring the stupid and unjust rules instead of fighting against them? How about not feeding this sick and inhumane combat system by obediently participating in so much but saying "no," perhaps through a general strike, through changed consumer behaviour, by refusing and living a new world, a new society, not by "fighting for it," but by simply living it?

How about next year at the Ramstein protest, ALL those who are against the war crimes and drone murders by Americans from German soil actually come to the protest, and instead of 1,000 people, ten million people gather there? How about on August 1st in Berlin, not the 500,000 people that the organizers hope for, but the 30% of the population who, according to official statistics, have doubts about the COVID-19 pandemic and the unfair measures, which means 25 million people?

There is no way to Peace, Peace is the way.

Just be the light you want to see in the world.

Darkness cannot be fought; that is foolish thinking, we have enough of it around us. You can't fight darkness, but you can ignite a light! And you know what's great about it? – When you light one light from another light, the giving light loses nothing! You can light hundreds of other candles from one candle without it getting weaker.

You can't do that with money! Money doesn't work that way, but it works with knowledge, with light, with Love, with Peace, with non-violence, with hope, and with health.

Fighting makes you weak. But when we go out, courageous, hopeful, in Love, in Peace, in light, we can keep strong and liberate hundreds, give hope to thousands, give courage to hundreds of thousands, and so on. Be the light in the world! Carry the truth, Peace, and Love in your everyday Life with courage.

Thank you for your existence!

Thank you for being there!

Go in Love with Peace!

76 About Dignity

Immanuel Kant, the renowned German philosopher, had significant insights into the concept of human dignity. He argued that human beings have intrinsic worth and should be treated as ends in themselves, not as means to an end. Kant's philosophy emphasized the moral autonomy and rationality of individuals. Here are some key points related to Kant's ideas on human dignity:

1. Inherent Dignity: Kant believed that human beings possess inherent dignity because they have the capacity for rational thought and moral autonomy. This intrinsic worth is not contingent on external factors, such as wealth, social status, or achievements. It is a fundamental characteristic of every human being.

2. Treat People as Ends, Not Means: Kant's famous formulation of the principle of human dignity is expressed in the Categorical Imperative, specifically the "Formula of Humanity." This principle states that we should always act in such a way that we treat people as ends in themselves and never merely as a means to an end. In other words, individuals should be respected and valued for their own sake and not exploited for the benefit of others.

3. Autonomy and Respect: Kant placed a strong emphasis on individual autonomy, the capacity for rational moral decision-making, and the ability to set one's own principles. Respecting human dignity, according to Kant, involves treating individuals as rational agents capable of making moral choices.

4. Moral Duties: Kant argued that it is our moral duty to respect the dignity of every human being. This includes refraining from using others for our own purposes, avoiding actions that degrade or dehumanize people, and upholding principles that promote the autonomy and moral agency of individuals.

5. Universal Application: Kant's philosophy of human dignity is grounded in the idea that moral principles should be universally applicable. The principle of treating people as ends in themselves is not contingent on specific circumstances but should guide ethical behaviour in all situations.

In summary, Immanuel Kant's philosophy highlights the fundamental importance of human dignity based on rationality and moral autonomy. He argued that we have a moral duty to respect the intrinsic worth of every individual and to treat them as ends in themselves, emphasizing the universality and autonomy of moral principles. Kant's ideas have had a profound influence on modern ethical and human rights theories, contributing to the development of the concept of human dignity as a central tenet of human rights and ethical discussions.

Article 1 of the Universal Declaration of Human Rights states:

All human beings are born free and equal in dignity and rights. They are endowed with reason and conscience and should act towards one another in a spirit of brotherhood.

This article of the Universal Declaration of Human Rights finds its counterpart and implementation primarily in Article 1 of our [German] Basic Law. This is not just a basic right but a right to existence.

The dignity of the individual shall be inviolable. To respect and protect it shall be the duty of all state authority. The German people therefore acknowledge inviolable and inalienable human rights as the basis of every community, of Peace, and of justice in the world. Maybe, focusing on basic rights is finally an occasion for more people to think about how human dignity is constantly being infringed upon beyond measures like those related to the pandemic, for example, due to unemployment, poverty, homelessness ... through an unfair and outdated education system, as well as through drone strikes from Ramstein, through the 14 wars the German army engages in around the world, through the intention to allocate 20% of the federal budget to defence spending, and so on and so forth.

In the official information on political education about basic rights from August 15, 2019, you can read the following:

The protection of human dignity is not only at the beginning of the text of the Basic Law; it also has overriding importance as the supreme constitutional value and a fundamental constitutional principle [...]. No law may thus authorize an encroachment on human dignity, no matter how high-ranking the reasons given for it may be.

I'll read it again: [...] No law may thus authorize an encroachment on human dignity, no matter how high-ranking the reasons given for it may be. To put it plainly, this Article 1 stands above all other laws, determining them as a principle and must never be restricted.

Unfortunately, the term "dignity" is hardly known in our everyday language. I also cannot recall this term being explained or discussed in schools. Perhaps, it is indicative that the opposite term, "degrading," does have significance for people.

The wording in Article 1 is also interesting. While other laws state how something should be, this article starts with a statement: "Human dignity is inviolable." The framers of the Basic Law deemed human dignity so important that they wanted to leave no room for interpretation and wrote it into the law as an unequivocal statement, as a fact. Why? In philosophy, there have been interpretations suggesting that dignity must be earned, and in the past, dignity was something that only men, not women, and especially only white men, not slaves, could earn. This view is outdated. Human rights and Article 1 unequivocally grant every human being dignity as an unalterable human quality and right that can never be denied. The dignity of the human being is inviolable, as stated in the German Basic Law. This law falls under the "eternity clause," which means it can never be changed or abolished as long as the Basic Law is in effect. In reality, however, human dignity is constantly encroached upon, so it should actually state that it must not be encroached upon or violated. For instance, the Swiss Constitution states, "Human dignity must be respected and protected." Here, everyone, including the state, is called upon to take action to protect dignity. Just the fact that a person is a human being obligates us to respect their dignity. Weighing one person's life and happiness against the lives and happiness of other people, as is common in politics today, is a violation of dignity. In his book "The Dignity is Vulnerable," Ferdinand von Schirach (2014) reminds us that governments have long begun "to circumvent this completely clear decision in favour of the equality of people with ever more complex constructions." And what is happening in the spring of 2020 and still now is an incredible assault on the inviolability of dignity.

When people are required to cover their faces for no reason and face covered individuals, that is undignified. When people are asked to consider how many people from how many households they may be with in what distance and in what space, that is an attack on their dignity. When people are locked away without breaking any laws and without being sick, that is a massive violation of their dignity, and so on and so forth. In fact, all the restrictions on basic rights that we are experiencing are not only an encroachment but a violation of human dignity.

Dignity has three dimensions:

1. One way I am treated by others: [...]. Here, dignity is something others determine" - What can be taken from someone if you want to destroy their dignity? Or also: What must never be taken away from someone if you want to protect their dignity... Regulations...

2. Dealing with others: "The guiding question is: Which patterns of actions and experiences towards others lead to the experience of preserving my dignity, and with which actions and experiences do I forfeit it. In this second dimension, the responsibility lies solely with me: I myself have the power to determine whether I lead a life with dignity or not ... doctor, police officer, politician ..."

3. Dealing with oneself: "The question one must ask oneself is: What kind of self-view, self-evaluation, and self-treatment allows me to experience dignity? And when do I feel like I am forfeiting my dignity through the way I behave towards myself?"... So, what do I do, for example, through blind obedience, to lose my dignity... or what do I do to protect and develop my dignity, for example, against injustice?

I once defined dignity as follows:

Respecting dignity means having respect for otherness, conceding the right to be vulnerable but never intentionally violating it.

Whenever we use other people as means to achieve ends, we violate their dignity. People want to determine their own purpose and not experience themselves as a means to someone else's end but as an end in and of themselves: as a being with inviolable dignity. This insight into the self-purpose of humans means that a self-set purpose can only be experienced by the subject itself.

And one can even say that humans have an inherent sense of dignity: From the perspective of neuroscience, Gerald Hüther speaks of an "inner compass that accompanies us from the beginning of our lives throughout our entire life. Thus, the idea of one's own dignity is deeply rooted and embedded in the inner conviction of what distinguishes us as human beings and in which our true humanity is expressed in our own actions.

And because obedience means that one cannot truly develop oneself, in my opinion, dignity and obedience are incompatible. Demanding obedience from a person is, therefore, a violation of their dignity.

How is it possible that politicians are no longer doing everything to protect our constitution, indeed, to defend it? How many hollowing out of Article 1 of the Basic Law are we willing to accept? [...]

We are here because great injustice is happening in our country, human dignity is being disregarded, and alarming developments that declare injustice to be just are still ongoing. And if our politicians and maybe even judges believe they can arbitrarily restrict and disregard Article 1 and other articles of our basic rights, then in return, we can only show disregard for the restrictions on basic and human rights and we must adhere to their inevitable implementation. Disregarding the unjust restrictions, we will live all the articles of our basic rights, especially Article 1, regardless of whether we face penalties or fines for it or not. As for Article 1, everyone is called upon to take self-responsibility and engage in civil disobedience, and they are required to refrain from encroaching upon the dignity of a person! I address this to all people in this country, especially to doctors, therapists, judges, and police officers who are asked to enforce coercive measures. You are responsible for your own actions. Because how can bureaucratic grievances and professional misjudgments be addressed? With the courage to go beyond standard regulations and recommendations if the dignity of those affected requires it. Courageous, autonomous decisions of each individual are needed.

I call on all people with the words of Gandhi:

Where the state has left the realm of law, civil disobedience becomes a sacred duty!

Resist!

77 The Pentecost Message, and about Compassion and Love

Speech given by Dr. Jörg Berchem, alias Jay B Joyful, during protests against the restrictions of fundamental rights and state violence during the so-called "Corona Pandemic" in May2020

Namasté

The gesture नमससस्ते (namaste), widely prevalent in many parts of the Middle and South Asia, is an expression of respect nurtured by compassion. Mahatma Gandhi translated it as: "I honour the place in you where the entire universe resides. I honour the place in you that is full of Love, truth, light, and Peace. When you are in that place within yourself, and I am in that place within myself, we are one."

Of course, we use this holing greeting to all critical individuals who attend demonstrations and vigils. But we also use it for people who fear getting infected and believe that all government measures are important and right. In regard to people who defame us, attack us, harass us, delete our videos, or add hate comments. In regard to people whom we believe to be destructive, dishonest and cruel.

Pentecost is a festival based on a biblical story related to communication.

The word "communication" comes from Latin, "*communicare*" = to participate ...

I wish we had developed a culture where communication still has the meaning of participation. What we see is more a rhetoric of persuasion and manipulation. Additionally, digital media often establish roles of sender and receiver. Someone posts something, an image, a text, a video, or the news... they become the sender. The receiver may like it or write a comment in response, but ultimately remains in the role of the receiver.

Then there are many people who seem to have no language of their own, who mechanically repeat what others have said. They become mere transmitting stations, often without a feedback channel.

Is it surprising that our society repeatedly drifts into polarization, defamation, and fighting rather than engaging in dialogue on important issues? Not really. From a psychological perspective, one could say that for those who only have one opinion, who only want to shout and persuade, there is almost an identification with the perpetrator, the aggressor. In this case, it's the government, which stopped communicating with the people a long time ago, stopped participating in their thoughts, wishes, concerns, and visions. Instead, it dictates dogmatically, interprets offensively, insults, fights, and issues orders. And a significant portion of the recipients of these messages without a feedback channel does exactly the same—just sending, dogmatically, combatively, insisting on one opinion.

In the Pentecost story, it is said at first: There was a rumbling, a thundering, and a commotion. We are familiar with this. We are currently living in a time of powerful commotion, with an enormous storm of news, regulations, speeches, internet videos, discussions, and persuasive podcasts. The problem is: Commotion makes us deaf! We no longer hear others. We no longer hear ourselves. We understand nothing. It is like in Babylon; people who actually speak the same language start speaking as if in different languages. And at Pentecost, this great miracle happens when people suddenly speak in "tongues," finding a new common language. What else can this common language be but what we call a feeling. Jesus speaks to the deaf in Aramaic: "*ipatah,*" which means "Open up!" "Open up" to communicate... to participate... For this, I must accept the other, accept them in their being. I must not exclude anyone... not be deaf and not silence others with labels and prejudices. Do not exclude anyone... [no right, left, green, red...] there are only people...

And the common language of all people, even all beings, is that of feeling. And to communicate in feeling means to develop compassion.

What is compassion?

Some believe that empathy and compassion are synonymous terms. However, they are not. Empathy is understanding another person by placing oneself in their shoes. However, no other goal is defined other than understanding the thought and behaviour patterns of the other person. Since there is no implied goal associated with this understanding, empathy can be used for anything, for example, to sell a product, manipulate people, or harm them. Empathy is, therefore, a neutral thought model. Compassion, on the other hand, always includes the goal of achieving something healing, empathizing rather than thinking, and being motivated to act. I define compassion as follows: Compassion means honouring the suffering and the suffering person and seeing in it a call to action based on Love, to bring about healing.

Compassion should definitely be distinguished from pity. In pity, the distance is lost; those who pity identify with the sufferer, so they suffer themselves. This naturally leads to even more and even one's suffering, and quickly to burnout.

Compassion is entirely different; it is a true source of strength, which in no way endangers one's own joy of life and positive outlook on life, but instead becomes a resource where these are lacking.

Where compassion and hope intersect, healing becomes possible.

It seems to me very important that compassion (and all associated qualities) is not only directed towards others but also towards oneself. Tenzin Gyatso, the Dalai Lama, describes it in these words:

> *May* I contribute in every moment of my life to liberating myself and others from suffering and its causes. May I (...) be able to help people experience happiness and its causes. May I always remember that compassion for all living beings begins with myself.*

The Dalai Lama explains: "This compassion for oneself has nothing to do with selfishness because 'all living beings' also means us." This is also in complete harmony with the Christian tradition: "Love your neighbour as yourself."

Fanaticism

Whenever we live only one pole and exclude the other, we project it onto others, judge others. For example, faith and unbelief: when I embrace disbelief in me, it challenges me to ask what do I really believe? - When I repress disbelief, I must project it onto others, fight against others, who are "unbelievers" (because they unsettle me and remind me of my repressed doubts, my repressed disbelief). One sign of all fanaticism is always a drastic lack of self-Love, as self-Love accepts inner contradictions and reconciles them. Love reconciles contradictions, also in us. This is something crucial. It is said: Love is the only force that can unite without destroying. Love connects us with the other without dissolving ourselves. Self-Love connects us with ourselves without repressing parts.

It goes even further: I am convinced that Love is the force of evolution. This contradicts, of course, the already incorrect translation of "survival of the fittest" as the "survival of the strongest" as the presumed principle of evolution. New evolutionary research shows what ecology has long known: not the strongest but the beings that have created relationships prevail and secure their existence. Nature shows us that life is only possible when we are connected with each other; and Love is the force that connects everything.

It is the source from which compassion and self-compassion are nourished.

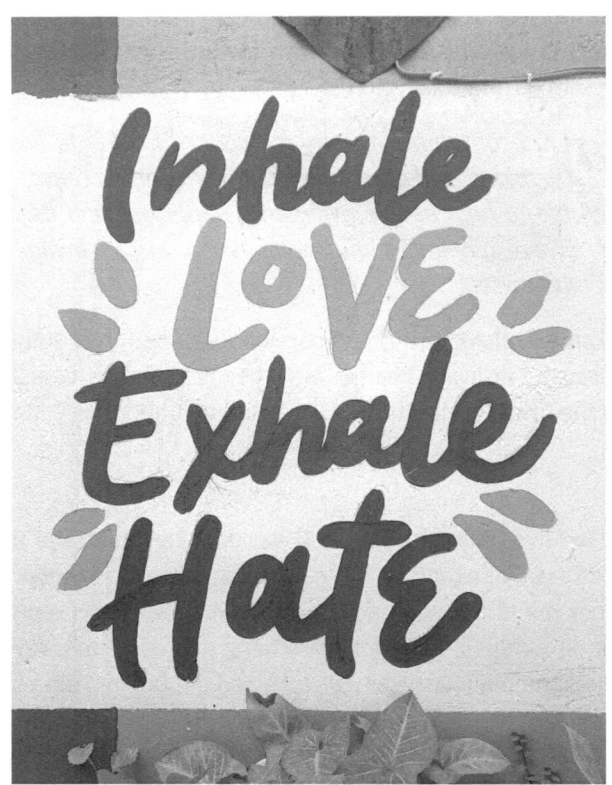

78 Neo-Myth Satanism

The revival of the Satanism myth as a simple explanatory pattern for misunderstood complex interrelationships and the justification for escalation, violence and retaliation

In times when complex connections remain hidden from people, leading to restrictions, upheavals, and uncertainties, many of them tend to turn to very simple (usually mono causal) theories that offer an easily understandable interpretation of the inexplicable. Because the seemingly inexplicable is perceived as so unlikely and unbelievable, the demands on simple interpretive models are low, and even the most incredible, bizarre, and entirely unsupported theories get a chance to find numerous followers. There are many examples of this throughout history and increasingly in the present.

Many of these theories are a constant revival of the myth of Satanism or a neo-mythological creation of a primitive world-view based on a simple interpretation pattern of the world, as described by Zarathustra, and originally found a visual representation in the game of chess. According to this view, there is light and darkness, white and black, good and evil in the world, which are constantly in a struggle that supposedly needs to be won.

In the book religions of Christianity, Judaism, and Islam, the so-called "evil" is personified as Satan or the devil, which threatens the world or at least humanity or society in the form of "satanic powers." Thus, a perceived threat can be easily interpreted and made bearable by clear blame attribution. Currently, this is most evident in the Q-Anon movement, which resurrects Satanism as a neo-mythos. The accusations made there are the same as in other Satanism myths throughout history, such as those against "heretics," Jews, or so-called "witches."

Ritual child murder, sexual violence, and ritual abuse, human sacrifice, and cannibalism are the classic accusations against a perceived evil power or group held responsible for suffering in society or the world as a whole.

The alleged worship of the devil by Satanists is not directed at the group of a few followers of a religion-like world-view, which only emerged in the second half of the twentieth century and counts mostly as followers of societal fringe groups. These followers are very heterogeneous but are increasingly fascinated, more or less seriously, by "malice," violence, and power, dark ritual acts, death, and magic. They partly turn traditional religions upside down in a counter-movement. Apparently, these individuals and groups are strongly influenced by corresponding films and horror stories that free the narratives of historical Satan myths from context and make them appear as historical reality. The increasing societal acceptance of sexual fetish practices like BDSM feeds the imagination and desire to believe that such practices are not only played, but also seriously and ritually celebrated somewhere. This is further fuelled by sensational media reports about individual cases of cannibalism and abuse victims and the depiction of paedophilia not as a treatable health disorder but as a malicious criminal offence. This recurring public discussion establishes credibility regarding the existence of Satanism, which forms a dangerous foundation for the current neo-myths.

In fact, the Satanism myths and the Q-Anon movement, in their blame attribution, do not target real diverse religious minorities but so-called "elite groups" as supposed Satanists, which neither self-identify as such nor consist of fringe groups but rather influential and affluent members of society.

There is also a parallel to historical Satanism myths, which is particularly evident in the case of the persecution of Jews and is partially directly connected to Q-Anon.

The authors and actors of the neo-myths, of which Q-Anon is just one, but the currently most widespread, use specific plausibility strategies based on dramatizations and myths. Public attention and concern are generated primarily by the brutality and enormity of the described experiences of abuse, indoctrination, and violence. These accounts mainly come from adult, mostly female victims. They report that they were (in their childhood) abused, tortured, and "programmed" for years in secret cult groups. Based on these reports, the assumption has emerged that secretly operating, highly developed, and internationally connected satanic organizations are responsible for this.

Satanism is not discussed as a real danger; instead, it is used as an element in the discourse for publicly disseminated perception and conception contexts.

The supposedly massive criminal processes are torn out of contexts usual in legal systems, and an alleged "evil force" is assumed, whose alleged followers, as "inhuman" and embodiments of "evil," deserve no trial, no accusation, and no legal process but should ultimately be "eliminated" through violence.

The same dangerous logic is increasingly adopted in "Western" intervention policies, where, for example, Muammar al-Gaddafi, Saddam Hussein, and Osama Bin Laden, as well as all the victims of drone strikes, do not receive accusations, trials, convictions, or acquittals but are considered appropriate and entirely legitimate to be executed and "neutralized" on the spot, even after prior pursuit, arrest, and torture.

Shockingly, the same thinking has also been adopted in many countries in the "fight against terrorism." The supposed terrorist, as the embodiment of evil, no longer needs to be prosecuted in a legal trial or convicted but may be immediately "neutralized" on the spot. This shows how the Satanism myth has become established beyond conspiracy ideological movements and has been established for political reasons.

One could say that this establishment is now taking revenge by applying the same supposed logic to those who once politically established it. It is not excluded that these movements, such as Q-Anon, are politically motivated and manipulated.

Moreover, the theory of the COVID-19 pandemic is also influenced by the ideas of the Satanism myth. The "story" of a thoroughly evil, destructive virus follows the same thought pattern. The assumption that there is something Satanic in nature has historically led to the extinction of animal species, such as bears and wolves, which were actually only competitors for food with humans. The fairy tales of the evil wolf are also a Satanism myth that justified the persecution of this species until extinction. It has been established as an archetype of evil in these tales.

Similarly, in recent decades, the myth of evil viruses has been framed to establish a satanic enemy, COVID-19, in 2020. Without a basic belief that something so destructive could exist in nature, the definition of this "pandemic" and the justification of destructive measures would not have been possible.

Similarly, in parts of the counter-movement/protest movement, this thought model can be found, but here, it is not the "evil" virus, but the "evil government/world government/elite."

Once established as a thought model and a real possibility, the myth increasingly leads to the creation and explanation of further scapegoats: "evil police," "evil Antifa," "stupid controlled masses," "evil pharmaceutical industry," "vaccination campaign with evil intentions," "evil intentions of Bill Gates."

How can a marginal theory and practice form like Satanism lead to a central interpretation theory of a movement, such as Q-Anon? This has obviously nothing to do with the relevance of Satanism as a real social and religious phenomenon. The significance lies in the inherent historical and symbolic reference system.

"Satanism" is used as a symbol for evil itself. "Satanists" embody the dark sides of society. Scenarios of demonization and dramatization and the involvement of specific groups of actors determine the constant reproduction of this Satanism myth in public discourse and in the political protest movement.

An essential feature of myths is their societal orientation. Since they convey something seemingly natural and unquestionable in their significance, they also serve to create certainties and as condensed stories in the construction of social contexts. This is used in the struggle for the assertion of different world-views and power interests.

In summary, the re-emergence and influence of Satanism myths can be attributed to various factors, including the human tendency to simplify complex problems and phenomena, the power of dramatic narratives, and their use by certain groups and movements to advance their agendas. While there is no substantial evidence to support these myths, they continue to persist and gain traction in some circles, which can have real-world consequences. Critical thinking, media literacy, and open dialogue are crucial tools for addressing and countering such myths.

79 Civil Disobedience - Definition, Conditions and Principles

Definition

Civil disobedience is a deliberate violation of rules or a conscious breaking of the law based on moral and ethical obligations (a matter of conscience).

Conditions

Civil disobedience is never selfish and always extends beyond the individual's interests. It is not motivated by selfishness or personal gain but rather serves the common good or the protection of minorities.

In addition to moral and ethical conflicts, a conflict of laws can also be a reason for civil disobedience. This can occur when two or more laws contradict each other. For example, a law may contradict the Declaration of Human Rights or fundamental rights laid out in the constitution. Under certain circumstances, such conflicting laws may make civil disobedience unavoidable, as taking action would mean disregarding one law or the other.

Civil disobedience assumes an acknowledgment of the legal system as a whole. This distinguishes it from resistance movements and revolutions.

Civil disobedience is always morally and ethically justified, never political.

Principles

Civil disobedience is always non-violent. This is done in the knowledge that non-violence is not the same as being entirely free from violence (non-harm). A peaceful, non-violent action may be perceived as an act of violence by others because it restricts their freedom or hinders their actions. However, non-violence is never intended to achieve violence as a goal. People have the freedom to refrain from violence and to use indirect forms of force through political or societal pressure or to prevent the enforcement of unjust measures (e.g., self-defence and protecting others).

Civil disobedience is always carried out publicly, usually with prior notice. This distinguishes it from a criminal act that is done in secret.

Civil disobedience involves the disregard of specific legal norms, never the entire legal system. The calculated violation of a particular rule [...] does not justify disregarding other rules, such as disrespecting the police as an institution or looting a supermarket, assaulting a bouncer or blocking life-saving measures.

Appendix 1: Erich Fromm

Erich Fromm points out that human history began with an act of disobedience. In the Hebrew myth, it was Adam and Eve who, against the prohibition, ate from the Tree of Knowledge and, due to this original sin, were expelled from the Garden of Eden. However, this did not corrupt them, but rather set them free "to learn to rely entirely on their own powers and to become fully human." The same is true in the Greek myth. Here, too, human history starts with an act of disobedience: Prometheus returns the fire, which was taken away by Zeus, to humanity. Fromm suggests that through the act of disobedience, by learning to say no to authority, a person can become free. Freedom and the capacity for disobedience are inseparable. The ability to be disobedient is a prerequisite for freedom, and, conversely, the courage to be free is a prerequisite for disobedience. Those who are afraid of freedom will not be disobedient. Therefore, for Fromm, any societal, political, or religious system that proclaims freedom but demands obedience or demonizes disobedience is a contradiction in itself.

From the beginning, humans have fought against authorities in the church, state, and family, and in doing so, they have continued to evolve, according to Fromm. Enlightenment philosophers and natural sciences embraced principles like "*sapere aude*" (dare to know) and "*de omnibus est dubitandum*" (doubt everything) in their struggle against tradition, superstition, customs, and power. These principles were characteristic of an attitude that allowed and promoted the capacity to say no. However, today, in a time of "hierarchically organized bureaucracies" that manage people as if they were objects, and where open authorities and rulers are absent, we have succumbed to the illusion of voluntarily acting according to our own will or at least rational authorities. Yet, Fromm questions, "Who can refuse obedience when they don't even realize they are obeying?"

(Quotes from: Fromm, Erich: "*Der Ungehorsam als ein psychologisches und ethisches Problem*" in: "*Über den Ungehorsam und andere Essays*"; Stuttgart: Deutsche Verlags-Anstalt 1982, S. 9-17)

Appendix 2: Jürgen Habermas

Civil disobedience plays a significant role in democratic systems. Jürgen Habermas, for instance, considers civil disobedience to be an "element of a mature political culture." He states, "Every constitutional democracy that is confident in itself regards civil disobedience as a normalized and necessary part of its political culture." It is often argued that civil disobedience should not be seen as a threat to the democratic order of a state but rather serves to expand and improve it, or, as suggested by Hannah Arendt, as a driver of societal change.

Appendix 3: Hannah Arendt

"Every human being is born as a member of a particular community and can only survive in it if they are accepted by it and can feel at home in it. The real situation of every newborn implicitly contains a certain form of consent, namely, an adaptation to the rules under which the great world theatre is performed in the particular group to which they belong by birth. We all live and survive through a kind of silent consensus, which can hardly be called voluntary agreement. How can we want what is already there? However, in the case where a child is born into a community where dissent is legally and de facto possible once they come of age, one could speak of voluntariness. Dissent includes consensus and is the hallmark of a free state; someone who knows they can dissent also knows that they, in a way, consent if they do not dissent." (Hannah Arendt)

(Quotes from Habermas, Jürgen: "Civil Disobedience – A Test Case for Democratic Constitutional State. Against Authoritarian Legalism in the Federal Republic." In: Glotz, Peter (Ed.): Civil Disobedience in the Constitutional State. Frankfurt a. M.: Suhrkamp, 1983, 29–53.)

80   Osho's Separation of Activity and Action

One of Osho's supreme understanding is his separation of activity and action, which relates, well, I think, to the notion of busyness we seem to be swamped by. Osho says:

> *Activity* is derived from the restless mind, which is equivalent to a state of mindlessness. While action is derived from the silent mind, a state of mindfulness.

Activity is the great escape from the self. It is a kind of drug to help us forget ourselves or our situation. It has become an obsession, with one of the greatest forms of activity in our self-development new age being the obsession with relaxation and meditation. How often do we hear 'I must relax' or 'You only need to relax', 'I must meditate' or 'You need to meditate more'.

Other forms of manic activity surround 'I should have a goal', 'You should have purpose', 'I must improve' and 'You need to grow'. These statements are all too familiar in the coaching setting, which often illustrate beliefs that are no longer serving us well. Yet, reaching the point where we start to recognize that activity is not the same as action can be a difficult transition, especially when we are too chronically busy to think clearly.

There is lots of debate over the word busyness. Is it being industrious, diligent, assiduous? It is certainly not showing idleness. But as we all know, you can only too easily be busy doing nothing of real importance.

However, too many of us still believe that the more we do, the more we are worth, irrespective of what it is we are doing or achieving. So busyness has perversely become a goal in its own right. But let's be clear. Busyness for its own sake is counter-productive. Busyness is a choice. But again, perversely, it is a choice we have given up. We make excuses for this. One of the great excuses of busyness is technological distractions. We blame technology, conveniently forgetting that we have the power to switch off our machines.

But the greatest contribution to busyness is autopilot. We allow ourselves to switch off and mindlessly roll with the blur of perpetual motion. Activity is our default reactions, based on past accumulations.

Action is a spontaneous yet purposeful response at the moment.

Most activity is not needed, or useful. They mostly tend to be reactions to situations that don't matter. Action, however, takes place when the situation truly demands it. But the mind convinces us that most situations demand a reaction. We convince ourselves that reactions are responses through a process of rationalisation.

This rationalisation is what Gurdjieff called 'buffers' – they blind us to our default reactions, so we carry on making the same kinds of default reactions over and over. We see this only too often in the so-called leadership space through the well-used mantra 'better to do something than nothing', or as Osho noted, the equally absurd mantra 'an empty mind is the devil's workshop'.

But this manic dash to do something has turned us from human beings into human doings. Indeed, this reflects Judith Butler's point when she questions the very question, 'what kind of doer am I', which she sees as a limiting question, where we have become no more than a repeated action. This is further reflected through Deleuze's point that most philosophy is based on "the conditions of our habitual experience".

Osho recognizes the need to understand the mechanisms of the mind, so we can cut the root. Not so much changing habits through changing activities, which can only create new habits, but transcending our habits and transforming activity into action. This means stop acting as a doer. And to do this, we need to stop identifying with things. Being identified is the root (this reflects much modern psychology, such as the work of Roberto Assagioli and psychosynthesis, which recognizes the need to dis-identify).

Busyness and limiting beliefs have become inextricably linked. Even the practice of mindfulness has become one of our manic activities. Is it not time to put on the brakes and stop? Unfortunately, we are mostly cognitive misers, as confirmed through research in the fields of neuroscience, and so for many it is easier to roll along on autopilot, ricocheting from one activity to the next.

But things don't have to stay that way. We have the choice.

81   Speech against Military and their Image Polish

As if it weren't bad enough that we are supposed to entrust our health to:

- A veterinarian who leads the state institute for human medicine, the "Robert Koch Institute,"
- A poor virologist who has been proven wrong and talked nonsense several times in the past,
- A banker who is known as a lobbyist for the pharmaceutical industry,
- A physicist who has never worked as one,
- A computer enthusiast who is megalomaniacal and equipped with unlimited money and power,

As if it weren't bad enough that this medical bunch of misfits wants to decide on our health and our living conditions, then the German army, commonly referred to as the "Bundeswehr" (i.e. "federal defence") in an endearing way, comes into play in this perfidious scenario ... The military has infiltrated the Ministry of Health since the beginning of the year, a situation typically associated with military dictatorships. What does the army, what do soldiers who have learned not to heal but to kill, have to do in the Ministry of Health? And by now, they are more and more everywhere: they have long been in our schools, the uniformed ones, to recruit minors with lies about the magic of scouting and alleged career opportunities in the army ... and teachers and parents look the other way! On television, they depict camaraderie despite increasing cases of bullying and right-wing extremism, a picture of a relief organization despite increasing military operations. One incompetent and corrupt Minister of War is replaced by the next for image polishing, and the military and the uniform are being reintegrated into society. Now they are at the airport, at train stations, going into kindergartens, sticking cotton swabs in people's throats, sitting in health offices ... I wonder what they are doing there. It is the same German army that conducted an illegal war of aggression against Yugoslavia; it is the same army involved in military actions in approximately fourteen countries, protecting dictatorships, enforcing German economic interests with force of arms, advising the worst war criminals like Saudi Arabia with know-how, and buying 45 nuclear-capable combat aircraft from the terrible Minister of War AKK in the spring. It is the same military that wants 20 percent of the German household budget, one-fifth, for preparation for killing, while in schools, two or more classes share textbooks, and a significant part of our society's seniors collect bottles to have enough to eat. Over 6,000 children and young people live on the streets in Berlin, but it seems more important that 16-year-olds learn to obey and kill.

And now, this army, these soldiers, are supposed to take on roles in a supposed health crisis. Army, military, soldiers... each of these words carries violence, authority, blind obedience. Dark scenarios are now imaginable, like those I only know from overseas countries: military roadblocks where people are questioned about their origin and destination, their luggage is searched, individuals singled out and taken away ... Authoritarian uniformed cap-wearers with more or less tinsel on their chests that one encounters in offices that are supposed to serve the people who finance them ... Military doctors who assess who still needs to be vaccinated, who gets a pass, an immunity certificate, and who does not. How can it be that in Germany in the 21st century, the majority of the population accepts, and possibly even approves of, the military taking on civilian tasks? How can it be that unqualified politicians with increasing powers, now the Minister of Health who is to receive new special powers... how can it be that it is accepted, that our democracy is being destroyed, the rule of law is being undermined, and the military is interfering in internal civilian affairs?

> *War is Peace*
>
> *Freedom is Slavery*
>
> *Ignorance is Strength* (George Orwell in: 1984)

In Orwell's 1984, these slogans originate from a mysterious entity known as "The Party," comprised of those in authority. They are prominently displayed in massive letters on the white pyramid of the Ministry of Truth. Considering their blatant contradictions, this placement seems peculiar.

The presence of these slogans on a government building, particularly within the Ministry of Truth, suggests an effort by those in power to convey their truth within the constructed society. These contradictions serve as an initial glimpse into the society's nature, illustrating how it is bound together by the functioning of opposing ideas.

George Orwell intentionally introduced his book in this manner to acquaint readers with the concept of Doublethink, enabling the citizens of Oceania to embrace constant contradictions. Doublethink is the ability to simultaneously hold two opposing ideas. The Party cultivates this skill by eroding individuality, independence, and autonomy while fostering an atmosphere of perpetual fear through propaganda. This strategic breakdown of rational thinking compels citizens to accept illogical ideas unquestioningly.

Throughout the book, similar contradictions abound, such as the Ministry of Peace overseeing war, the Ministry of Love engaging in torture, and the Ministry of Truth manipulating historical and news content. These contradictions keep citizens unsettled, dependent on the Party for guidance, and unsure of themselves and others.

The national motto of Oceania, like other contradictions, underscores the Party's success in psychological mind control. The government maintains the apparent truth of these opposing statements through their societal functions, making them a reality in Oceania.

Exploring the meaning of "War Is Peace," the people believe it implies enduring the horrors of war to attain Peace. However, the war is fabricated by the Party, occurring far from Oceania. The contradiction serves to distract citizens from the Party's control, creating a shared enemy that unites them and diverts attention from internal issues. This mentality, orchestrated for the Party's benefit, facilitates governance by providing an external scapegoat for societal problems.

For me, who sees the greatest mistake in post-war German history in rearmament, it is clear: soldiers should be locked away in barracks in their own country, where they can play their disgusting games. If it were up to me, they would all be pacified and retrained, and then they can work as healthcare and elderly caregivers, which we urgently need, in a truly meaningful and non-violent job: the general as a nursing assistant, so he learns humility, the ordinary soldier as a care service manager so that he learns self-responsibility.

The credibility of the so-called pandemics of our time is reflected in the fact that independent NGOs like the Red Cross, the Technical Relief Agency, etc., are not send out, but soldiers!

There is no right to obedience! Take personal responsibility! Say NO!

FORGIVENESS is healing. And true LOVE sets you free.

Forgiveness is the only path we have to better fairness in an unfair world; it is the unexpected turnaround of Love against pain, and forgiveness alone offers strong hope for healing the hurts we feel so unfairly.

Forgiveness is looking at the future, not the past. When you give and receive forgiveness, focus on restoring the relationship, on coming together and letting the past be past.

Forgiveness does not mean setting the record straight. It means leaving behind emotional baggage, guilt, shame and the feeling of being right.

False Love is pain and bondage,

True LOVE sets you free!!!

83   The Ego is the Mask worn by the Inner Child

What a powerful piece of art: Two people turn their backs on each other after an argument and close themselves off. But their inner child longs to meet and connect.

As a child, we are open to the world and absorb everything without judgements and evaluations. This part of our being has not disappeared, but is mostly split off by hurts and fears.

The ego arises from this splitting off in the first place.

We often read that it is important to heal the inner child. But how can the ego do this, since it is, so to speak, the personified injury?

It really needs a higher entity.

To do this, one has to understand that ultimately it is neither about healing the ego nor about healing the inner child, which is only a metaphor. The goal of healing work is another: to make accessible the higher consciousness, the real truthfulness that we actually are. It is the healing self that, through the becoming one of inner child and ego, makes it possible to turn to our neighbour through loving attention to ourselves.

This is how Peace is created ... within and without.

84 The Power of Compassion - About the Healing Power of Love, Forgiveness, and Blessings

For those who have not delved deeply into the topic, it is easy to get lost in assuming that empathy and compassion are synonymous terms. However, they are not. Until just a few years ago, psychology relied on "professional empathy" and categorically rejected the additional qualities of compassion. It took the respect for Buddhism and the influence of Buddhist psychology to make compassion socially acceptable and to rediscover this essentially Christian value for therapeutic practices.

In the Christian-European context, this value was perhaps considered too "church-laden," making it easier to borrow it from Buddhism. This phenomenon, where one's own grounded culture is rejected due to the perception that it is not genuinely or honestly lived, only to rediscover and redefine it as pure and honest in a foreign culture, is quite common. It is primarily explained by the fact that knowledge of the foreign culture does not extend far enough to reveal the equally superficial and often insincere reality behind the ideal.

For those who have witnessed how compassion is idealized and genuinely lived in Buddhist countries, or observed the discipline, asceticism, and rigour, including physical self-discipline, in a Buddhist monastery that rivals that of a Christian monastery, it becomes apparent that ideals are just that—ideals. Christian compassion is no better or worse than Buddhist compassion.

But first, let's return to the conceptual distinction:

Empathy is the act of understanding another person by putting oneself in their shoes. However, no other goal is defined except to "understand" the thought and behaviour patterns of the other person. Since no implied goal is associated with this understanding, empathy can be used for anything, including selling a product better, manipulating people, or even harming them. Therapeutic empathy is, therefore, a neutral thinking model.

Compassion, on the other hand, always includes the goal of bringing about something healing, emphasizing feeling over thinking, and being motivated to take action.

I define therapeutic compassion as follows:

> ## *Compassion* *means to acknowledge suffering and the suffering individual and to see in it a call to action rooted in Love, to bring about something healing.*

Compassion is by no means limited to the feelings, thoughts, and actions of the therapist but should also be understood as a resource for the patients when we succeed in helping them develop compassion for others and themselves (compassion and self-compassion).

Experiments conducted by Tanja Singer also scientifically confirm that empathy and compassion are two fundamentally different things, which are reflected in different brain activities. It is essential to differentiate between these two. In the case of compassion, a certain distance is maintained; the one feeling compassion empathizes with the suffering but does not fully identify with it, thus avoiding becoming overwhelmed. On the other hand, compassion is about empathy and a call to action rooted in Love to bring about something healing.

Compassion should not be confused with pity. In the case of pity, the distance is lost, and the one feeling pity fully identifies with the suffering, causing them to experience suffering themselves. This naturally leads to even more suffering and can quickly result in burnout (often erroneously referred to as "compassion fatigue" among therapists).

It becomes very challenging when therapists or healers act out of pity, are trapped in systems of doubt and fear. Ultimately, one cannot help anyone in this way. It takes compassion and a Love that "believes everything," including the possibility of healing. It requires a Love that "hopes for everything" [1 Corinthians 13:7], believing that everything is ultimately "good" as part of an interconnected whole, in the sense of a higher order.

Even empathy, which often involves struggling against internal resistance, quickly leads to exhaustion and can often negatively impact one's own self-image. Many traumatized patients suffer from the empathy they receive. No one can truly empathize with what a traumatized patient has endured and feels. Expressing that one can "empathize" or "understand the feelings and suffering" of a victim of sexual abuse or a refugee who has suffered indescribable horrors in their homeland and during their flight may sound like mockery to many trauma patients. Nobody can do that except the individuals themselves. Therefore, it is essential to respect and honour the uniqueness of each person's personal story and individual suffering. Empathy can be insincere and inappropriate in such cases.

In contrast, compassion is a true source of strength. It does not jeopardize one's own joy of life or positive outlook, and can become a resource in situations where it is lacking.

| *Where* compassion and hope meet, healing and Peace become possible.

Currently, books and courses on mindfulness are widespread. However, mindfulness can only be a first step, and often, the goal is missing. Why should I be mindful? For many patients, learning mindfulness is essential, but quite a few can end up in a dead end and experience a motivational block if a clear direction is not added soon. Without a sense of purpose, mindfulness alone can lead to even more self-blame and despair.

That's why Buddhism, for example, teaches the path of mindfulness as a way to perceive what is, in order to reach a state characterized by compassion, kindness, equanimity, joy, and ethical behaviour.

One should not assume a linear sequence of path and goal but rather that the path of mindfulness is increasingly characterized by compassion, kindness, equanimity, and joy. Ethical behaviour is not an option for Buddhism or Christianity; it is inherent to compassion and an essential prerequisite for healing. However, many books and therapists omit the aspect of ethical behaviour, as it may be uncomfortable and demanding for the modern mindset. This omission can reduce mindfulness and compassion to mere wellness products.

Mindfulness alone makes sense for the patient to perceive themselves and their situation, and it makes sense for the therapist to develop empathy. However, therapeutically, it is only the beginning and becomes valuable when mindfulness leads to compassion, the desire for change, and ethical behaviour.

Interestingly, you can make yourself very unpopular, especially among many psychotherapists and psychologists, by using the term "ethical behavior." This is rooted in a confusion between "ethics" and "morality." I define the difference (also to my patients) as follows:

Ethics is purely value-based and formless, meaning how these values are implemented remains open. Ethics is unchangeable, deeply rooted in the universal human being.

Morality, on the other hand, prescribes very clear forms and behaviours considered right and wrong. Morality is changeable; it is time- and culture-dependent and often defined by authorities.

The Buddhist concept of equanimity, which is often overlooked in discussions of mindfulness, or is blended into "perceiving without judgment," is also frequently misunderstood. It can be confused with "indifference" and "fatalism." However, it is not about passively enduring suffering, as this would be completely counterproductive to effecting change. "Equanimous" means that all states are equally "equally valid," so everything is an option to the same extent. "Equanimity," on the other hand, means that you separate the apparent connection and imagined causality between an external state and your inner emotional world. "*Mut*" is an old German word for "feeling" (for example, *Hänschenklein* is "*wohlgemut*"). Compassion separates the apparent connection between a state and a specific emotion. Therefore, well-intended therapist questions like "What does it do to you?" are entirely counterproductive in this sense because "nothing does anything to us," but we "respond" with an emotion to something. So, compassionate questions are, "How do you feel about it?" (mindfulness) and "How would you prefer to feel?" (goal orientation) and "What is necessary for that?" (action).

Equanimity means that you no longer react pattern-dependent, giving you the opportunity to decide on a reaction and action "equanimously" for the better (joy and kindness, also towards yourself).

A crucial aspect, in my opinion, is that compassion (and all associated qualities) are not only directed towards others but also towards oneself. This is immensely important for patients but equally important for us therapists.

Tendzin Gyatso, the Dalai Lama, describes it in these words, which therapists could indeed make their mantra:

> *May* *I in every moment of my life contribute to freeing beings from suffering and its causes. May I always be able to help beings experience happiness and its causes. May I always remember that compassion for all that lives begins with myself.*

The Dalai Lama explains, "This compassion for oneself has nothing to do with selfishness because when we say 'all living beings,' we also include ourselves." This sentiment aligns perfectly with the Christian tradition: "Love your neighbor as yourself" (Mark 12:31, Galatians 5:14, James 2:8, Leviticus 19:18, and others).

As mentioned repeatedly, the topic of "Love" is often uncharted territory for our patients. It's a terrain where, similar to continental drift, various emotional and personal expectations drift apart and collide, leading to volcanic eruptions.

In the complex causality of our patients' illnesses, the theme of Love and self-Love tends to resurface sooner or later. Therefore, it's worth investigating this matter more closely, both in terms of terminology and the phenomenon itself. This exploration requires us to contemplate our understanding of healing, ultimately realizing how powerful a resource compassion can be in therapeutic work.

Often, it's insightful to turn to the ancient Greeks. For Plato, Love is the force that holds everything together, connecting all things. We are familiar with the concept of connecting in the field of medicine, where we use a "bandage" to bind wounds. The word "healing," despite its historical baggage, refers to something that is whole, connected as a unity.

In childhood language, it was common during my time to say that we would "make something whole" when trying to mend or fix something that was broken. The Mainz Carnival song "Heile, heile Gänschen" promised the people in a city destroyed by war, regarding rubble and suffering, that "in a hundred years, everything will be gone," and it has remained a comforting lullaby for children to this day.

It's not surprising that the term "healing" was once a form of greeting. In many languages, people greet each other using words related to "healing." The

Arabic "salaam" and Hebrew "shalom," both meaning "Peace," have origins in a Semitic word for "unity," "connection," and "wholeness." After all, what is Peace if not the connection of different elements into a unified whole?

Healing is indeed related to "connecting" and "making whole," and Love "connects" and "unites." Every person longs to Love and be loved. However, in every experience of Love, we encounter both light and shadow: fulfilment and disappointment, enchantment and hurt.

The pain from injury and disappointment can become so great that a person can no longer feel Love, believing only hatred remains. Like no other Gospel in the New Testament, that of John aims to make people who have become estranged from Love capable of loving again. Right at the beginning, it says, "For God so loved the world, that he gave his only Son, that whoever believes in him should not perish but have eternal life." [John 3:16] — Thus, the essence of the incarnation is Love. God is, by His very nature, Love: "God is Love, and anyone who abides in Love abides in God, and God abides in him." [1 John 4:16]

In philosophy, it is similarly said that Love is the foundation of everything. It is the foundation of all existence. John presents images of Love, such as the cross, the death on the cross. Originally, it is not about atonement and suffering, but rather initiation into the mystery, called "*telos*" in Greek. "*Telos*" also means a wedding: Love connects everything that is otherwise separate, life and death, heaven and earth. The cross is a symbol of initiation into the mystery of a Love stronger than hate, stronger than death.

In fact, the symbol of the cross is not the instrument of torture as many people believe (in Roman times, it actually looked like an "X"), but a symbol that originates from the ancient Egyptian ankh, which symbolizes eternal life through two intertwined cords.

The cross is the unity of opposites. In this sense, John uses it: The cross symbolizes an embrace. ("And I, when I am lifted up from the earth, will draw all people to myself." [John 12:32]) The cross and the gesture of the crucified call us to embrace the opposites within us. This is an important image of Love.

Whenever we only live one pole and ignore the other, we project it onto others and condemn them. For example, faith and disbelief: When I embrace the disbelief within me, it challenges me to ask what do I truly believe? - If I repress disbelief, I must project it onto others, fight against those who are "unbelievers" (because they unsettle me and remind me of my repressed doubts and unbelief).

A sign of religious fanaticism (but also of fanatical atheism) is always a drastic lack of self-Love because self-Love accepts internal opposites and unites them. Love unites the opposites, even within us. This is something crucial. It is said that Love is the only force that can connect without destroying.

Love connects us with others without dissolving ourselves. Self-Love connects us with ourselves without repressing parts of ourselves. C.G. Jung is skeptical about the oceanic feeling of merging with everything (today we might talk about the concept of "flow"), but according to C.G. Jung, Love means connection, union, without losing our own identity, so we remain ourselves.

It goes even further: I am convinced that Love is the driving force of evolution. This contradicts the often misinterpreted translation of "survival of the fittest" as the "survival of the strongest" as a presumed principle of evolution. New evolutionary research shows what ecology has long known: it is not the strongest but the beings that have created relationships that prevail and ensure their existence.

Nature shows us that life is only possible when we are interconnected, and as we have seen, Love is the force that connects everything.

It is certainly no coincidence that in a time when humans believe they can detach themselves from nature, Love is also increasingly suffering, as evidenced by divorce rates and the local and global social development in almost every aspect.

Disease is a complex, multi-causal phenomenon. But all diseases ultimately arise from an injury, a breakdown of wholeness, which is a connection, a union of differences. Psychologically, for example, illness arises from the repression of certain aspects or from traumatization, and physically from accidental injuries, imbalances (remember: "medi" in "medicine" or "medication" means "middle") or from the breaking of DNA strands, and so on.

No two people are alike in anything, except in their loneliness. Wars, hatred, and envy all stem from our loneliness, the desire to be needed and loved. The only way to overcome our loneliness is through encounters filled with compassion.

In my experience, unresolved grief plays a significant role in neoplasms (abnormal tissue growth), indicating a loss that has not been healed: an injury, a lost connection.

Grief is an important emotional resource to maintain this connection beyond death and transform it into a new level. Diagnosing grief lasting longer than two weeks after the loss of a loved one as an "adjustment disorder" to prescribe psychotropic drugs or psychotherapy overlooks its healing power.

To understand the functioning of compassion and Love, we need to clarify that the common interpretation of our world as composed of opposing forces is not in line with reality, even from a physically demonstrable perspective.

We often talk about light and darkness, heat and cold, as if both are equal and opposing forces. However, in actuality, heat is a reality, and cold is merely the absence of heat. At -273.15°C, there is no heat whatsoever; it can't get any colder than that. On the other hand, there's no limit to how much heat we can have; we can always have more heat. Similarly, we can create light with lamps, but there are no devices that generate darkness because darkness is just the absence of light. It can't get darker than having no light.

The Zoroastrian bipolar view of the world, embodied in the game of chess where light and shadow battle, is an illusion. The same goes for the concept of the battle between good and evil ...

Hatred is nothing else, than the absence of Love, the power that connect everything.

Fear is the absence of courage.

Doubt is the absence of trust. etc.

Soldiers and other murderers often talk about the "inner emptiness" they felt. Upon closer examination, wars are not waged out of hatred but out of greed and fear, which are also forms of emptiness. Wars are, of course, also driven by extensive lies and manipulation, stemming from a lack of knowledge, honesty, and self-awareness.

Polarities are just one way to describe the world, but there's no scientific evidence for polarities as real entities.

Joy and sorrow, for example, are not polarities; they are independent emotions that can coexist and are allowed to do so. The absence of joy is called depression, not sorrow.

It becomes clear that combating emotions like fear and hatred is not effective and doesn't lead to positive development. To apply this understanding to our concept of health and disease, we can view disease as the absence of health.

This perspective allows us to recognize the destructive and futile nature of much of modern combat-oriented medicine.

One cannot fight a deficiency or an injury. We can see this clearly in the decades-long "fight against hunger." Sharing and fairness would be appropriate here, but not a battle against a non-existent enemy.

Isn't it the same with the "fight against cancer"? After all, these are your own body cells that have lost their connection to the system, fallen out of the cell association, and "degenerated"... How can you restore this connection through a fight? And doesn't "cancer" only become an entity when I make it so through language and thought? - I leave it to the reader to consider the therapeutic implications that arise from this question.

We can illustrate this model as follows:

The healthy (whole) human is filled with Love, trust, vitality, and more. These resources are nourished from an inner source of strength (Buddhists refer to it as the inner Buddha).

In case of injuries, they can heal on their own from the inner source as long as they are minor injuries.

Larger injuries, accordingly, take longer to heal or persist and can play a role in a multifactorial disease process.

Deep wounds almost reach the inner source. For example, this can lead to an anxiety disorder (resource of courage, trust) or a lack of self-awareness and self-Love.

To fill the gap created by injury and to heal, after mindfulness (assessment of the condition, avoiding further injuries, connecting with the inner source), compassion and/or self-compassion are needed as a healing resource.

The active ingredient in this medicine is ultimately always Love. The goal of the longing for Love is not that we are only loved but that we are Love. Through compassion, we come into contact with the inner source of Love that resides within us.

When we feel the quality of Love at the core of our soul, we are one with God; we are "in God." That's when healing from injuries can occur.

Jesus calls on us to rediscover the world with the heart of Love, essentially to feel this source of Love in our souls and let it bubble forth.

Compassion also gives us the ability to forgive ourselves and others. Judgment is essentially the lack of compassion. A significant misconception needs to be clarified here: I do not forgive for the sake of the other but for myself, for my own healing. Forgiveness can be a powerful therapeutic resource, but it must be built on self-compassion above all.

At this point, a thought on loving one's enemies from my therapeutic perspective: Enmity arises from projection. Someone cannot accept themselves or parts of themselves and projects what they cannot accept onto others.

Loving the enemy means understanding enmity, recognizing that enmity is not rooted in the other but in oneself. How torn apart must someone be to want to tear me apart? How broken must they be to feel the need to break me? Through compassion and enemy Love, I see in them the person who longs for their unity, and when they come into harmony with themselves, they won't need this enmity.

A great potential for healing lies in blessing the people you hold grudges against. This is essentially the pinnacle of (self-)compassion. When blessing, I rise above, step out of the victim role, and connect with my inner strength. I no longer give power to the other. My Love for my enemies benefits me. In this is the wisdom of Jesus' words: "Love your enemies, bless those who curse you." [Luke 6:27]

Let me explain: In this article, I will focus on Love in terms of self-Love, Love for others, and universal Love (ἀγάπη). I will address the themes of friendship Love (φιλία) and romantic Love between two individuals (ἔρως) in another article.

Another aspect of Love deserves closer examination, especially to deepen the understanding of self-Love: Plato already connects Love with beauty. Beauty awakens Love, and Love expresses itself through the beautiful. In a world of photo-shopped supermodels and consumer-defined beauty ideals, along with the resulting long lists of modern people's self-criticism, Plato's statement may initially be shocking. It becomes even more challenging with Dostoevsky, who speaks enthusiastically: "Beauty will save the world." - How can we understand this?

For this, we first need to look at the etymology of "beautiful." "Beautiful" actually comes from "to behold" or "to look." The disassociated person believes that beauty is what allows them to lovingly gaze. In reality, something is beautiful when we look at it with Love. I am beautiful when I look at myself with Love. And I discover the beauty in others when I look at them with Love. I become ugly when I hate myself.

Etymologically, "beautiful" is likely also related to "to spare" or "to spare from harm." Beautiful is the one we spare, the one we let be as they are, the one we do not judge, criticize, or find fault with. I am beautiful when I "spare" myself, meaning I do not judge but accept myself lovingly as I am.

The gesture नमस्ते (namaste), widely used in many parts of Middle and South Asia, is an expression of respect nurtured by compassion. Mahatma Gandhi translated it as "I honour the place in you where the entire universe resides. I honour the place in you of Love, truth, light, and Peace. When you are in that place in you and I am in that place in me, we are one."

Prayer of Love

O Divine Source of all Love,
You who are the essence of all that is pure and true,
Fill our hearts with the boundless Love that knows no condition,
The Love that asks for nothing, yet gives everything.

Teach us to love as You love –
Without judgment, without expectation,
With open hands and an open heart,
Seeing Your divine spark in every soul we meet.

Let our Love be patient, even in trial,
Let it be kind, even in the face of hatred,
Let it be strong, even when the world is weak.

May we love those who bless us with joy,
And even more, may we love those who challenge us,
For in them, too, is the face of Love,
Calling us to rise above ourselves.

Let our love mend the broken,
Comfort the lonely,
Lift the weary,
And heal the wounded.

May we be vessels of Your love,
Pouring it into the world
Like a river that never runs dry,
A light that never fades.

O Eternal Love,
Let us be Your hands,
Your voice,
Your heart in this world,
So that all may know
That Love is the highest truth,
The deepest calling,
The greatest gift.

Amen.

85　Ritual of Compassion

To prepare for the ritual, you are asked to perform a random act of charity, a casual act of compassion, the day before or on the same day. For example, giving 5 euros to the next person who asks for money and immediately moving on without judging or determining how the money will be used; buying small gifts and placing them in a spot where passers-by can take them; paying in advance for the next unknown person at the cinema or supermarket checkout, etc. We will use this energy for the ritual. Of course, it can also be performed as an exercise.

Stand in a place where you have enough space and won't be disturbed. Position yourself so that you have a secure footing.

Close your eyes.

Feel your body's centre.

Slowly, let your attention descend over your legs to your feet. Feel how the earth supports you, how you are rooted in it. Be aware of this in a metaphorical sense:

How the earth nourishes you,

How she supports you,

How she provides stability.

Now, slowly move your attention up from your feet (or proceed through your chakras, if you're familiar with them). Once you reach the top (crown chakra), raise your hands and arms with each inhalation, stretching them upwards until they lightly open, reaching towards the sky (Worship gesture).

Pay attention to your breath and realize how your breath connects you to all living beings and fellow creatures.

This gesture is also one of blessing. So, bless all people, including those you hold grudges against, and all creatures, nature, animals, and plants. (...)

May all people be happy.

May all people be free from suffering.

"All" means everyone, including myself.

Slowly lower your arms until they are extended horizontally (Cross gesture). Dare to symbolize a cross with your body. Free yourself from the notion that this is a gesture of suffering. Take a moment to feel how it feels to take up this space. The cross connects all opposites, joining the vertical with the horizontal, two lines that would never meet otherwise.

Feel the openness of this gesture, the acceptance, devotion. The devotion of yourself and the acceptance of everything else. Feel the connection of all with all.

The cross is also a symbol of a key. The cross is the key to the inner space of silence, the space of Love, the space where we are whole, authentic, original, just being.

Love is pure being, free from justification, free from performance pressure, free from guilt, free from shame.

Just enjoy being.

Imagine how you embrace the whole world in this way.

Then, bring your arms forward and embrace yourself. (Self-Love gesture)

Embrace yourself in your entirety, embrace your own contradictions.

I embrace the strong and the weak within me,

... the healthy and the lack of health, the sick,

... what I've lived and what remains unlived,

... what has succeeded and what has failed,

... what has remained whole and what has broken,

... what is conscious and what is unconscious.

I embrace the trust and the lack of trust, the doubts,

... the courage and the lack of courage, the fear,

... the hope and the hopelessness,

... the Love and the lack of Love, the hatred,

... the Peace and the lack of Peace, the aggression,

... the faith and the lack of faith, the disbelief,

... the living and the lifeless, the frozen,

... all that is bright and the lightless darkness.

I feel how my arms, in the embrace, connect everything within me.

In this connection, there is healing.

This embrace is an expression of Love, Love for myself.

This embrace creates a space of Love, free, whole, original, authentic, pure, and clear... and completely at home... myself.

I release the embrace, place my hands on the solar plexus...

I connect with my perfect, whole core, my inner Buddha ... my source of Love, connected to the all-encompassing divine Love, which is eternal.

I feel how I can fill myself with it until I overflow with Love and radiate it...

I take a deep breath and a deep exhalation, solidifying these connections with everything ... — And conclude this ritual.

V. Handbook of Non-Violence and Civil Disobedience

86   Foreword

We have forgotten and buried non-violent resistance and civil disobedience. We have forgotten and buried its successes, and our trust is lost. I hear people lamenting that "those up there" control, steer, and lead the world, while we, as ordinary people, are powerless. "Those up there, they do whatever they want!" is the rhetoric of our times, and it is not new because this rhetoric has existed for years and is just another unreal scapegoat of humanity. In Western democracies, the signs of crisis are caused by the rapid decline of civil courage and, above all, by the weakening of civic responsibility. It is not the supposedly overpaid, detached politicians who work too little who are to blame, but serve some excellently as scapegoats. The fact that "those up there" is a figment of the imagination is revealed by a simple look at history. Human history testifies to people with pure hearts, noble intentions, and powerful actions. History tells of our strength and our influence in shaping the world. It speaks of the possibility of commanding the good and proves the possibility of preventing injustice solely through the realization of the good. We, as people, together and collectively, have shaped the world as it is. With all the poverty and injustice, misery, but also the beauty, prosperity, and small and great happiness, with all the wealth, waste, violence, and need, and everything in between. It was us. Not "those up there." We are all just human beings. Through and through. Equal and the same.

So "those up there" or "others up there" will not take over our tasks for us. It is not necessarily required to think directly in the "big we." Self-responsibility begins with the individual. The behaviour of people is positively influenced by good role models. Distinguished role models, good deeds, and the practice of virtues stimulate human reflection. Perhaps, by observing and following a good example, people reflect and follow suit. A good role model is transferable and has the potential to spread like a pandemic. As soon as the spotlight is focused on the individual, we recognize the importance of the individual. The whole is based on the small and individual.

87   *Ahimsa*

Ahimsa, in its modern interpretation following Gandhi's understanding, means "respect for all Life and the avoidance of harm and violence."

Ahimsa has often been referred to as "non-violence," but it must be literally translated from Sanskrit as "absence of harm" and is closest in meaning to "Peacefulness" in German. *Ahimsa* is an ancient concept with its origins in the Vedas, a spiritual and philosophical wisdom from India dating back to around 1900 BCE, making it nearly 4,000 years old. The Vedas, which roughly translate to "divine knowledge," were originally passed down orally over centuries and were considered authorless. The four Vedas, from which the Bhagavad Gita is derived, were eventually compiled and written down in Sanskrit by a sage named *Vyasa*. Another sage, Patanjali, is said to have studied these Vedic texts and developed what we now know as the Yoga Sutra, the foundation of the eight limbs of classical yoga.

Ahimsa is part of the first of the eight limbs, known as Yama, or practices of self-regulation, which free us from being victims of our own human impulses. *Yama practices* are likened to cleansing techniques for our mind, body, and spirit, enabling us to lead a more conscious and liberated Life. Ahimsa is not just a Yama in yoga, but is also a fundamental principle of Hinduism, Buddhism, and Jainism.

Great leaders like Gandhi lived by the principle of *Ahimsa parama dharma*. "Non-violence is our greatest duty."

Practice and Path

The word "practice" implies that something is learned and applied, and "path" suggests something that requires effort, time, and refinement. Ahimsa, as a practice of not causing harm to others, may seem simple in theory: Of course, one shouldn't lose their temper when they don't get their way. Of course, one shouldn't bully others to gain advantages or assert their will. Of course, one shouldn't lie. We readily recognize that this theory is often much harder to put into practice and maintain than it initially seems.

"Harming" doesn't only mean physically hurting other people. Words, sounds, loudness, behaviours, and even our thoughts can become weapons when used destructively. Even if our intention is peaceful and non-violent, it can be perceived differently by others and cause harm. In the Vedas, the ways of causing harm are *kayaka* ("by hand" or through physical actions), *vācaka* ("expressive" or through words), and *manasika* ("by the mind" or through thoughts).

While we may consider physical, word-based, or thought-based forms of violence as separate, we should understand that they are all interconnected.

Ahimsa-based practices of restraint, foresight, compassion, and good choices bring us closer to a stress-free and peaceful Life. When we have nothing to hide or regret and live this as a practice, we live simpler and freer. That is yoga.

The Vedas encourage us to honour our own dharma (righteous Life) or our own path while following principles like *Ahimsa*.

"I believe and try to teach that *Ahimsa* is fundamental in yoga, but it is also a fundamental principle of the other four *Yamas*. For example, in *yama satya*, or truthfulness, the truth is relative and embodies *Ahimsa*. Be honest, but not if it causes unnecessary pain or harm. Ask yourself: Do I want to speak my truth at all costs, or should I stop when I might cause harm at that moment? Another way *Ahimsa* is practised in the yoga community is becoming vegan or vegetarian. While a predominantly vegetarian diet is good, complete abstinence from meat and dairy does not work easily for everyone. A friendlier option is to teach people to recognize what is best for their bodies and health, and not to shame them for their choices." (Sangeeta Vallabhan, Yoga Teacher)

The principle of *Ahimsa* can be found in the teachings of Jesus as well as in naturopathy: *Primum non nocere*, which means "first, do no harm."

88   Non-Violence

Many people think that non-violence is simply refraining from violent actions. As a fundamental concept, that's not bad, but it's not that simple in theory and practice. "Non-violence," "non-violence," and "non-violence" are quite different things. Non-violence is based on a philosophical and theoretical concept that must be understood in order to live non-violence or to effectively and honestly implement it as a political and social movement and as a means of protest.

For other people, non-violence often remains mysterious, controversial, or a completely foolish and unrealizable ideal.

We want to attempt an "introduction to non-violence" here to clarify some of the misunderstandings, basic problems, and controversies and to help understand the concept of "non-violence" so that there is no disappointment or failure in trying to live it or apply it as a means.

In my opinion, non-violence has always existed because there have always been pacifists and people who abhor violence or have recognized the inevitable destructiveness of violence. Historically, however, the theoretical elaboration and organized implementation of non-violence are relatively young. It has already proven itself several times as a significant form of political and social engagement. Its nature and potential deserve better understanding.

Non-violent action does not rely on the goodwill of the opponent but is designed to be used even against determined resistance or violent suppression.

Non-violence is not just any method of action that is non-violent. Non-violence is, first and foremost, a state of mind.

And then it is a form of action that goes beyond the normal institutionalized political methods (voting, lobbying, letter writing, verbal expressions), without harming or attacking opponents. Non-violent action, like war, is a means of conflict resolution. It requires a willingness to take risks and endure suffering without retaliation. Sometimes it is a means by which people discover their social power, with the danger of leaving the path of non-violence based on that feeling. This must not happen, which is why a high level of mindfulness and discipline is required.

Non-violence vs. Non-harm vs. Renunciation of Violence

To understand, it is necessary to distinguish between "non-harm," "non-violence," and "Enunciation of violence." Non-harm is the avoidance of any form of violence. A roadblock is not non-violent if someone wants to use that road and to pass is prevented by force. Therefore, such an action cannot be "non-harm".

Non-violence is aware that an action that does not use violence may be perceived as violence by others. Therefore, in non-violence, while direct violence is avoided, the decision is made freely about how much indirect violence may be accepted in a non-violent action, e.g., because it is unavoidable. This indirect violence generally serves to avert greater violence, which also includes significant injustice: in Schopenhauer's sense:

| *Injustice is a form of violence.*

In contrast, "Renunciation of violence" should be further defined. Renunciation of violence is the renunciation of any direct and indirect violence. Actions are chosen that do not involve direct violence and also do not trigger indirect violence (e.g., coercion of others). In addition, in the case of renunciation of violence, no response is made to a violent reaction to non-violent action, so even a blow is not parried but received without defence.

In the case of non-harm, a violent response is not met with direct violence. However, defending oneself, such as blocking a punch, is still a form of indirect violence, as it impedes the attacker from carrying out their action. This obstruction or prevention can be perceived as an act of violence. Nonetheless, abstaining from violence actually means not defending against a violent response, including not blocking a punch but allowing oneself to be struck.

True pacifism and non-violent resistance are the courageous confrontation of evil with the power of *love.* (Martin Luther King)

For non-violent actions to be conducted safely and effectively, good planning and mental preparation are required. When combined with civil disobedience, non-violence necessitates a willingness to endure injustice, punishment, and violence.

The seven principles of non-violence are derived from two fundamental guidelines that we must always keep in mind:

(A) We are never against other people, but only against what they do.

(B) Violence is a perception of the other, which is why non-violence requires a high degree of empathy.

Non-violence is based on seven basic ideas:

(1) Alternatives are possible

One can confront injustice without resorting to violence.

(2) Empathy and sympathy

Non-violence seeks to win the friendship and understanding of the perceived opponent, not to harm them, but to also win them over to non-violence.

(3) Differentiation

The separation of the act from the actor: The protest is not directed at the individuals committing wrongdoing but at the wrongful action or rule.

(4) Capacity for suffering

To act non-violently, one must be willing to endure suffering because it is not retaliation but suffering and silent protest that bring redemption.

(5) Thinking and feeling

Non-violence avoids not only "external physical violence" but also "internal mental violence." Those who practice non-violence not only refuse to combat their counterpart but also refuse to hate them.

(6) Motivation

The motivation for non-violence is driven by Love in the sense of the Greek word Agape, which also means "understanding" and "good will, good intentions towards every human being."

(7) Vision

Those who practice non-violence must have a deep faith in the future, being convinced that the universe is ultimately evolving correctly, meaningfully, and according to a divine order.

90 The Seven Core Principles of Non-Violence

Non-violence is much more than just refraining from hitting.

Non-violence is guided by seven essential principles of non-violence:

(1) Respect everyone, including yourself.

The more we respect others, the more effectively we can persuade them to change. Never use humiliation as a tool, and never accept the humiliation of others.

Injustice anywhere is a threat to justice everywhere.
(Martin Luther King Jr.)

When it comes to yourself, remember that no one can degrade you if you do not allow yourself to feel humiliated.

(2) Constructive programs are more important than protest.

Concrete actions are always more powerful than mere symbolism, especially when these concrete actions are constructive; therefore, they should always be part of non-violence. The advantages of concrete constructive actions are evident: first, you are not just reacting to oppression, but you are actually taking responsibility. This helps shed passivity, fear, and helplessness. Second, it provides continuity to a movement, as it can evolve, especially when direct resistance is not advisable. Third, it builds a community with shared goals. Studies have shown that collaborative creative work is the most effective way to unite people. Constructive programs also create sympathy and reassure the public. They demonstrate that your movement is not a threat to social order, and, most importantly, creative programs offer solutions and build structures needed when the oppressive regime falls. Many an uprising has been successful, only to find that a new group of oppressors rushed into the vacuum. So, a good guideline is to be constructive wherever possible and obstructive only when necessary.

(3) Be aware of the long term.

Non-violent action always yields positive results, sometimes more than we intended. But we need patience. Violence may sometimes appear to "work" quickly because it forces certain changes, but in the long run, it leads to more misery and disorder. Violence does not improve relationships! Remember: we have no control over the ultimate outcomes of our actions, but we always have control over the means we employ, and, if we choose, over our feelings and state of mind.

(4) Seek "win-win" solutions that satisfy the real needs of all parties.

Remember that, whenever possible, your goal must be to restore relationships, not to achieve "victories." In a conflict, we may feel that for one side to win, the other must lose, but that is not true. We should move away from such notions and categories. Therefore, in non-violence, we do not seek to be winners or to elevate ourselves over others; rather, we strive to learn and make things better for everyone. The "psychology of winners" is part of the age-old war dynamic of "me against you," but the non-violent person views Life as a respectful "co-evolution" toward a loving community where all can thrive. Only by pursuing "win-win" solutions can a minority in a democracy realize their rights and ideals. And only then are they entitled to assert and enforce them.

(5) Power does not come from violence but from truth.

We are conditioned to think that power "grows from the barrel of a gun." There is indeed a form of power that comes from threats and brute force, but it is powerless if we refuse to obey it. There is another kind of power that arises from the truth. In Gandhi's sense, this means: Let's say you have advocated for the removal of an injustice; perhaps you have expressed your feelings in polite but determined acts of protest, but the other party does not respond. Then, as Gandhi said, you must "address not only the head but also the heart." And we can do that by taking on the suffering inherent in the unjust system to make it evident. This is known as Satyagraha, or the "Law/Force of Truth." In extreme cases, we may have to do this at the risk of our lives (hence, it is important to be very clear about our goals!). Do this with caution! History has shown that even bitter hostilities can melt with this kind of persuasion aimed at "moving the other's heart" rather than forcing them.

(6) Non-violence is not always non-action, which is just a theory.

However, there are times when we must use forms of coercion, for example, when a regime refuses to stop using violence and abuse, and we must act immediately to end the immense human suffering caused by the abuse of power. Even then, it requires strategic thinking and non-violent care to do it right. But when time allows, we use the power of patience and persuasion, enduring rather than inflicting suffering. Changes brought about through persuasion are enduring: someone who is convinced remains convinced, while someone who is forced only waits for the chance to return or seek revenge.

(7) Everything is interconnected.

Non-violence is based on the belief that all Life is interconnected, and when we understand our true needs, we do not compete with anyone. Always be aware that if you apply non-violence with courage, determination, and a clear strategy, you are more than likely to succeed: whether you achieve all your goals or not, you will contribute to a great transformation of human relationships that shapes our future. Martin Luther King said,

> *I can never be what I ought to be until you are what you ought to be. And you can never be what you ought to be until I am what I ought to be.*

91   Structure and Methods of Non-Violent Action

The Structure of Non-Violent Action

(1) Analysis of the conflict: Uncovering the injustices and gradually approaching the actual extent of the problem.

(2) Preparation of grassroots groups, information, and education.

(3) Action steps of the appropriate method of non-violence.

Methods of Non-Violent Action

Dialogue and negotiation are the cornerstones of non-violent action. Trust in people and their capacity for justice and truth are the hallmarks of this form of action, characterized by constant readiness for dialogue and respect.

The strength of dialogue is found in its truthful components:

- Revealing the truth of the opponent
- Exposing one's own complicity in the conflict
- Presentation of the injustice
- Constructive proposals from those affected by injustice

Direct action becomes necessary when the conflict opponent has broken off dialogue. Direct action brings the dialogue into the public eye. The goal is to prepare the groundwork and resume the dialogue. Grassroots groups with a clear strategy are necessary to carry out meaningful direct actions.

One of the most powerful forms of action is civil disobedience and non-cooperation. Mass refusal to cooperate paralyses the unjust system.

In constructive programs, the desired goal is partially anticipated. Models are created in which the desired justice is realized.

It's not about defending the status quo or possibly a part of the territory; it's about defending the values of the people who live there.

There is little to gain from ruling a country where people practically reject you. Complete non-cooperation with the unjust "ruler" paralyses their power.

People must be trained for this.

Non-violence and civil disobedience are also counter-models to militarization.

The non-violent actor always places people at the centre of events.

They don't want to destroy the enemy/opponent/oppressor, but to win them over. Only when that succeeds is the conflict resolved: both emerge from the conflict liberated, in a state of truth. There are no winners and losers, only reconciliation in justice.

It's also not advisable to isolate oneself from others or instil fear in them. Winning over the other cannot be accomplished with hatred.

92 Forms of Non-Violent Action

Non-violent action has three main forms:

1. Protest and persuasion
2. Civil disobedience and non-cooperation
3. Intervention

Protest and persuasion

The first category includes activities like speaking, picketing, petitions, vigils, street theatre, marches, rallies, and teach-ins. When practised under conditions of state tolerance, these methods can be relatively insignificant. If the expressed views are unpopular, controversial, or against government policies, even the mildest of these methods may require great courage and can have a strong impact.

Civil disobedience and non-cooperation

The second category involves active non-cooperation. In the face of institutional injustice, people may refuse to act as "normal" - to work, buy, or obey. This largest category of non-violent actions includes refusing to pay taxes, withholding rent or utilities, civil disobedience, conscientious objection, fasting, and more than fifty different types of boycotts and strikes. Non-cooperation can effectively disrupt the normal functioning of society, depending on the nature of the action and how widespread its application is. The most potent expression of non-cooperation is the general strike, in which a majority refuses to engage in usual social functions.

Intervention

Finally, there is non-violent intervention, which can be defined as the active interference and disruptive presence of people in the regular processes of social institutions. This can include sit-ins, occupations, disruptions of "business as usual" in offices, on the streets, or elsewhere.

In special cases, this also includes the creation of new social and economic institutions, including the establishment of parallel governments competing with the old order for sovereignty. These methods tend to represent a more direct and immediate challenge than the other methods described earlier, and may either lead to quicker success or harsher repression. The potential for escalation in them is obvious. Therefore, very good preparation and public relations are crucial to avoid misunderstandings: it's not about destroying a state to bring it back to the right path; it's about temporarily taking over an unjust legal order until it is restored.

Non-violence is not blind activism

To keep all forms of non-violent protest and civil disobedience truly non-violent, it is essential to cultivate non-violent thinking and feeling and engage intensively with the philosophy of non-violence.

93   Non-Violence and Pacifism

Many people confuse "pacifism" with "non-violence." Some reject pacifism and therefore believe that "non-violence" is merely "refraining from violence." This is not correct. Non-violence is much more than refraining from violence, and pacifism is a mindset that goes beyond non-violence. Even people who are not pacifists can participate in non-violent actions and learn non-violent thinking.

Pacifism as a fundamental attitude or conviction undoubtedly facilitates understanding and implementing non-violence. Non-violence is oriented toward the ideals of pacifism, and it's pacifists who have shaped and developed non-violence. Non-violence shows that pacifism does not mean "inaction," as is often misunderstood.

Although religious teachers have often imagined a world without violence and hatred, this ideal has appeared unattainable to most. The first notable groups in the modern world that attempted to live their non-violent ideals were small "non-resistant" Christian sects such as the Mennonites and Anabaptists, who, during times of war, refused military conscription and endured the penalties imposed on them without resistance. Apart from military service, such groups were generally law-abiding and desired to be left alone. Their focus was clearly on their personal spiritual well-being. Where such groups still exist today, they are politically disinterested and prefer a withdrawn, untroubled Life that allows them to live according to their ideals. We rarely observe such groups using non-violent methods.

Another, more secular, "non-violence,' which can be called "active reconciliation," is practised by many Quakers and individual pacifists. Their aim is particularly to reconcile parties in conflict, do Peace work, and assist victims of war and poverty. Alternative strategies for conflict resolution are to be developed, publicized, and implemented through education and example rather than coercion.

Parts of the German Peace movement have been involved in Peace work for decades in this way, and in some cases, they are also active in crisis areas with programs of mediation and aid to war victims, without attracting much public attention.

It is often observed that those who follow the approach of "active reconciliation" prefer a quietist approach to social problems. Rejecting war and violence may be acknowledged and possibly condemned, but what is related to "disturbance" or "trouble" is rather avoided. In this regard, it can be seen that "non-violence" does not mean "non-violence," as a boycott, blockade, or strike, for instance, inherently involves an element of violence, even though active violence is not exercised.

The Quakers and advocates of "non-violence" and "active reconciliation" have clearly emphasized this conflict. Nevertheless, this tradition has made important contributions to the philosophy of non-violence and non-violent action. Their views are less widespread today among pacifists and in the Peace movement in general than in the past.

Of significant importance in the development of non-violence is a movement that can be called "moral resistance." Advocates and followers of this path propagate and engage in education and projects to promote human cooperation. However, they often lack a comprehensive analysis of society or a comprehensive program for social change. 19th-century Americans who worked for the abolition of slavery articulated such "moral resistance." Many activities of the civil rights and anti-Vietnam War movements, such as sit-ins, marches, refusal of military service, blockade of ammunition deliveries, and disruption of draft centres, reflected this attitude, which focuses on a specific situation perceived as unjust but does not imply a (pacifist) fundamental attitude or a specific social understanding.

The women's rights movement in America in the 19th century used civil disobedience, tax refusal, and public demonstrations. Alice Paul's Woman's Party used vigils and hunger strikes to exert pressure for women's suffrage. During the Great Depression of the 1930s, sit-down strikes were employed to secure recognition of labour rights. Less known but highly significant was the battle plan called the Continental Association, adopted in America in October 1774. Delegates from the thirteen colonies agreed on a program that included economic boycotts (non-consumption, non-importation, and non-exportation) as well as social boycotts and other sanctions against those who refused to comply. Their program was the largest before the Gandhian campaign, which included a planned strategic phasing of the struggle.

"Non-violence" developed from and with these ideas in the 20th century. Social oppression, a commitment to national independence, and conflicts between labour and capital were often the motives. The concept of civil disobedience and the value of non-violent resistance were highlighted by writers such as Thoreau and Tolstoy. Until then, pacifists had not abolished war or injustice. They lacked an effective method for actively pursuing their goals, one that could harness human courage, energy, idealism, and solidarity and express itself in action.

The attention received by Mohandas Gandhi (1869-1948) marked a turning point in the development of non-violence. Gandhi began to resist British imperial oppression and initiated Indian independence. He was the first to develop and implement a variety of explicitly non-violent forms of action in a strategic plan aimed at long-term goals. This was not lacking in a philosophical basis and spiritual conviction influenced by ancient Vedic texts. Deeply religious, practical, and experimental in temperament, Gandhi was a shrewd, tireless, and efficient organizer who combined cheerfulness and humility with unwavering determination. He was less a political fighter than a social visionary.

Gandhi's non-violence had three main elements:

1. Self-improvement; i.e., the effort to develop oneself into a better person

2. Constructiveness; i.e., concrete programs and work to create the desired new social order

3. Campaigns of resistance against injustices blocking progress, such as the caste system and British colonial exploitation

Gandhi's success in linking mass action with non-violent discipline demonstrates the enormous social power that this form of engagement could generate. His experimental, unsystematic approach and his personal charisma, the special situation of Indian society, and Gandhi's eccentricity make it difficult to view his non-violent actions as universally applicable. Nevertheless, they are a significant inspiration for all forms of non-violence since then.

94   Examples of Non-Violent Activism

During World War II and shortly thereafter, militant pacifists in the USA successfully demanded the end of segregation in the prisons in which they themselves were incarcerated and participated in the first "Freedom Rides" to end segregation in transportation. The most dramatic non-violent actions of the 1950s were several voyages to atomic test areas by small ships with pacifist crews. At a time when nuclear war loomed as a fate that humanity seemed helpless to prevent, these actions expressed the widespread desire to act against the madness of tests and arms races. Although the boats were prevented from reaching their goal in each case, their powerful symbolism strengthened the morale of the anti-nuclear movement and gave the public a genuine impetus, eventually leading to the 1963 Nuclear Test Ban Treaty.

Thus, non-violent activists have repeatedly inspired by examples of courage and by taking personal responsibility for institutional injustice.

The Importance of the Grassroots

However, it was the Black civil rights movement and the struggle to end racial oppression, which, after Gandhi had already gained international attention, not only impressed the idea of non-violence upon the American consciousness but also garnered worldwide recognition. The Montgomery bus boycott in Alabama, which began in December 1955 when Rosa Parks refused to give up her seat to a white passenger, grew into an alternative transportation system and ended with the desegregation of the entire bus system. An articulate young pastor, Dr. Martin Luther King Jr., gained international fame as the spokesman for the struggle. He demonstrated that non-violence could lead to significant victories not only in India but also in the USA and everywhere. He achieved this despite racist violence and intimidation, which, unfortunately, as with Gandhi, led to his assassination but, in both cases, did not halt the initiated development but rather drove it forward.

In both cases, it was not one person who brought success but rather the emerging popular movement, which is often not adequately recognized and valued.

So, in 1960, a new wave of activities began when the first "sit-in" by four Black college students in Greensboro, North Carolina (one of them had just read a comic about the Montgomery campaign by the pacifist Fellowship of Reconciliation), decided to non-violently protest the denial of service at a local lunch counter. The action quickly spread and spurred a wave of similar actions, including those in front of public facilities. Under the pressure of actions by many small activist groups whose demands were widely perceived as just, new court decisions began to legitimize the changes people were fighting for. Meanwhile, the campaigns were carried out in many places, either spontaneously or loosely coordinated by groups like the Southern Christian Leadership Conference (SCLC) and the Student Non-violent Coordinating Committee (SNCC). King's important role as the speaker and moral symbol of the struggle has often led to an underestimation of the importance of the movement's decentralized base.

The heart of the movement was definitely the decision of thousands of people to risk their safety, often their lives, for the cause and their willingness to sacrifice their well-being for the greater fulfilment in the pursuit of justice and human community.

Revolution Through Non-Violence

The civil rights movement in the USA had enormous and lasting impacts. It influenced both Black and White people through the legal and institutional changes it brought about. It also created a group of people with a shared moral and political background from which they could address other injustices, such as the Vietnam War, imperialism, poverty, and sexism. This achievement was often downplayed by those who radicalized out of the movement when they shifted their focus to what still needed to be achieved and impatiently departed from the path of non-violence in thought and action.

"Pacifism is necessarily revolutionary," wrote Paul Goodman in 1962. "We will not have Peace unless there is a profound change in the social structure." But this conclusion was by no means evident to everyone, or at least most pacifists shied away from the magnitude of the task it implied. A. J. Muste (1885-1967), perhaps the most significant pioneer of revolutionary non-violence in America, had a position in an article from 1928 titled "Pacifism and Class Struggle." Muste, a minister who lost his position because he spoke out against World War I, had become a key leader in labour struggles. He called on pacifists to "acknowledge the violence upon which the current system is based" when some criticized the violence in certain labour actions. This is a recurring and current objection in non-violent actions when pacifism is only understood as the renunciation of violence but not as a belief intended and lived. When faced with the violence of the "opposing side," doubts arise about non-violence and non-violent resistance.

> *As long as we do not deal honestly and adequately with these ninety percent (of violence) of our problem, our concern for the ten percent of the problem becomes something ridiculous and perhaps hypocritical. In a world built on violence, one must be a revolutionary before one can be a pacifist.*

For these reasons, Muste turned away from pacifism for a while. He and his followers played a crucial role in organizing the unemployed, and he was, for a time, a highly respected ally of the Trotskyist movement. But he became convinced of the inadequacy of Marxism-Leninism and ultimately sought a policy that should be both revolutionary and non-violent.

Non-violent action, therefore, always requires trust and understanding of non-violence. This is precisely what defines non-violence: to remain non-violent in the face of violence.

A concise expression of such a policy, remarkably contemporary in tone, came in 1945 from the Committee for Non-violent Revolution in the USA: "We favour a decentralized, democratic socialism that involves workers and consumers in the management of industries, utilities, and other economic enterprises. We believe that workers themselves should take steps to control factories, mines, and shops. ... We advocate such methods of group resistance as demonstrations, strikes, organized civil disobedience, and underground organization where necessary. We view non-violence both as a principle and as a technique. In all actions, we eschew the methods of punishing, hating, or killing human beings. We believe that non-violence allows for such methods as sit-ins, strikes, and factory occupations. We believe that revolutionary change is only possible through direct action from below and not through deals or reformist proposals."

The Heyday of Non-Violent Actions

Groups advocating fundamental social change based on their experiences in the 1960s and early 1970s continued many of the focuses of earlier non-violent movements. They worked on changing fundamental economic and social systems and aimed to change themselves to eliminate the ways in which personal behaviour perpetuated gender, race, class, and other oppressions. They rejected the Western notion of the "good Life" based on compulsive consumption in favour of a richer way of Life rooted in higher self-awareness, fun, and greater social satisfaction – a way of Life that can only be realized through fundamental changes for all. Additionally, they advocated non-hierarchical organization and consensus-based decision-making and sought better ways to educate people through training programs, including group dynamics and peer counselling, and workshops. This political work included educational efforts to spread an analysis of society, a vision of a better society, a strategy for getting from here to there, and the organization of non-violent campaigns as part of this strategy.

Campaign Movements

In Germany, non-violence has particularly stood out through the actions of environmental activists, the Peace movement, and the anti-nuclear movement.

It is important to note that, except for some religious groups and pacifist elements of the Peace movement, most non-violent actions were not initiated or sustained by principled non-violence.

"The greatest advances in non-violence have not come from people who pursued non-violence as an end in itself, but from people who passionately sought to free themselves from social injustice" (Dave Dellinger: "The Future of Non-violence"). The typical structural conditions that lead to a turn to non-violent struggle are that conventional political and legal channels appear blocked, but people are unwilling to abandon their goals, as was clearly the case in the fight against nuclear power. Out of their own creativity or, more often, through hearing about or remembering relevant events, people discover a way to act.

However, this process does not have to be spontaneous but can be consciously promoted. In 1972, William Moyer, co-founder of the Movement for a New Society, proposed a strategy for a nationwide and transnational movement against nuclear power in a speech titled "De-developing the U.S. Through Non-violence." Instead of forming a national coalition of supporting groups (a process with several disadvantages, which he described in his article), "the campaign movement approach encourages groups to organize what they find creative and important. Small groups begin small projects in different locations and only join others when their interests coincide. The key here is not the size of the initial numbers but the ability to organize local campaign-focused socio-dramatic projects with drama, crises, and other socio-dramatic elements. Even if all these ingredients are present, there is no guarantee that a project will become a full-fledged movement. The strategy of the campaign movement approach in national efforts is that if enough independent socio-drama projects are started, there will soon be enough public and interest." This is exactly what happened in the worldwide struggle against arms, nuclear energy, and other social movements. Another example of this strategy is "Third World" attention to Fair Trade. Local small groups set up so-called "Third World shops," took their message to the public through information stands, boycotted unfair companies, and more. This led to general attention to the issue, the formation of companies and quality seals, and an agenda for international policy. The international protest movement against apartheid in South Africa is another such movement and can probably be considered one of the most successful. Locally, groups of people who wanted to do something about apartheid in South Africa formed. There was no common organization, and networking was rare. Countless such groups dedicated themselves to an issue that did not directly affect them. They organized festivals and informational events, concerts, and protest rallies, there were bank account closure campaigns and boycotts of South African goods. Companies were confronted and exposed through sit-ins and other actions, postcard campaigns and signature collections called on politicians to take a stand and no longer support the regime in South Africa. International pressure grew so great through these numerous action groups and initiatives that the apartheid regime in South Africa had to give up and release Nelson Mandela. It is probably the most peaceful, non-violent, largest, and most successful movement of its kind that we know of, and it received little media recognition.

There are several other examples in history where non-violent actions and movements played a significant role in ending or hindering violent conflicts. Here are a few notable examples:

- Indian Independence Movement (1942-1947): Led by Mahatma Gandhi, the Indian independence movement used non-violent civil disobedience and protests to gain independence from British rule. The movement ultimately contributed to the end of colonial rule in India.

Civil Rights Movement in the United States (1950s-1960s): Advocates such as Martin Luther King Jr. employed non-violent resistance tactics, including boycotts, sit-ins, and marches, to fight against racial segregation and discrimination. The movement played a crucial role in the enactment of civil rights legislation and significant social changes.

People Power Revolution in the Philippines (1986): The non-violent uprising in the Philippines ousted the long-time dictator Ferdinand Marcos. Millions of Filipinos engaged in peaceful protests, including the famous "EDSA Revolution," which led to Marcos fleeing the country.

Velvet Revolution in Czechoslovakia (1989): A series of non-violent protests, led by dissident groups and individuals like Vaclav Havel, contributed to the overthrow of the communist regime in Czechoslovakia. The Velvet Revolution marked the end of communist rule in the country.

- Northern Ireland Peace Process (1990s): The Peace process in Northern Ireland involved negotiations between conflicting parties and communities, as well as the inclusion of paramilitary groups in the political process. The Good Friday Agreement of 1998 helped bring an end to decades of sectarian violence.

- "Arab Spring" (2010-2012): While the outcomes of the "Arab Spring" uprisings were mixed, some movements, like the one in Tunisia, achieved success through non-violent means, leading to the overthrow of authoritarian regimes.

These examples demonstrate that non-violent actions, including civil disobedience, protests, and negotiations, can be powerful tools in resolving conflicts and achieving social and political change.

I will be non-violent because I see this as the answer to humanity's problems. (Martin Luther King Jr.)

95   Non-Violence as an Indicator of Strength and Power

The conventional view of power is that it's something some people possess and others don't. Power is often associated with soldiers, authority, ownership of wealth, and institutions. The non-violent theory of power, on the other hand, is quite different. Instead of viewing power as something you possess, it argues that power is a dynamic social relationship. Power usually depends on sustained obedience. When people refuse to obey rulers, the power of those rulers starts to crumble. This fundamental truth is, in some ways, obvious, yet it took the dramatic historical episodes of Gandhi's civil disobedience campaigns to establish a new model of power. In everyday social Life, this truth is often obscured, but events like the fall of the former Shah in Iran or the oppressive regime in Bolivia in 1978 can't be understood without it.

From the conventional view of power, heavily armed rulers hold all the cards. They can arrest demonstrators or, in extreme cases, have them shot. However, reality is more complex. Instead of just two societal actors - the rulers and the opposition - a whole range of intermediary forces can be crucial. What if new demonstrators keep appearing? What if influential societal groups or individuals begin to condemn acts of brutality? What if troops or the police, or their officers, decide to disregard orders? The overthrow of dictators in Guatemala and El Salvador in 1944 (described by George Lakey in "Strategy for a Living Revolution") and the fall of repressive regimes in Iran (1978-1979) and Bolivia (1978) show that such events are historically possible. There have also been changes in political systems in Eastern Europe that can essentially be attributed to non-violent resistance by the people as the rulers.

In a planned non-violent campaign, it's essential to lay the foundations. This means defining goals, selecting strategy and tactics, creating de-escalation and emergency plans, training, and so on. Non-violence is neither magic nor chance; it's a way to mobilize the power we have for maximum effectiveness.

Regardless of whether non-violent actions begin as a grass-roots initiative that authorities respond to or if it's an improvised public response to an event, the above outline shows that the initial "action and reaction" is just the beginning. Taking the example of occupying a nuclear power plant site, there are not only the main actors in conflict with each other but also anti-nuclear activists who do not commit civil disobedience but play an active support role; potential participants who didn't feel enough urgency or feel needed to take part in the action; people who would like to see an end to nuclear power but have no intention of doing anything about it; people who are not aware of the issue; people who are hostile to "environmentalists delaying necessary progress"; people who say "lawbreakers should be punished" but limit themselves to complaining; right up to the utility company executives, the governor's staff, bank presidents, and so on. There are also police officers and other security forces whose job is to counteract the demonstrators, but whose personal attitudes may vary along the spectrum.

The following diagram shows how activists try to influence and engage people with various viewpoints along this spectrum.

The actions of the key societal actors potentially affect all these people. The outbreak of the conflict draws attention to the issue. In a crucial sense, the two sides do not "fight" each other directly, but also compete for the support and allegiance of third parties or "the public."

To achieve their desired outcome, the agents of repression must convince activists to lose their solidarity and abandon their goals. However, if they maintain their solidarity and discipline, this form of repression becomes ineffective. Solidarity alone doesn't ensure success; it can be complemented by a kind of "political jiu-jitsu" where the repressive efforts themselves tend to shift the balance of power in favour of non-violent activists. People on the side of the activists increase their commitment, while those aligned with the oppressive power reduce their support or switch sides. Changes in attitudes are just as important as changes in behaviour because both sides base their actions on how they perceive their support.

While conventional power-holders like to exaggerate and overstate the ratio of their supporters, the tendency exists among non-violent activists as well. However, caution is needed. An honest assessment of the actual circumstances is crucial to develop the right strategy and not neglect important steps in building a foundation.

Non-violent action isn't dependent on the opponent being repressive or making mistakes. It isn't hindered if the opponent is moderate and conciliatory. Most methods mobilize political power regardless of the opponent's reaction.

Non-Violence Uses Intelligence

For non-violence to be successful, it's important to learn and understand the philosophy and methods.

Mindless activism doesn't align with non-violence, and it often unfairly tarnishes the term, making activists vulnerable and hindering success. To be effective, every approach to social change has certain requirements. Because most people fear and disapprove of violence, any action perceived as violent undermines the dynamics that gain allies and lead to success. Organizers have a responsibility to insist on training and common discipline to minimize violent outbreaks. "Opponents" consistently try to "use" any violence to discredit activists and divert attention from their message. Seasoned working-class organizers have long recognized this.

96 Truthfulness of Non-Violence

Public Relations and Openness

Good public relations and the courage to distance oneself from activists who don't adhere to non-violent rules are essential. It is also crucial to openly and honestly discuss plans from the beginning, as this can prevent misinterpretation by the "opposition" or expose it as such. Deception or secrecy may seem advantageous, but openness is vital for non-violent actions.

Secretiveness leads to inefficiency, authoritarianism, and distrust because it necessitates hiding much of what is planned from allies. Dependence on secrecy opens a movement to disruptions by infiltrators and informants. This secrecy fosters fears of betrayal, and movements towards secrecy often occur when a movement loses confidence, further weakening the movement by reducing its numbers and attracting people with a secretive, conspiratorial mindset.

On the other hand, the positive effects of openness are significant. It aligns with the goal of educating the public on issues and the kind of society we hope to build. Openness presents a positive image to the public, showing that we consider our actions legitimate and expect others to think the same, which encourages them to adopt this view. Openness boosts the morale and self-esteem of participants. Our style contrasts sharply with the secrecy and self-importance of our opponents. No matter what the short-term appearance may be, when all pros and cons are weighed, long-term effectiveness clearly requires openness.

Police and Authorities

One aspect deserves special attention: relations with the police and other authorities. It can be argued that the police are not impartial enforcers of the law, but rather agents of an unjust system whose authority should not be respected. "Cooperating" with the police by informing them about our plans can be seen as facilitating their work, accepting their authority, and thus supporting the system we should be fighting against. The first point is valid, but not the conclusions. Because police violence often results from fear and ignorance in tense conflicts (even if it is often ordered from above), it is in our interest to engage in precise communication.

Moreover, although agents of a system sometimes symbolize and seem to embody that system, they should not be confused with the system itself or the actual power structure. The police, no matter how brutal some may behave, is a plaything from which we should demand not to act against their own interests. Hostility towards the police is misplaced.

In my view, slogans like "Join us!" make no sense when they call for an attitude that I cannot be sure is also held by them. Demanding that someone join a counter-opinion is undemocratic and violent. It also doesn't consider that, while on duty, police officers can express their opinions only under significant sanctions. Thus, the bar for remonstration is very high.

Leaving the decision to recognize their authority and integrity and fostering empathy is much more effective and sustainable.

97   Non-Violence is not a Peace Movement

Does using non-violent actions automatically turn a protest movement into a Love and Peace movement? No, absolutely not. — The use of non-violence is indeed a step towards a more loving world, but it is too far to reach in one leap. If "Love" is understood as a prerequisite for non-violent action (and not just as a helpful refinement), the demand for "Love" can lead to violence, especially for people who have done cruel things or who are rightfully embittered and unable to Love their adversaries. Loving each other means accepting one another. However, non-violent action is a protest movement that does not want to accept the actions and attitudes of the other side. Adorning oneself with "Love" and "Peace" in a non-violent protest can provoke the opposite of what is desired because "Love" and "Peace" cannot be decreed but arise from the feelings of the observer or the other party. A movement that perceives itself as "loving" and "peaceful" but takes non-violent actions can be seen as violent and rejecting by others. An example is the 1970s hippie scene, which was characterized by a self-perception of "Love" and "Peace" but was perceived as aggressive, provocative, and "dangerous" by wide parts of society.

An eye for an eye will leave the whole world blind.
(Mahatma Gandhi)

Why is non-violent action not only justified but also sensible against a violent oppressor?

There is no painless path to liberation. Given the inevitability of suffering, it is both ennobling and pragmatic to present non-violent discipline and suffering (as Martin Luther King, Jr. and Gandhi did) as imperatives. "Venting anger" in a way that costs a group of allies is a luxury that serious movements cannot afford. What a movement that wants to achieve good must never afford is escalation and getting sucked into a spiral of violence.

For women who are concerned that non-violence could make them victims and for men who fear that non-violence could make them cowards, it is important to emphasize self-assertion, which is associated with non-violent action. Feminist theorist Barbara Deming wrote that non-violent actions are inherently androgynous. In them, the two impulses traditionally treated as different, "masculine" and "feminine," the impulse of self-assertion and the impulse of compassion, are clearly combined. The brilliance of non-violence is that it shows they are indivisible and thus restores human community: One asserts one's rights as a human, but one asserts them with consideration for others, asserting them as rights that belong to every person - mine, and therefore yours, yours, and therefore mine. Non-violence does not exclude self-assertion. On the contrary, it is the most powerful tool that individuals and the masses possess. Through non-violent actions, women, children, and vulnerable groups can mobilize power without reinforcing the predominant power of violent domination.

Property Damage

Now, let's consider whether non-violence allows property damage or destruction.

The risk of property destruction is that it moves toward the logic of violence. If we are determined to destroy property, will we be willing to hurt a person who stands in our way? The dangers of property destruction are significant. It can provide a convenient pretext for repression. It can be a way to slide toward violence by reflecting a loss of confidence in the chosen means and an inclination to waver between two conflicting strategic decisions. Such ambiguities lead to violence by other participants and prove fatal to success. Property destruction can be an effective tactic under certain circumstances, but must always be evaluated on whether it is primarily understood as "a challenge in human terms from humans to other humans" (Shaw).

The effective use of property destruction is appropriate only when random and undisciplined destruction is avoided, and any destruction is entirely public and subject to careful and deliberate control. Under special circumstances, it may be necessary to prevent violence or acute danger. For example, targeted destruction of weapons, barricades, or unlawful surveillance equipment can be a meaningful non-violent action if (1) the action is public, (2) the reason and symbolism are revealed and communicated, (3) no one is harmed, and (4) the use is proportional or unavoidable.

Violence in Response to Non-violence?

Non-violence can also provoke violent responses. Sometimes people believe that if they use non-violence, the other side will also refrain from using violence. That is not necessarily the case. However, it should not be thought that non-violence has not worked in such cases. De-escalation and avoiding counter-violence are just a minor aspect of non-violence.

Unrealistic hopes for a quick "victory" hinder the development of any effective strategy. Non-violence does not guarantee success any more than armed struggle. It is crucial to apply similar criteria when evaluating the effectiveness of these approaches, which is not usually done. Failures of armed struggle are usually attributed to a poor strategy, insufficient resources, and low morale. In contrast, the failure of non-violence is usually attributed to non-violence itself, not to how the action was carried out. Similarly, the value and significance of non-violent successes are downplayed, while violent successes are exaggerated without fully weighing their costs and losses.

99   Civil Disobedience

Those who say it can not be done, should not interrupt those doing it. (Chinese Proverb)

Civil disobedience is a deliberate violation of rules or a conscious breaking of the law based on moral and ethical obligation (a matter of conscience). Civil disobedience is never selfish; it always extends beyond an individual's interests. It is not about egoism or personal gain but rather serves the common good or the protection of minorities. In addition to moral and ethical conflicts, a conflict with the law can also be a reason for civil disobedience. Two or more laws may contradict each other; for example, a law may contradict human rights declarations or fundamental rights laid out in the constitution. Under certain circumstances, laws may conflict in such a way that civil disobedience becomes inevitable because adhering to one law would mean violating another. Civil disobedience presupposes the recognition of the legal order as such. This sets civil disobedience apart from resistance movements and revolutions that do not acknowledge just constitutions and the rule of law.

Civil disobedience is always morally and ethically motivated, never political.

Civil disobedience is always non-violent. This is done in recognition that non-violence is not the same as passivity. A peaceful, non-violent action can still be perceived by others as an act of violence because it interferes with their freedom or the exercise of their actions. However, non-violence never seeks the use of physical violence as an objective. People have the freedom to abstain from violence and to employ indirect violence through the exercise of political or societal pressure or the prevention of the implementation of unjust measures (e.g., self-defence and the protection of others). Civil disobedience is always conducted publicly, usually with prior notice. This sets it apart from criminal acts carried out in secrecy. Civil disobedience disregards specific legal norms but never the legal order as a whole. Engaging in a specific calculated rule violation, such as not wearing a face mask when such a rule is in place, does not justify disregarding other rules, like disregarding the police as a whole or looting a supermarket or assaulting a bouncer.

100 222 Methods of Non-Violent Action

This is a collection of potential and actual non-violent actions. Some of these actions may, under certain circumstances, be considered illegal. The mere mention of such actions is not an incitement to commit a crime. Local laws should be observed. Each individual is responsible for their own actions or inaction.

I. Methods of Non-violent Protest and Persuasion

Formal Declarations

1. Public Speeches, Speaker's Corner
2. Approving or Disapproving Letters
3. Declarations by Organizations and Institutions
4. Public Declarations with Signatures
5. Complaints and Statements of Intent or Will
6. Group or Mass Petitions, Online Petitions
7. Communication with a Wider Audience
8. Slogans, Caricatures, and Symbols
9. Banners, Posters, and Displayed Communications
10. Leaflets, Pamphlets, and Books
11. Independent Newspapers and Magazines
12. Advertisements in Newspapers, Radio, Television, Media
13. Recordings (e.g., Songs or Speeches), Broadcasting, and Television
14. Writing in the Sky and on the Ground
15. Songs, Concerts, Street Music

Group Actions

16. Delegations

17. Satirical and Parodic Awards for the Opposite Side

18. Flash Mobs, Spontaneous Theatre

19. Influence through Interest Groups

20. Picket Lines and Blockades

21. Mock Elections

Symbolic Public Acts

22. Displaying Flags and Symbolic Colours

23. Wearing Symbols

24. Prayer and Worship

25. Supplying Symbolic Objects

26. Public Undressing in Protest

27. Dressing Uniquely in Protest

28. Conscious Destruction of One's Property

29. Symbolic Lights (Torches, Candles, Lasers, etc.)

30. Window Displays, Signs in or Outside of Windows

31. Display of Portraits

32. Protest Painting

33. New Signs and Names (e.g., for Streets)

34. Symbolic Sounds (e.g., Bell Ringing)

35. Symbolic Reclamation (e.g., of Certain Territories) for Another Purpose

36. Rude Gestures

Pressure on Individuals

37. "Persecution" of Government Representatives

38. Mocking of Government Representatives

39. Fraternization

40. Vigils Outside Homes or Offices

Theatre and Music

41. Sketches and Satire

42. Performance of Plays or Music

43. Symbolic Display as a Flash Mob

Processions

44. Marches

45. Parades

46. Religious Processions

47. Pilgrimages

48. Motorcades

Cult of the Dead

49. Political Mourning

50. Symbolic Funerals

51. Funerals as Demonstrations

52. Honouring at Gravesides

Public Meetings

53. Protest or Solidarity Meetings

54. Demonstrations, Rallies

55. Vigils

56. Protest Gatherings

57. Covert Protest Gatherings

58. Teach-ins

Withdrawal and Rejection

59. Leaving a Conference, Meeting, Discussion, etc.

60. Silence

61. Declining Honours

62. Turning One's Back on Someone

63. Obtrusive/Verbal Disruptions of the Opposite Side's Rallies

64. Infiltration of Meetings

65. Abuse/Manipulation of Question-and-Answer Sessions, Discussions

II. Methods of Social Non-cooperation

Boycott of Persons

66. Social Boycott (Ostracism)

67. Selective Social Boycott

68. Non-cooperation in the Manner of Lysistrata (Sexual Refusal)

69. Exclusion, Excommunication

70. Interdict

Non-cooperation in Social Events and Customs and with Institutions

71. Suspension of Social and Sports Activities

72. Boycott of Social Events (e.g., Receptions, Banquets, Parties)

73. Student and Pupil Strike

74. Social Disobedience

75. Withdrawal from Social Institutions

Withdrawal from the Social System

76. Stay-at-Home

77. Civil Disobedience

78. Complete Personal Non-cooperation

79. Workers' Flight

80. Sanctuary Flight (e.g., Church)

III. Methods of Economic Non-cooperation

Economic Boycotts

Actions by Workers and Producers

Actions by Middlemen

Actions by Owners and Managers

Common Strikes in Industry

> 121.Company Strikes (within a Company)
>
> 122.Sector Strikes (within a Sector or Industry)
>
> 123.Solidarity Strikes

Limited Strikes

> 124.Piecemeal Strikes (Workers Leave One by One)
>
> 125.Selective Strikes (Refusal of Specific Work)
>
> 126.Slowdown Strikes
>
> 127.Working to Rule
>
> 128.Sick-ins
>
> 129.Work-to-Order Strikes
>
> 130.Limited Strikes (No Complete Stoppage)
>
> 131.Selective Strikes (e.g., Refusal of Certain Activities)
>
> 132.General Strikes
>
> 133.General Strikes

Combinations of Strikes and Shutdowns

> 134.Hartals (Temporary Stoppage of Economic Life in a Region)
>
> 135.Economic Shutdowns

V. Methods of Political Non-cooperation

Rejection of Authority

> 136.Withdrawal of Cooperation on a Large Scale (Withdrawal of Authorship)
>
> 137."Hit and Run" Actions (Temporary Acts of Refusal)
>
> 138.Mutiny

Non-cooperation by Citizens with the Government

Alternatives to Obedience

Actions by Government Personnel

VI. Methods of Non-violent Intervention

Physical Intervention

183. Sit-in (Occupation of Rooms or Buildings)

184. Stand-in (Standing Still, e.g., at Counters or Entrances, Even After Being Denied Entry)

185. Ride-in (Using Public Transportation in Seats Reserved for Others)

186. Wade-in (Using Public Beaches Despite Racial Segregation)

187. Mill-in (Protesters Keep Moving, Unlike Sit-in)

188. Pray-in (Attempt to Attend a Service from Which One Is "Officially" Excluded)

189. Non-violent Symbolic Seizure

190. Non-violent Invasion

191. Non-violent Intrusion

192. Non-violent Obstruction

193. Non-violent Occupation

Social Intervention

195. Establishment of New Social Patterns

196. Deliberate Overloading of Public Facilities

197. Stall-in (Social Actions, e.g., Banking Transactions, Performed as Slowly as Possible)

198. Speak-in (Disruption of Meetings with Speeches on Issues Not Necessarily Related to the Agenda)

199. Guerrilla Theatre

200. Building Alternative Social Institutions

201. Alternative Communication Systems

Economic Intervention

202. Reverse Strike (Workers Work Harder and Longer than Required)

203. Stay-in Strike (Workers Strike but Remain at Their Workplace)

204. Non-violent Land Seizure

205. Ignoring Blockades

206. Politically Motivated Forgery (of Money or Documents)

207. Purchase of Certain Goods to Prevent Their Availability to an Opponent

208. Confiscation of Property

209. Dumping (Selling Goods on the World Market at a Lower Price to Deplete Another Country's Revenue)

210. Patronage of Selected Companies

211. Alternative Markets

212. Alternative Transportation Systems

213. Alternative Economic Institutions

Political Intervention

214. Deliberate Overloading of Administrative Systems

215. Revealing Identity of Agents

216. Seeking Arrest Intentionally

217. Civil Disobedience Against "Neutral" Laws

218. Work-to-Rule Without Collaborating

219. Alternative Judicial Processes

220. Double Sovereignty and Parallel Government

Constructive Intervention

221. Help and Protection for Refugees

222. Psychological, Social, Legal Support for the Oppressed or Suffering

Particularly constructive interventions can be creatively developed in various ways.

101 Contemplation

The mind perceives a problem, but consciousness sees a task.

All too often, people entrust the conduct of their lives to the mind, and thus, to the ego. Yet, the ego pursues its own goals, lives its own Life, and in this state, we don't truly live our lives ourselves.

Only when your Self, your consciousness, leads your Life, does true Life begin from "inner wisdom."

Difficulties, all suffering, and any deficiency arise from the illusion of the self.

Consciousness knows no problems, knows no suffering or deficiency; it simply is.

There's no such thing as "awakening" because consciousness is always awake and present.

It's merely a matter of perception.

Take a moment to realize:

Who thinks when I think?

Who acts when I act?

Who feels when I feel?

Who hears when I hear?

Who sees when I see?

Who speaks when I speak?

Who experiences what I experience?

Do you think it's your body and your mind?

Or do you perceive what is as yourself, as your consciousness?

Through intuitive perception, you experience what is, always in the present moment.

When the ego and the mind vanish, so do rumination and thought, making room for the wisdom of consciousness.

Judgment and condemnation vanish.

Foes and fears disappear.

In your Life, there are only situations and events. You realize that all "problems" are actually just "tasks."

To walk your path, you need a clear goal because a clear goal leads to clear priorities, the path, and the right steps.

And you'll find this clear goal nowhere else but within yourself.

When you mentally feel the goal beforehand, you can't possibly miss it.

There are no hopeless situations. There's always a way and a solution.

Never give up.

Sometimes you have to take a leap because you can't cross an abyss with small steps.

Keep your attention constantly focused on your goal and the achieved success until it becomes a reality.

Don't lament the present, as in the next moment, it becomes the past. What's the value in complaining about the past?

Shape the present because it creates the future.

Resistance only begets resistance.

Instead of complaining and suffering about the undesirable, devote your thoughts to the desired and the longed-for.

Reality is created within, in consciousness, and manifests outwardly. However, if something doesn't exist within, it can't become a reality externally.

Everything requires an inner mental counterpart as a form for the manifestation of reality in the external world.

We live in a unique time with unprecedented changes in all aspects of human existence: technically, socially, politically, and economically. These are the birth pangs of a new era. What happens is not as important as how we deal with it, what we make of it, and that's decided by each individual in each moment. This is the great opportunity of our time, your personal opportunity for the better.

Everything you pray and ask for—believe that you have received it, and it will be yours. "
(Mark 11:24)

In what's commonly known as the Sermon on the Mount, Jesus provided an instruction for happiness that can guide us through all crises. In the translations by Eugen Drewermann, it reads something like this:

Blessed are the people who know of their poverty and embrace it.

Blessed are those who weep, for their hearts will be pure.

Blessed are the defenceless, for only they will be able to make Peace.

Blessed are those who hunger and thirst for the right Life.

Blessed are the merciful.

Blessed are the pure in heart.

Blessed are the Peacemakers.

Blessed are those who suffer persecution for the sake of the right Life before God.

VI   Building Peace

In times of crisis intelligent people look for solutions,
Idiots for the guilty.

102　The Necessity and Importance of Universal Human Rights

The quest for Peace has been a perpetual aspiration of humanity, reflecting the collective yearning for a world free from conflict, oppression, and injustice. At the heart of this pursuit lies the indispensable role of universal human rights. Enshrined in international agreements and declarations, these rights serve as the linchpin for fostering Peace on a global scale. The necessity and importance of universal human rights for Peace are profound, as they provide a common ethical foundation that transcends borders, cultures, and political ideologies.

Universal Rights in a Multi-Cultural World

Some Islamic countries have criticised universal human rights. They claim that they are one-sidedly Christian or "Western" orientated and do not take into account cultural differences between nations, different value systems and other religious norms.

They have even drafted their own alternative version of a declaration of human rights. However, if you look at this exclusively Islamic declaration, you realise that it is less about the rights of human individuals and more about the supposed rights of the Islamic God. Almost every article is about respecting God and that this takes precedence over everything else. All aspects of dignity, equality, etc. are thus subject to religious interpretation and possible restrictions by (religious) authorities. But this is exactly what the Universal Declaration of Human Rights tries to avoid.

Other criticisms that the Universal Declaration of Human Rights focusses too much on the individual, while in some cultures the common good or the interests or authority of a social group take precedence over individual freedom, also do not apply, since the aim of the Universal Declaration of Human Rights is precisely to protect the individual from the harmful decisions of an authority.

Dignity as a Path to Peace

Universal human rights begin with the recognition of the inherent dignity of every individual. The acknowledgment that all humans share a fundamental and equal worth lays the groundwork for peaceful coexistence. When societies uphold the dignity of their citizens, they cultivate an environment that values mutual respect, tolerance, and understanding. Peace flourishes in societies where individuals are treated with dignity, as it creates a sense of belonging and shared humanity that transcends divisive factors.

Equality as a Catalyst for Harmony

The principle of equality embedded in universal human rights is a catalyst for social harmony and, consequently, global Peace. The recognition that everyone is entitled to the same basic rights, regardless of their background, fosters a sense of fairness and inclusivity. By dismantling discriminatory practices and promoting equal opportunities, societies can mitigate social tensions and reduce the potential for conflict. Inequality, on the other hand, is a breeding ground for resentment and discord, posing a direct threat to Peace.

Freedom as a Guarantor of Stability

The preservation of Peace hinges on the protection of individual freedoms. Universal human rights encompass a spectrum of civil and political liberties that empower individuals to express their opinions, assemble peacefully, and participate in the decision-making processes of their communities. Societies that safeguard these freedoms create spaces for dialogue, constructive dissent, and the resolution of conflicts through peaceful means. In contrast, the suppression of basic freedoms often leads to social unrest, discontent, and, ultimately, upheaval.

Justice as the Foundation of Lasting Peace

Universal human rights underscore the importance of justice as the foundation of lasting Peace. By ensuring access to fair legal systems and promoting accountability for human rights violations, societies can address grievances and rectify historical injustices. Justice serves as a deterrent to violence, offering a non-violent avenue for resolving disputes. When individuals believe they have recourse to a just system, they are more likely to trust in the institutions that govern them, fostering stability and the conditions for peaceful coexistence.

It seems to be very import to define the meaning of justice, as it could be pointed out, that many wars are justified for reasons of justice and that "justice" is often used in a sense of "revenge".

The Universal Declaration of Human Rights (UDHR) does not explicitly provide a detailed definition of justice. However, the principles outlined in the UDHR imply a commitment to justice as a fundamental value within the context of human rights. The document emphasizes equality, fairness, and the rule of law, all of which are integral components of a just society.

Several articles in the UDHR contribute to the understanding of justice:

1. Article 7: Equality Before the Law: 'All are equal before the law and are entitled without any discrimination to equal protection of the law." This article underscores the principle of legal equality, an essential aspect of justice.

2. Article 8: Right to Remedy by Competent Tribunal: "Everyone has the right to an effective remedy by the competent national tribunals for acts violating the fundamental rights granted him by the constitution or by law." This article recognizes the importance of access to justice and legal remedies for individuals whose rights have been violated.

3. Article 10: Right to Fair Public Hearing: "Everyone is entitled in full equality to a fair and public hearing by an independent and impartial tribunal, in the determination of his rights and obligations and of any criminal charge against him." This article reinforces the principles of fairness and impartiality in legal proceedings.

4. Article 21(1): Right to Participate in Government: "Everyone has the right to take part in the government of his country, directly or through freely chosen representatives." This article highlights the importance of participatory justice, where individuals have the right to be involved in decisions that affect their lives.

5. Article 28: Social and International Order: "Everyone is entitled to a social and international order in which the rights and freedoms set forth in this Declaration can be fully realized." This article suggests that justice extends beyond the national level to the international arena, emphasizing the need for a just global order.

While the UDHR does not provide a comprehensive definition of justice, it establishes a foundation for a just and equitable society by promoting principles such as equality, fairness, access to legal remedies, and the rule of law. The interpretation and application of these principles contribute to the broader understanding of justice within the context of human rights. In no way "justice" is supposed to be understood as "as "revenge" nor can the forced introduction of "justice" justify violence or war, because these means do violate human rights themselves.

Global Cooperation and Solidarity

The interconnected nature of our world necessitates global cooperation in the pursuit of Peace. Universal human rights provide a shared framework that transcends national boundaries, fostering international cooperation and solidarity. Nations that prioritize human rights in their foreign policies contribute to the creation of a global community built on mutual understanding and collaboration. Through diplomacy, dialogue, and respect for universal values, nations can work together to address the root causes of conflicts and build a more peaceful world.

Is there a Human Right to Peace?

While there is no specific international human right explicitly termed the "right to Peace," the concept of the right to Peace is indirectly addressed in various international instruments and declarations. The right to Peace is often considered a fundamental aspect of the broader framework of human rights that contribute to creating conditions for Peace and security.

The Universal Declaration of Human Rights (UDHR), adopted by the United Nations General Assembly in 1948, emphasizes the importance of Peace in several articles. For instance, Article 3 states that "Everyone has the right to life, liberty, and security of person," and Article 28 asserts that "Everyone is entitled to a social and international order in which the rights and freedoms set forth in this Declaration can be fully realized."

Additionally, the International Covenant on Civil and Political Rights (ICCPR) and the International Covenant on Economic, Social and Cultural Rights (ICESCR) recognize the right to self-determination (Article 1, ICCPR and Article 1, ICESCR) as a key element for promoting conditions that contribute to Peace.

Several international declarations and initiatives, such as the Declaration and Program of Action on a Culture of Peace (1999), also underline the importance of fostering a culture of Peace through education, dialogue, and respect for human rights.

While the explicit recognition of a stand-alone "right to Peace" may not be present in international law, the various human rights instruments collectively contribute to the establishment of conditions conducive to Peace and the prevention of conflicts. The promotion of human rights, justice, equality, and social well-being is considered essential for building a world where Peace can thrive.

Human Rights and Inner Peace

In conclusion, the necessity and importance of universal human rights for Peace are evident in their capacity to cultivate dignity, equality, freedom, and justice. Societies that respect and implement human rights and make them the basis of their laws and actions create a foundation and environment for avoiding trauma and violence. This is also an important prerequisite for each individual to develop inner Peace, which can lead to social and ultimately global Peace.

Conclusion

By embracing the principles of human rights principles, societies lay the groundwork for harmonious coexistence and contribute to the broader goal of global Peace. As we navigate the complexities of the contemporary world, the commitment to upholding universal human rights remains not only a moral imperative but also a pragmatic approach to fostering a world where Peace is not merely an aspiration but a tangible reality.

103 The One-Sided Presentation of History and the Evidence of Non-Violent Societies

We often hear that aggression and war are an expression of deeply rooted human behaviour, that they are "written into our DNA", so to speak, and are therefore completely natural and legitimate behaviour. Our own history seems to be a continuous succession of wars and cruelty, we are told of warring tribes in Africa and America, cannibalism as an expression of unrestrained cruelty and savagery, Asia does not come off well either, because apparently only cruel and belligerent rulers have made it into the history books. The image of early human history is characterised by club-wielding half-savages who are in a constant state of readiness to fight for food and sexual partners.

This gloomy picture can be questioned. How would humanity have survived through fighting if the relatively tiny populations had not regularly wiped themselves out? Wounds and disease would also have carried off most of the victors, and the additionally decimated populations would have been weakened by incest and probably too small to enable survival or even technological development.

The misunderstanding or unquestioning acceptance of Darwin's theory of evolution dismisses the belief in humanity as a sense of cooperation rather than competition, compassion instead of hatred, and peaceful living rather than the cries of war. The "survival of the fittest" is understood as the survival of the stronger.

The word "fit" in the English language has multiple meanings, and its interpretation depends on the context in which it is used. Here are some of the common meanings of the word:

- In Good Physical Health – Example: "After regular exercise, she felt fit and energetic." Meaning: Physically healthy, in good condition, or physically prepared for a particular activity.

- Suitable or Appropriate – Example: "This outfit is not fit for a formal occasion." Meaning: Suitable, appropriate, or conforming to a particular standard or purpose.

- Matching or Properly Aligned – Example: "The puzzle pieces fit together perfectly." Meaning: To be compatible or properly aligned; pieces or parts that come together harmoniously.

- In a State of Agreement or Harmony – Example: "Their ideas about the project fit well together." Meaning: To be in harmony or agreement, often used to describe compatibility or a good match.

- Being of the Right Size or Shape – Example: "Make sure the furniture is the right fit for the room." Meaning: The right size or shape to be suitable for a particular space or purpose.

- Conformity to a Standard or Specification: Example: "The documents must fit the required format." Meaning: To conform or meet the specified standards or requirements.

- To Install or Connect: Example: "He will fit the new tires on the car tomorrow." Meaning: To install, attach, or connect, especially when referring to mechanical components.

"Strong", "violent" or even "brutal" are obviously not a meaning of "being fit". So the "Survival of the fittest" means rather the "Survival of the most adapted".

If we look at human history, warmongering and violence have never led to a prosperous society in which it seems attractive to want to live. The opposite is true:

Several cultures and empires throughout history faced decline or ultimate collapse, and some scholars argue that their emphasis on warmongering and glorification of violence played a major role in their downfall. Here are a few examples where militarism and glorification of violence have been implicated in the decline of cultures or empires:

- Roman Empire: The Roman Empire, known for its military prowess and conquests, faced internal decay and external pressures. The constant state of war and the strain on resources due to maintaining a vast empire contributed to economic decline. Additionally, internal conflicts, political instability, and reliance on military solutions to complex problems played a role in the fall of the Western Roman Empire.

- Mongol Empire: The Mongol Empire, under leaders like Genghis Khan and his successors, achieved unprecedented military conquests. However, the empire's over-reliance on conquest and militarism, coupled with internal conflicts and succession struggles, contributed to its eventual fragmentation.

- Ottoman Empire: The Ottoman Empire, while a powerful military force for centuries, faced challenges as it entered a period of stagnation. The empire's militaristic policies, territorial expansion, and internal strife contributed to its decline. The glorification of military achievements and resistance to innovation also played a role in the Ottoman Empire's inability to adapt to changing geopolitical realities.

- Sparta (Ancient Greece): Sparta, a city-state in ancient Greece, was known for its militaristic society and emphasis on military training. While its military might was formidable, its focus on warfare led to neglect in other areas, such as arts, culture, and economic development. This lack of balance is said to have contributed to Sparta's relative decline compared to other Greek city-states.

- Aztec Empire: The Aztec Empire in Meso-America, known for its militaristic expansion and human sacrifices, faced internal dissent and external pressures from rival groups. The empire's military-centric policies and the discontent of subjected populations contributed to its vulnerability, eventually leading to its conquest by the Spanish conquistadors.

- Nazi Germany: While not an empire in the traditional sense, Nazi Germany's aggressive militarism and glorification of violence were central to its ideology. The pursuit of expansionist policies and engagement in World War II ultimately led to the downfall of the regime. The devastation caused by the war and the moral repudiation of Nazi ideology marked the end of this militaristic regime.

It is difficult to comprehend, but history books somehow only report on war-faring nations and "great emperors" and "conquerors", such as "Alexander the Great", or "Napoleon", who, in-spite of their glorification, were mass murderers, just like Hitler etc.

Why don't history books name them as such and why don't they give the same attention to non-violent cultures and nations?

Could it be that, with the passage of time, a kind of transfiguration occurs that leads to the celebration of clearly megalomaniacal and brutal warmongers like "Alexander the Great" as heroes of history and to make their armies look like victorious Olympic athletes, "victorious heroes" who massacred entire peoples, destroyed cultural treasures, robbed, plundered and raped?

And why do history book only mention the leaders, but do not remind us, that the cruelties were not committed by those who ordered them, but by those who carried them out? The killings, the mutilations, the torture, the abuse, were not committed by Nero or Hitler, but by the conscientious collective we, those who "only carried out orders", those who supposedly "had no choice", those who "were loyal subjects".

I remember my Latin lessons: apart from Nero, who was portrayed with a little smirk as crazy, all Roman emperors seemed to be well-educated heroes who created a marvellous cultural empire. The enslavement and subjugation of entire peoples, the appropriation of their culture and cultural treasures, slavery, etc., all seemed to be permissible, non-condemnable means of teaching great empire. Not a word about those who carried out their orders, those who took part, those who were actually responsible for all this horror, those who murdered, pillaged, enslaved and raped. Not a word about those who lit the pyres and those who cheered it on. Not a word about the soldiers, the torturers, the yes-men.

The fact that the hero-worshipping texts of the entire European history should be questioned and the fact that they are often demonstrably falsified or fictitious is something that historiography still refuses to recognise today.

Whereas in the past, peaceful behaviour usually led to sustainable prosperity, such as in my home town of Cologne, Germany, which was never fought over until the world wars. When Napoleon's troops marched outside the city and fired a shot, so the story goes, the city guards shouted, "Hey, can't you see that people are standing here?" and opened the gates. While other fighting cities were devastated, Cologne flourished. When the French troops withdrew, they kept what they found useful, e.g. the house numbers that the French introduced (4711 got its name from this) or umbrellas, which still bear the French name in dialect today.

In the past, a military campaign might promise short-term gains and wealth to the stronger party, and Europe, which fell behind in its development through centuries of wars, owes its wealth, not least, to brutal colonial exploitation.

In today's system, one doesn't even need to "win" wars to economically benefit. The preparation for wars, the escalation of conflicts, and the mere act of waging war itself are already a huge business, benefiting the military-industrial complex and sustaining or possibly reviving some economies.

After the war, during which resources of the affected country are already exploited, there is also significant profit in the reconstruction efforts. Hundreds of thousands of deaths, or 1.5 million as in the Iraq War, become a "renewable resource" and are not perceived as a loss in a world that believes the lie of overpopulation and has previously vilified the "enemy" as "non-human."

Nothing in this behaviour is evolutionarily justified or natural. No other being on this planet sends its offspring to war and then is proud when they die or are traumatized and maimed. In the animal kingdom, we observe social behaviour related to foraging and protection, but nowhere is there observable warlike behaviour. A hunting animal, often inaccurately labelled as a "wild animal" or "predator," does not kill out of aggression. It is highly concentrated and focused, which is the opposite of what triggers aggression. A hunting animal does not kill out of a desire for profit or greed. A pride of lions captures a wildebeest from a herd. The pride never attempts to kill the entire herd or more than one animal.

Aggressive behaviour in the animal kingdom does exist naturally, often for territory defence and in some species to assert claims on sexual partners. However, in these cases, the battle is fought between the two contenders, but no animal sends an army of sons and daughters into battle to celebrate themselves as heroes.

Hans Peter Dürr, the German physicist, has repeatedly explored the question of what "holds the world together at its core". His conclusion: love. In his opinion, this not only provides clear instructions for peaceful coexistence, but also for dealing with the whole of creation.

We must not see nature as our enemy to be dominated and overcome, but rather learn to co-operate with

nature again. It has four and a half billion years of experience.
Ours is much shorter. (Hans Peter Dürr)

For thousands of years, culture and religion have had the task of regulating the destructive possibilities that humans have and emphasising their individual responsibility for their actions. Sometimes, however, they have been misused to justify atrocities.

But besides from all this history and presence of war and violence, is there a history of Peace? Are there examples of societies that live(d) peacefully, without violence and without war?

Numerous traditional societies and cultures around the world are known for promoting non-violent behaviour and conflict resolution through peaceful means. It's important to note that generalizations about any society may oversimplify the diversity within that group, and individual practices can vary even within a single community. However, some societies have historical or cultural attributes that emphasize non-violence. Here are a few examples:

The Khoisan of South Africa

The Khoekhoe and San people, also known as "Bushmen", have often been described as having relatively low levels of interpersonal violence within their traditional societies. Many anthropologists and researchers suggest that the San traditionally exhibited cooperative and egalitarian social structures, which contributed to a relatively peaceful way of life.

Key characteristics of San societies that have been associated with non-violence or low levels of conflict include:

1. Egalitarianism: San societies traditionally lack hierarchical structures, and decision-making tends to be based on consensus rather than centralized authority. This emphasis on equality may contribute to reduced interpersonal conflicts.

2. Cooperative Living: San communities traditionally rely on cooperation for survival, sharing resources such as food and water. This cooperative lifestyle fosters a sense of interdependence, potentially reducing the likelihood of violent disputes over scarce resources.

3. Nomadic Lifestyle: The San historically led a nomadic lifestyle as hunter-gatherers. Their mobility may have contributed to lower population densities and reduced competition for resources, potentially lowering the likelihood of violent conflicts.

4. Humour and Culture: Humour, sharing stories of wisdom, music and dance play an important role in San culture. Traditionally they are laughing a lot. Rituals honouring and restoring the "world order" have a meaningful impact on conflict resolution and avoidance.

A notion of "pacifism" may not align precisely with the way indigenous societies conceptualize conflict. But many do not have anything like an army or class of "warriors". Traditional conflict resolution methods within San communities often involve dialogue, negotiation, and consensus-building rather than resorting to physical violence that is .is generally rejected, also in child education.

The Aka of Central Africa

The Aka people are indigenous groups in Central Africa, primarily found in the Congo Basin. They have been studied by anthropologists for their unique social structures, cultural practices, and conflict resolution strategies.

Aka culture and social life are characterised by:

1. Egalitarian Social Structure: The Aka are known for their egalitarian social structure, where there is a lack of hierarchical leadership. Decision-making is often communal, and conflicts are resolved through discussion and consensus.

2. Sharing and Cooperation: Aka communities emphasize sharing and cooperation. Individuals are expected to share resources, and cooperation is valued over competition. This communal approach helps prevent conflicts related to resource scarcity.

3. Humour and Playfulness: The Aka people often use humour and playfulness to diffuse tension and resolve conflicts. Laughter is seen as a way to address issues without resorting to aggression.

4. Avoidance of Direct Confrontation: Direct confrontation is generally avoided, and individuals may withdraw temporarily from a situation to allow emotions to cool down. This helps prevent escalation of conflicts.

The Ngandu of Central Africa

Anthropologists described the Ngandu as a non-violent people with amazing techniques to address conflicts.

Ngandu culture and social life are characterised by:

1. Consensus Decision-Making: Similar to the Aka, the Ngandu people often employ consensus decision-making. Community members come together to discuss issues, and decisions are reached through dialogue and agreement.

1. Mediation and Elders' Involvement: Conflicts are often addressed through mediation, involving respected community members or elders. These individuals play a crucial role in facilitating discussions and finding solutions that are acceptable to all parties involved.

2. Ceremonial Rituals: Ceremonial rituals and communal gatherings may serve as platforms for conflict resolution. These events provide opportunities for individuals to express grievances and seek resolutions within a supportive community context.

3. Restorative Justice: Ngandu communities may prioritize restorative justice, focusing on repairing relationships and reintegrating individuals rather than punitive measures. Offenders might be expected to make amends to the community.

It's essential to recognize that the descriptions above are descriptions of a traditional way of life, rarely found nowadays. External factors such as modernization and influences from the broader society may impact traditional conflict resolution methods over time.

Ancient India and Ashoka's Mauryan Empire

Ancient India, during the time of Gautama Buddha, witnessed the rise of philosophies and religions that advocated non-violence and compassion.

Buddhism, in particular, teaches the principle of *ahimsa* (non-violence) and advocates for compassion towards all living beings.

Emperor Ashoka, who ruled the Mauryan Empire in India from 268 to 232 BCE, is renowned for adopting Buddhism and embracing its principles, including non-violence. After the Kalinga War, Ashoka experienced a change of heart and committed to ruling his empire based on compassion and tolerance.

Jainism, an ancient Indian religion, places a strong emphasis on non-violence (*Ahimsa*) as one of its core principles. Jains follow a strict vegetarian diet and practice non-violence not only towards humans but also towards all living beings.

The Baining in Papua New Guinea

The Baining people are known for their avoidance of violence and conflict. Their cultural norms emphasize cooperation and communal living, and they seek to maintain harmony within their community.

The Hopi in Northern America

The Hopi people, a Native American tribe, have a long history of valuing Peace and harmony. Their cultural teachings emphasize the importance of living in balance with nature and maintaining good relationships with others.

The Inuit in the Arctic Regions

Indigenous Inuit communities traditionally practised conflict resolution through communication and consensus-building. Their emphasis on maintaining harmony within the community helped them survive in the challenging Arctic environment.

The Amish in the United States and Canada

The Amish, a Christian religious group, are known for their commitment to non-violence and pacifism. They avoid military service and are committed to resolving conflicts peacefully within their communities.

The Quakers in the United Kingdom and USA

The Religious Society of Friends, commonly known as Quakers, advocates for Peace and non-violence. Quakers historically played a role in various Peace movements and have been active in promoting social justice.

Tibetan Buddhist Culture

Tibetan Buddhism, with its spiritual leader the Dalai Lama, promotes principles of non-violence, compassion, and mindfulness. Despite facing political challenges, the Tibetan culture emphasizes inner Peace, meditation, and the avoidance of harm to others.

There are many more less known people and communities who traditionally live without army, without war, solving conflicts in a non-violent way.

They never produced weapons or bombs. They never had prisons or rules on corporal punishment. Their education of children is free from invasive bodily modifications, such as circumcision, or beating. They do not engage in competition or permanent changes in their natural environment.

And our culture used to call them "wild"!

104   Countries without an Army

In a world often defined by geopolitical tensions and military conflicts, a handful of nations stand out as anomalies, choosing to navigate the turbulent waters of international relations without maintaining a standing army. These countries have adopted unique approaches to national defence, relying on alternative strategies to ensure the safety and security of their citizens. This essay explores the characteristics and motivations of countries without standing armies, shedding light on the factors that influence such decisions.

Costa Rica: A Pioneering Path to Peace

> *Here,* conflicts are resolved at a negotiating table. (Oscar Arias Sanchez, former president of Costa Rica, and Nobel Peace Prize Laureate)

Costa Rica is a notable example of a country that has long embraced a commitment to Peace by forgoing a standing army. The decision to abolish its military forces in 1949 was enshrined in the country's constitution, and Costa Rica has since become a symbol of demilitarization and pacifism. Instead of investing in traditional military capabilities, Costa Rica allocates resources to education, healthcare, and social programs. This deliberate choice reflects the nation's dedication to fostering a culture of Peace and stability.

Iceland: A Strategic Absence

Iceland, situated in the North Atlantic, is another nation without a standing army. Its strategic location, nestled between Europe and North America, has historically allowed it to avoid the need for a military force for territorial defence. Instead, Iceland relies on the collective security provided by its NATO membership and the absence of significant military threats in the region. The nation's emphasis on diplomacy and international cooperation further reinforces its commitment to maintaining a peaceful existence.

Panama: A Post-Conflict Transformation

Panama is a unique case where the absence of a standing army is a result of historical circumstances. Following the invasion by the United States in 1989, Panama underwent a process of demilitarization. The Panama Canal Treaty, signed in 1977, also stipulated the withdrawal of U.S. military bases from the country. As a consequence, Panama's constitution explicitly prohibits the establishment of a standing army. The focus on rebuilding the nation's infrastructure and fostering economic development has taken precedence over traditional military capabilities.

Mauritius: A Commitment to Development

Mauritius, an island nation in the Indian Ocean, is celebrated for its economic prosperity and political stability despite lacking a standing army. The country has chosen to prioritize development, education, and social welfare over military expenditures. Mauritius demonstrates that sustainable progress can be achieved without a substantial military presence, challenging conventional notions about the necessity of standing armies for national security.

Other countries without a standing army are Monaco, Solomon Islands, Tuvalu and Vatican City.

Countries without standing armies challenge the prevailing paradigm that military might is the cornerstone of national security. Whether driven by historical circumstances, strategic considerations, or a commitment to Peace and development, these nations offer alternative models for navigating the complex landscape of international relations. While the absence of a standing army does not guarantee immunity from external threats, these countries demonstrate that there are diverse paths to ensuring the safety and well-being of their citizens, contributing to a more nuanced understanding of security and Peace in the global arena.

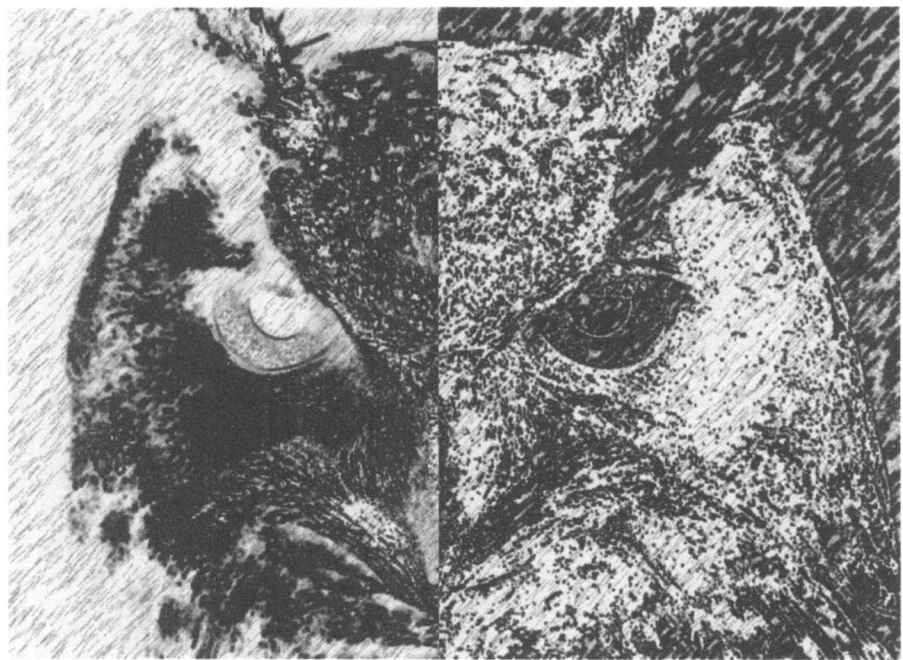

Education and spirituality play crucial roles in Peace-building by fostering understanding, empathy, and a shared sense of humanity. They can promote inner Peace, mindfulness, and emotional well-being. Individuals who have a strong sense of inner Peace are more likely to contribute positively to their communities and engage in constructive dialogue, reducing the likelihood of conflict.

The Crucial First Years: Shaping Responses to Conflict

The early years of life lay the foundation for a person's cognitive, emotional, and social development. The experiences during this formative period play a pivotal role in shaping an individual's responses to conflicts. This essay explores the impact of early-life experiences on the development of both violent and non-violent responses to conflicts, emphasizing the importance of nurturing environments and positive influences during these critical years.

In many societies today, pregnancy and birth are seen as an illness, an emergency, or at least a process and an event that requires medical intervention. Birth trauma is spoken of as if it were a matter of course. Alternative birth methods teach us the opposite. If pregnancy is a process of constant uncertainty and fear, the first neurones are laid prenatally, the first experiences of self-uncertainty and lack of trust.

In many countries, shortly after birth or even later, a trauma follows in which the most sensitive part of the body is removed, often without or with inadequate anaesthesia: circumcision. Circumcision of girls has now been widely recognised as a barbaric act and banned. But what about the circumcision of boys? The foreskin is several times more sensitive than the glans of the penis. There is no medical reason to remove it and change its natural state, even if there are repeated attempts to invoke such reasons. The fact that such an operation represents a deep trauma is concealed.

The unspeakable practice of dumping children in crèches and daycare centres at an early age, which is now accepted almost everywhere, leads to further confusion and loss of trust. Who is the reference person? Why are children no longer allowed to experience their early childhood development with their parents?

During the first years of life, the establishment of secure attachments with the parents (and nobody else) is fundamental. Children who experience consistent love, care, and responsiveness develop a secure base for emotional regulation. This emotional stability is crucial for managing stress and conflicts later in life. Conversely, those with insecure attachments may struggle with emotional dysregulation, increasing the likelihood of aggressive responses during conflicts. The establishment of secure attachments with caregivers is fundamental. Children who experience consistent love, care, and responsiveness develop a secure base for emotional regulation. This emotional stability is crucial for managing stress and conflicts later in life. Conversely, those with insecure attachments may struggle with emotional dysregulation, increasing the likelihood of aggressive responses during conflicts.

The development of trust and self-confidence, acceptance and self-acceptance, love and self-love, as well as the experience of justice and dignity, should not be underestimated in their significance. In later life, they are difficult to catch up on.

Parenting styles significantly influence a child's understanding of conflict and its resolution. Authoritative parenting, characterized by warmth, responsiveness, and clear boundaries, tends to foster non-violent conflict resolution skills. Conversely, children raised in environments with authoritarian or neglectful parenting may resort to aggression or violence as a learned response to conflicts, lacking effective models for peaceful resolution. But in many societies children are still being beaten, not just by their parents, but also by caretakers and teachers.

Experiences of trauma during the early years can have profound and lasting effects on an individual's responses to conflict. Children who witness or experience violence may internalize it as a legitimate means of resolving disputes. On the contrary, a nurturing environment that prioritizes safety and emotional well-being can serve as a protective factor, mitigating the risk of resorting to violence in response to conflicts.

Early interactions with peers, best of different ages, contribute significantly to the development of social skills and conflict resolution strategies. Children who experience positive peer relationships learn to navigate conflicts through communication, empathy, and cooperation. On the other hand, those who struggle with peer interactions may be more prone to resorting to aggression as a means of conflict resolution.

Early education programs hinder natural socialization. Locking up exclusively same-aged children in playgroups and school classes is equally unnatural and prevents learning from older individuals and consideration for younger ones. Even before entering school, a sense of competition and comparison often begins today. Social media usually soon completes the rest.

Early cognitive development, including the development of problem-solving skills, shapes how individuals approach conflicts. Children provided with opportunities to explore, question, and solve problems creatively are more likely to develop non-violent conflict resolution strategies. In contrast, a lack of cognitive stimulation and problem-solving experiences may hinder the development of adaptive conflict resolution skills. The cognitive development cannot be forced, neither can it be replaced by the learning of knowledge.

Cognitive development is a process best supported by observation, experiment and playing.

Children are highly influenced by the behaviours they observe in their immediate environment. If caregivers and significant adults model healthy communication and non-violent conflict resolution, children are more likely to internalize these skills. Conversely, exposure to aggressive or violent behaviour at a young age can normalize such responses, leading to a higher likelihood of resorting to violence in conflicts.

Many children around the world continue to be exposed to violent patterns of aggression or direct violence in armed conflicts. Other children experience these (re-)action patterns through the internet and television. For the unconscious, there is no difference between reality and virtual environments. Only the conscious mind, which is still developing, helps to make this distinction, but it shapes our entire life, our behaviour patterns and our feelings far less than the unconscious mind.

The fact that there is any discussion at all about whether there is a connection between violent behaviour patterns and violent video games - and even the virtual shooting of ducks or hitting a virtual opponent is violent - is inconceivable.

Numerous psychologists and studies have sufficiently proven these correlations. Nevertheless, such games, some of them developed or sponsored by the military, remain on the market and many parents shrug their shoulders as their children go to war virtually, have armies fight each other or try to win violently in other scenarios.

The experiences during the first years of life lay the groundwork for how individuals respond to conflicts throughout their lives. Early attachments, parenting styles, exposure to modelling behaviour, trauma, cognitive development, and peer interactions collectively shape whether an individual is more inclined towards violent or non-violent responses. Recognizing the critical role of early experiences in influencing conflict resolution strategies is essential for fostering environments that promote Peace, empathy, and healthy interpersonal relationships.

The Impact of Alternative Education for Peace

Education serves as a powerful instrument not only for transmitting knowledge but also for shaping societal values and fostering Peace. Conventional education systems often follow a standardized curriculum, but alternative education approaches have emerged, emphasizing inclusivity, creativity, and the promotion of Peace.

Alternative education prioritizes holistic development, recognizing that Peace is not merely the absence of conflict but a state of well-being and harmony. Social Emotional Learning (SEL) is a key component, addressing the emotional intelligence of individuals. SEL equips students with the skills to manage their emotions, empathize with others, and develop healthy relationships. These competencies lay the foundation for peaceful coexistence.

Alternative education emphasizes inclusive pedagogies that celebrate diversity. By acknowledging and embracing different cultures, perspectives, and backgrounds, alternative education creates an environment where students learn to appreciate differences rather than fear them. This fosters a sense of unity and understanding, reducing the likelihood of prejudice and intolerance.

However, this inclusion first requires a secure development of ego identity. This is another reason why young children need familiar caregivers and social groups who can give them an identity through their mother tongue and culture. Without this, an attempt at inclusivity quickly leads to uncertainty about one's own identity, which can later lead to peer groups trying to determine identity. Intolerant and violent behaviour can arise in the attempt to defend one's own pseudo-identity.

Peace education within alternative frameworks often incorporates explicit teaching of conflict resolution skills. Students learn to navigate disputes peacefully, fostering a culture where disagreements are viewed as opportunities for growth rather than sources of hostility. These skills are crucial for developing a generation capable of addressing global challenges collaboratively. If Peace education only includes methods of conflict resolution, this will not be enough. This denies the fact that Peace within the individual is a central prerequisite for realising sustainable Peace on the outside. In this respect, Peace education must also include philosophical, religious/spiritual and (self-)awareness training.

Alternative education empowers students to think critically and question the status quo. This ability is fundamental for challenging systems that perpetuate inequality and violence. By encouraging independent thought and a questioning mindset, alternative education equips individuals to contribute positively to society, advocating for peaceful and just solutions.

How do we get the imagination to rise again? We need to change our education system. In my opinion, we need to reduce the content extremely so that young people can experiment with their thinking again. (Hans-Peter Dürr)

Alternative education does not focus on key qualifications, but it promotes individual talents and recognises the value of culture and art for dealing with the world around us and developing better ways of living together and our with all creation and phenomena in and around us.

Many alternative education models emphasize environmental and social responsibility. This connection between personal actions and broader global consequences encourages a sense of interconnectedness and interdependence. Students learn about the impact of their choices on a global scale, fostering a sense of responsibility for the well-being of the planet and its inhabitants.

Alternative education often incorporates elements of global citizenship education. This perspective encourages students to see themselves as part of a larger global community, emphasizing shared values and a commitment to social justice. Through understanding and appreciating diverse global perspectives, individuals are better equipped to contribute to a more peaceful world.

Alternative education is a catalyst for nurturing a culture of Peace by fostering holistic development, inclusivity, conflict resolution skills, empowerment, spirituality and a sense of global responsibility. As we navigate an increasingly interconnected world facing complex challenges, alternative education models provide a pathway to create compassionate, critical-thinking individuals capable of promoting and sustaining Peace. By embracing these innovative approaches, societies can work towards building a more harmonious and equitable future.

The Impact of Spirituality and Religion on Non-Violent Responses to Conflicts and the Building of Peace

Spirituality and religion have long played influential roles in shaping human behaviour, ethical frameworks, and societal values. The impact of spirituality and religion on responses to conflicts and the promotion of Peace is profound and multifaceted.

Spiritual and religious traditions often emphasize the importance of compassion and empathy. Believers are encouraged to treat others with kindness and understanding, fostering an attitude of empathy even in the face of conflict. These teachings cultivate a sense of shared humanity, emphasizing that every individual, regardless of differences, is deserving of compassion and respect. This mindset becomes a foundation for non-violent conflict resolution.

Many spiritual and religious traditions place a high value on forgiveness and reconciliation. The idea of forgiveness as a transformative and healing process is often central to these traditions. The promotion of forgiveness encourages individuals to move beyond grievances and grudges, creating an environment conducive to reconciliation. This, in turn, contributes to the resolution of conflicts without resorting to violence.

Spiritual and religious teachings often provide individuals with ethical guidelines that shape their decision-making processes. These principles guide believers in choosing non-violent paths even in challenging situations. The ethical compass offered by spirituality and religion helps individuals navigate conflicts with a commitment to principles such as justice, mercy, and fairness, ultimately contributing to Peace-building efforts.

Some religions in the past and present confused ethics with morality: they defined, with a raised index finger, code-of-conduct rules akin to laws. Ethics, on the other hand, prescribes universally applicable values, allowing individuals to decide on their own behaviour based on their understanding of these values. The book religions of the Torah, the Quran, and papal Christianity are examples of religions in which moral legal texts have emerged. The words of Jesus, however, as well as Buddhism, are examples of religions that convey an ethics while also respecting the freedom of the spirit. Morality is always dependent on culture and epochs, thus it changes over times, while ethics is universal and immutable.

Many religious traditions emphasize the importance of dialogue and understanding in resolving conflicts. Interfaith dialogue and respectful communication are seen as essential for building bridges between diverse communities. The commitment to dialogue encourages individuals to seek common ground, fostering understanding and appreciation for differences. This approach stands in stark contrast to violent conflict resolution methods.

Spiritual and religious perspectives often delve into the root causes of conflict, addressing issues such as inequality, injustice, and poverty. By acknowledging and addressing these systemic problems, believers contribute to sustainable Peace-building efforts. The emphasis on social justice within many spiritual traditions motivates individuals to work towards creating equitable societies, reducing the conditions that give rise to conflict. Many spiritual practices focus on cultivating inner Peace and mindfulness. Individuals who have a sense of inner tranquillity are more likely to approach conflicts with a calm and rational demeanour, reducing the likelihood of resorting to violence. This inner Peace becomes a reservoir of strength, empowering individuals to face challenges and conflicts with resilience and a commitment to non-violent resolutions.

In conclusion, spirituality and religion play pivotal roles in influencing non-violent responses to conflicts and contributing to the broader efforts of peace-building. By promoting compassion, forgiveness, ethical guidance, dialogue, addressing root causes, and fostering inner Peace, these traditions offer valuable resources for individuals and communities striving to create a world characterized by harmony, understanding, and enduring Peace. Embracing the positive aspects of spirituality and religion can contribute significantly to the transformation of conflicts and the building of a more just and peaceful global society.

106 Advocating a Rethink and a (R)evolution

In a world often marked by discord and conflict, the pursuit of Peace stands as our noblest endeavour. History has borne witness to the devastating consequences of war, both in terms of human suffering and the irreversible damage inflicted upon societies. It is incumbent upon us, as global citizens, to rise above the allure of aggression and embrace a path guided by understanding, compassion, and cooperation.

The essence of Peace lies not merely in the absence of armed conflict but in the presence of justice, equality, and respect for one another. True Peace is not a passive state but an active pursuit of dialogue and diplomacy. It requires us to engage in open conversations, to listen to the grievances of others, and to seek common ground where our differences can be resolved through understanding rather than force.

True Peace also means facing your own demons and feelings, accepting vulnerability and self-responsibility. It means exposing manipulation and lies and refusing to hate. Peace on the outside must always begin with Peace on the inside.

Pacifism, often misconstrued as a stance of weakness, is, in fact, an embodiment of strength and moral courage. It calls upon us to break the cycle of violence and retaliation, recognizing that there is no lasting victory in the ashes of war. The true victors are those who can overcome animosity, reconcile differences, and build bridges of cooperation. The real heroes are those who refuse to fight. They are those who expose the lies of war. They are those who turn swords into ploughshares. They are those who follow only their conscience and reject ideologies. They are those who, with patience, humility and compassion, never stop working for a non-violent world, even if it costs them their lives.

In the face of adversity, we must resist the allure of militarism and instead invest in education, dialogue, and the promotion of human rights. By fostering a culture of Peace, we sow the seeds of a future where conflicts are resolved through negotiation and understanding and not through the destructive force of arms.

It is crucial to acknowledge that the scars of war extend far beyond the battlefield. They linger in the hearts and minds of generations, perpetuating cycles of hatred and vengeance, guilt, shame and fear. By championing Peace, we break this cycle, offering the prospect of a brighter, more harmonious future for all.

Let us not underestimate the power of diplomacy and international cooperation. Through forums such as the Internet and genuine non-governmental organisations, we have the opportunity to build alliances, foster mutual understanding, and address the root causes of conflicts, even without the consent or support of governments. It is through collaboration that we can create a world where the dignity and rights of every individual are upheld and where nations work together for the greater good.

Let us never underestimate the power of the people. No commander, no dictator, no president can ever lead a war if the people refuse to believe his lies, refuse to dream his fantasies of violence, and refuse to do the dirty work for him. - We are used to talking about "the powerful", "the rulers" and even "the elites" - but in fact this is a lie: the power lies with the people, and that is us, each and every one of us. The people have the power, but most of them don't believe it.

In conclusion, I urge you, high-minded reader, to reflect on the profound responsibility we bear as a conscious part of this world. Let us be architects of Peace, not purveyors of discord. By embracing pacifism, we choose a path that leads to a more just, compassionate, and sustainable world for ourselves, for our co-creation* and for generations yet unborn.

* I highly recommend avoiding words like "environment", as they express a distance that does not correspond to reality. We should rather speak of a "co-world", of which we are simply an equal part.

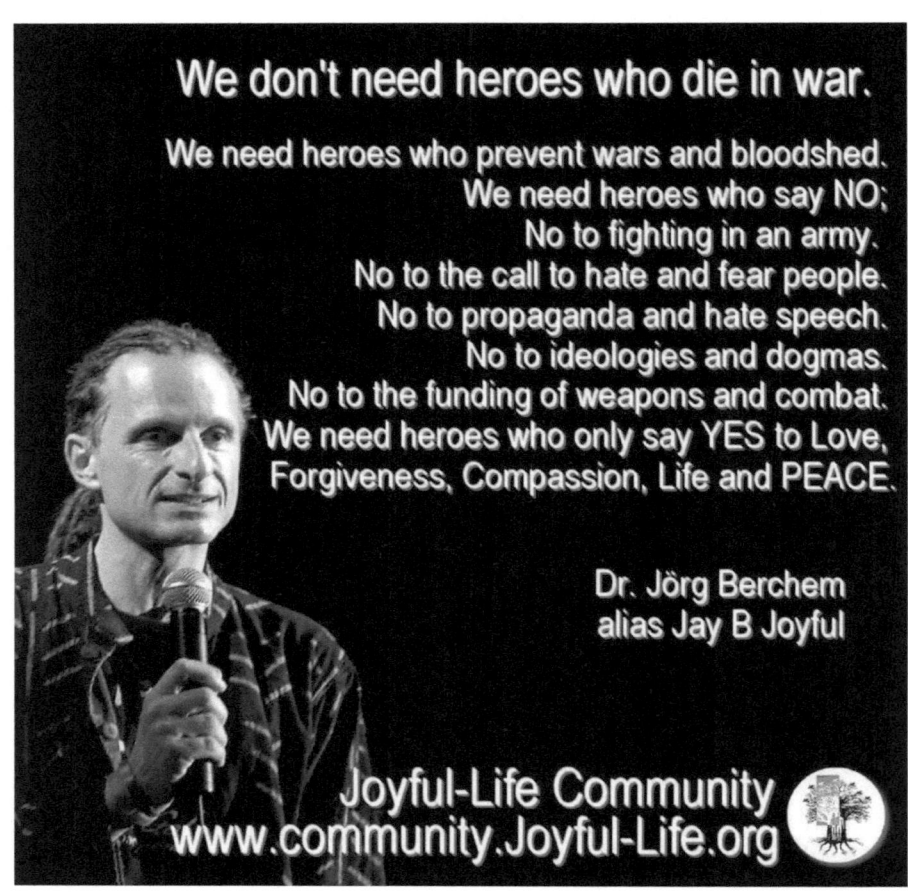

We don't need heroes who die in war.

We need heroes who prevent wars and bloodshed.
We need heroes who say NO;
No to fighting in an army.
No to the call to hate and fear people.
No to propaganda and hate speech.
No to ideologies and dogmas.
No to the funding of weapons and combat.
We need heroes who only say YES to Love,
Forgiveness, Compassion, Life and PEACE.

Dr. Jörg Berchem
alias Jay B Joyful

Joyful-Life Community
www.community.Joyful-Life.org

346

VII   Appendix

List of Symbols of Peace

The use of the dove as a symbol of Peace has ancient origins and is deeply rooted in various cultures and religions. The most well-known association comes from the biblical story of Noah and the Ark. In the Book of Genesis in the Bible, after the great flood, Noah sent out a dove to find dry land. The dove returned with an olive branch, signalling to Noah that the waters were receding and land was nearby. This image of the dove carrying an olive branch became a powerful symbol of hope, Peace, and renewal.

The biblical connection established the dove as a representation of Peace, and this symbolism has transcended religious boundaries. Over the centuries, the dove has been adopted by various cultures and movements as a universal symbol of Peace, purity, and Love.

In addition to its biblical roots, the dove also has a long history in ancient Greek and Roman cultures, where it was associated with the goddess of Love and beauty, Aphrodite (Venus in Roman mythology). The Greeks and Romans saw the dove as a symbol of Love, fidelity, and the renewal of Life.

In the 20th century, the dove gained further prominence as a Peace symbol during the anti-nuclear and Peace movements. Artist and activist Pablo Picasso famously used the image of a dove in his work for the World Peace Congress in 1949, solidifying the dove's association with Peace in the modern era.

Overall, the dove as a symbol of Peace has a rich and diverse cultural history, drawing on both religious and secular traditions from around the world.

The use of an olive branch as a symbol of Peace dates back to ancient times and has roots in various cultures. The most well-known association is from ancient Greece, where the olive tree was considered sacred and its branches were used to symbolize Peace, prosperity, and goodwill.

In ancient Greek mythology, the goddess Athena was said to have gifted the olive tree to the city of Athens, and it became a symbol of wisdom and Peace. The olive tree was highly valued for its economic importance, providing not only olives for food but also olive oil for various purposes, including lighting lamps and anointing the body. The cultivation of olive trees was associated with fertility and abundance. The Olympic Games in ancient Greece further contributed to the association of the olive branch with Peace. Winners of the Olympic Games were crowned with wreaths made from olive branches, emphasizing the connection between victory and Peace.

The Romans also adopted the olive branch as a symbol of Peace, and it was often included in the imagery associated with the goddess Pax, the Roman goddess of Peace.

The biblical story of Noah and the Ark also plays a role in the association of the olive branch with Peace. According to the Book of Genesis, after the great flood, Noah sent out a dove, and it returned with an olive leaf, indicating that the waters had receded and Life could be sustained once again.

In more recent history, the olive branch has continued to be a powerful symbol of Peace, and it was incorporated into the design of the United Nations flag, symbolizing the organization's mission to promote international cooperation and prevent conflicts.

Overall, the use of the olive branch as a symbol of Peace has a rich history that spans various cultures and carries with it the associations of prosperity, wisdom, and reconciliation.

The Peace sign, often represented by the symbol ☮, has its origins in the anti-nuclear and anti-war movements of the mid-20th century, particularly in the 1950s and 1960s. It is also known as the "Peace symbol" or "Peace emblem." It is also often referred to as CND Symbol (Campaign for Nuclear Disarmament).

The design of the Peace sign is credited to Gerald Holtom, a British artist and designer. It was created in 1958 for the Campaign for Nuclear Disarmament (CND) in the United Kingdom, which was advocating for the peaceful resolution of the Cold War and the end of nuclear weapons testing.

Holtom designed the Peace symbol by combining the semaphore signals for the letters "N" and "D," which stand for "nuclear disarmament." Semaphore is a system of sending messages using flags or lights to convey letters or numbers. The "N" is represented by two flags held down at an angle, and the "D" is represented by one flag held straight up and one pointing straight down. Together, they form the circle with three lines that we recognize today as the Peace sign.

The symbol was first used in a protest march from Trafalgar Square to the Atomic Weapons Research Establishment at Aldermaston, England, in 1958. Over time, it gained international recognition and became a powerful emblem of the broader Peace and anti-war movements.

The Peace sign was quickly adopted by various counterculture and Peace movements around the world during the 1960s, especially during protests against the Vietnam War. It has since become a widely recognized and enduring symbol of Peace, non-violence, and the call for a world without nuclear weapons. The simplicity and universal nature of the Peace sign contribute to its continued use as a symbol of Peace and activism.

The V-sign, often also referred to as the "Peace sign," has a fascinating and varied history. The most well-known usage of the V-sign as a symbol for Peace originated in the 20th century and became particularly prominent during the 1960s.

The V-sign made its first major public appearance during World War II. In 1941, Winston Churchill, the Prime Minister of the United Kingdom, started using the V-sign with his index and middle fingers extended in a V shape. This gesture was meant to symbolize "V for Victory" and became a rallying symbol for the Allied forces. It quickly gained popularity and was widely used to boost morale and convey a sense of optimism during a challenging time.

After World War II, the V-sign became more and more associated with Peace, rather than victory. As the 1960s unfolded, the symbol became particularly linked with the anti-war and Peace movements of the time, especially during protests against the Vietnam War. Activists and counterculture figures adopted the V-sign as a gesture of Peace, Love, and solidarity. The symbol was often accompanied by the slogan "Make Love, Not War."

The V-sign's association with Peace and counterculture expanded beyond political movements. It became a ubiquitous symbol of the 1960s and 1970s, representing a desire for social change, non-violence, and a break from traditional norms. The symbol found its way into art, fashion, and popular culture, further solidifying its connection with Peace.

Over time, the V-sign for Peace transcended its origins and became a global symbol for non-violence and pacifism. It is now recognized and used around the world to convey a message of Peace and goodwill.

The white poppy is a symbol that emerged in the USA as an alternative to the traditional red poppy symbol, which is commonly associated with Remembrance Day and honouring military veterans. The white poppy has its origins in the pacifist and anti-war movements, with a focus on promoting Peace and remembering all victims of war, civilians and soldiers alike. Here is a brief overview of the origin and meaning of the white poppy symbol:

The white poppy was first introduced by the Women's Co-operative Guild in the United Kingdom in 1933. The Women's Co-operative Guild was a feminist and pacifist organization that sought to promote Peace and social justice. The white poppy was conceived as a symbol of remembrance that emphasized the need for lasting Peace and the prevention of future wars.

The primary meaning of the white poppy is rooted in a commitment to Peace and opposition to war. It represents a pacifist stance, advocating for non-violent conflict resolution and the pursuit of diplomatic solutions to international disputes.

Unlike the red poppy, which is often associated specifically with military personnel who lost their lives in armed conflicts, the white poppy is intended to honour all victims of war, including civilians and those who suffered as a result of the social and economic consequences of war.

Wearing or displaying a white poppy is often seen as a statement against the glorification of war and a call for the prevention of future conflicts. It is embraced by individuals and organizations that actively work towards disarmament, conflict resolution, and the promotion of a more just and peaceful world.

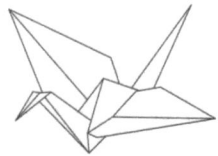

In Japan, the crane, specifically the origami crane, has deep cultural and historical significance as a symbol of Peace, hope, and healing. The most well-known story associated with the crane as a Peace symbol is the ancient Japanese legend of the "Thousand Origami Cranes."

The Thousand Origami Cranes legend is inspired by the life of a young Japanese girl named Sadako Sasaki, who was exposed to radiation from the atomic bombing of Hiroshima during World War II. Sadako developed leukaemia as a result of the exposure, and while in the hospital, she heard a traditional Japanese belief that folding a thousand origami cranes could grant a wish, particularly for health and longevity.

Sadako embarked on the task of folding one thousand paper cranes with the hope of recovering from her illness. Tragically, she passed away before completing the thousand cranes, but her classmates and friends completed the project in her memory. In the years following Sadako's death, the origami crane became a symbol of Peace, nuclear disarmament, and a tribute to all victims of war.

The crane, as a Peace symbol, carries several layers of meaning:

1. Hope and Healing: The act of folding one thousand cranes is seen as a gesture of hope, healing, and resilience. It symbolizes the power of the human spirit to overcome adversity and tragedy.

2. Wish for Peace: In the context of Sadako's story, folding the origami cranes is associated with a wish for Peace. The tradition has since been adopted as a universal symbol for Peace, transcending cultural and geographical boundaries.

3. Anti-Nuclear Movement: The origami crane, particularly in the context of Sadako's story, is closely linked to the anti-nuclear movement. It serves

as a poignant reminder of the devastating impact of nuclear weapons and a call for nuclear disarmament.

4. Global Symbol: Over time, the origami crane has become a global symbol for Peace, symbolizing not only the specific historical context of Hiroshima but also a broader commitment to a world free from violence and conflict.

Today, people around the world fold origami cranes as a symbol of Peace and solidarity. The tradition has extended beyond the context of Hiroshima and Nagasaki to encompass a general desire for global harmony and the end of all forms of violence. The crane's elegance and the symbolism associated with its folding make it a powerful and widely recognized emblem of Peace.

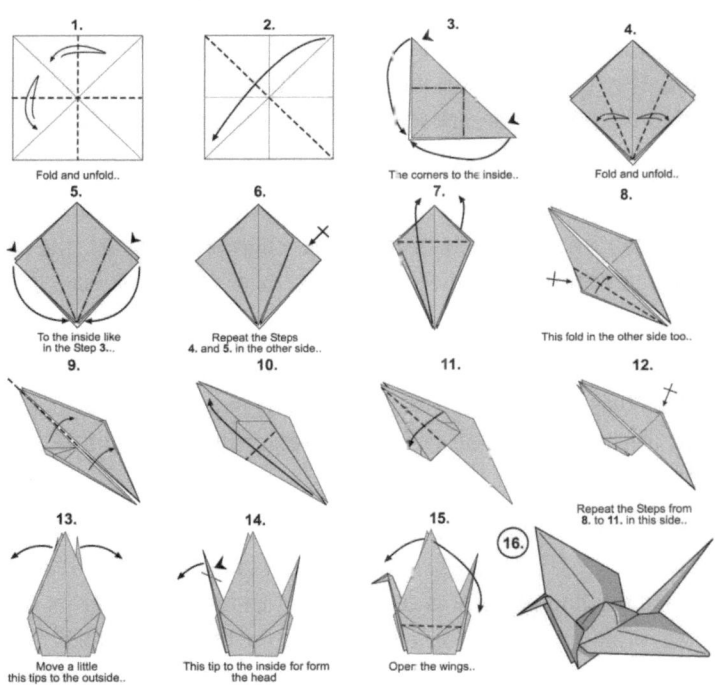

The rainbow and the rainbow flag have been used as a symbol of Peace and hope in various cultural and historical contexts. While it might not have a single origin, its association with Peace often stems from its positive and colourful representation. For sure the individual experience of seeing the phenomena of a rainbow over the sky and the resulting astonishment and joy have contributed to its popularity.

In Judeo-Christian traditions, the rainbow has a significant symbolic meaning. In the Bible, particularly in the story of Noah's Ark (Genesis 9:8-17), a rainbow appears as a sign of God's covenant with humanity, promising not to flood the Earth again. This biblical association with divine promise and protection has contributed to the positive and peaceful connotations of the rainbow.

During the 1960s and 1970s, the rainbow gained prominence as a symbol of Peace and unity. It became closely associated with various Peace movements, including the anti-war movement and the counterculture of the time. The rainbow flag, in particular, gained popularity as a symbol of Peace, Love, and inclusivity during this era.

The rainbow's vibrant and varied colours are often used to represent the diversity of cultures, ethnicities, and people coming together in harmony. The idea is that, like the colours of the rainbow, diversity is a beautiful and integral part of the human experience.

In recent years, the rainbow flag, consisting of multiple colours, has become an iconic symbol of the LGBT rights movement. Designed by artist Gilbert Baker in 1978, the rainbow flag represents diversity and inclusivity. While its initial focus was on gay pride, it has since evolved into a broader symbol of equality, acceptance, and the pursuit of a peaceful coexistence among diverse communities.

The white dove on a blue background is a popular symbol in various Peace movements and campaigns, especially in Europe. It is frequently employed in art, posters, and banners to convey a universal desire for Peace, regardless of cultural or religious differences.

In summary, the white dove on a blue background as a symbol of Peace has deep historical roots, drawing inspiration from biblical narratives and Christian traditions. Its enduring and cross-cultural significance makes it a powerful and widely recognized emblem of hope, reconciliation, and the aspiration for a world free from conflict.

The broken rifle symbol, often depicted as a rifle or gun broken in half, is a powerful and globally recognized symbol of Peace. This symbol has its roots in the anti-war and Peace movements of the 20th century, particularly in the context of conscientious objection to military service.

The broken rifle symbol was initially created by a British artist and pacifist named Eric Austin Gill. In 1958, Gill designed the symbol for the first Aldermaston March, a series of anti-nuclear weapons demonstrations in the United Kingdom. The original design featured a stylized, broken rifle against a white background.

The broken rifle symbolizes the rejection of war, violence, and the destructive power of weapons. The act of breaking the rifle signifies a conscious decision to refuse participation in armed conflict and a commitment to Peace. The symbolism goes beyond mere opposition to war; it conveys a positive message of actively working toward disarmament, conflict resolution, and the promotion of non-violent solutions to conflicts.

The broken rifle emblem gained popularity and became associated with conscientious objection to military service, particularly in the face of nuclear weapons proliferation during the Cold War. It was adopted by various Peace organizations and movements globally, reflecting a shared commitment to a world free from the threat of war and the use of military force.

Today, the broken rifle symbol remains a poignant representation of pacifism and the pursuit of Peace. It is often used by individuals, Peace activists, and organizations advocating for disarmament, the prevention of war, and the promotion of alternative, non-violent approaches to resolving conflicts. The symbol resonates with the idea that breaking the cycle of violence and rejecting the use of weapons is essential for building a more peaceful and just world.

The heart-shaped Peace sign, often referred to as the "heart Peace sign" or "heart hand gesture," is a modern variation of the traditional Peace sign. Its origins are rooted in the broader Peace and Love movements, particularly those that gained momentum during the 1960s and 1970s.

The specific origin of the heart-shaped Peace sign is not attributed to a single individual or event. Instead, it evolved organically as an expressive and artistic variation of the traditional Peace symbol. During the counterculture movements of the 1960s, which were characterized by a rejection of mainstream values and an emphasis on Peace, Love, and social change, individuals began to experiment with alternative symbols and gestures to convey their messages.

The heart-shaped Peace sign combines two powerful symbols: the heart and the Peace sign.

The heart is universally recognized as a symbol of Love, compassion, and emotion. Its inclusion in the Peace sign emphasizes the connection between the pursuit of Peace and the values of Love, understanding, and empathy.

The Peace sign itself, with its inverted "V" and a circle, is a symbol that emerged in the 1950s and became synonymous with anti-war movements. It represents the letters "N" and "D" in semaphore, which stand for "nuclear disarmament." Over time, the Peace sign has evolved to represent a broader commitment to Peace, non-violence, and social justice.

The heart Peace sign, with its combination of the heart and Peace symbols, conveys a message of Love, compassion, and a heartfelt commitment to Peace. It is often used in a variety of contexts, including protests, artwork, and social media, to express solidarity with Peace movements, advocate for Love over conflict, and call for positive change in the world.

Index of Names

Further Reading

The Gospel of Love and Peace

Essene Books I - IV

Jörg Berchem (Hrsg.)

Spiritualität & Esoterik
Hardcover
420 Seiten
ISBN-13: 9783739241692
Verlag: BoD - Books on Demand
Erscheinungsdatum: 31.08.2016
Sprache: Englisch
Schlagworte: Essener, Qumran, Gospel, Essenes, Friedensevangelium

★★★★★

erhältlich als:

| BUCH 29,00 € | E-BOOK 16,99 € |

Order from any bookshop, or https://GLP.Joyful-Life.org

Also available in German.

The Sevenfold Peace

Contemplations for Universal Peace According to the Essene Gospel of Peace

Jörg Berchem

Spiritualität & Esoterik
Paperback
148 Seiten
ISBN-13: 9783758329517
Verlag: Books on Demand
Erscheinungsdatum: 23.01.2024
Sprache: Englisch
Schlagworte: Essenes, Peace, Meditation, contemplation, Gospel

★★★★★

erhältlich als:

| BUCH 16,99 € | E-BOOK 9,99 € |

Order from any bookshop, or https://bod.Joyful-Life.org

Also available in German.

The Teachings of the Essenes

From Enoch to the Dead Sea Scrolls

Edmond Bordeaux Székely, Dr. Jörg Berchem (Hrsg.)

Gesellschaft, Politik & Medien
Paperback
148 Seiten
ISBN-13: 9783758300127
Verlag: Books on Demand
Erscheinungsdatum: 01.11.2023
Sprache: Englisch
Schlagworte: Essenes, Essener, Qumran, Jésus, Gospel

★ ★ ★ ★ ★ 0 Bewertungen

erhältlich als:

BUCH 16.00 €   E-BOOK 5,99 €

Order from any bookshop, or https://bod.Joyful-Life.org

Also available in German.

Meditations of the Children of Light

Communions with the Angels according to the Essene Gospel of Peace

Jörg Berchem

Spiritualität & Esoterik
Paperback
148 Seiten
ISBN-13: 9783758326561
Verlag: Books on Demand
Erscheinungsdatum: 10.01.2024
Sprache: Englisch
Schlagworte: Essener, Székely, Angels, Meditation, Engel

☆ ☆ ☆ ☆ ☆

erhältlich als:

BUCH 18,99 €   E-BOOK 9,99 €

Order from any bookshop, or https://bod.Joyful-Life.org

Also available in German.

Be Peace – Say No to War is a heartfelt and powerful music album that calls for unity, compassion, and non-violence in a world yearning for change. Through soulful melodies and compelling lyrics, this collection of songs becomes a musical protest against war and a passionate tribute to peace. Each track weaves messages of hope, love, and resistance, urging listeners to reflect on the power of peace and their role in creating a better world. From uplifting reggae rhythms to contemplative ballads, the album offers a rich musical landscape, inspiring listeners to stand firm in their beliefs and say "no" to war.

This album is more than just a collection of songs — it's a musical movement, calling everyone to embrace the power of peace and reject the destructiveness of war. With every beat and lyric, this album invites you to tune into the frequency of peace, empowering you to say "no" to war and "yes" to love, compassion, and unity. Because peace isn't just a dream — it begins with us.

🌐 🎵 *"Be the peace you wish to see. Say no to war. Together, we can change the world."*

Available on all well-known streaming platforms.

"Gospel for Peace" – A Journey of Harmony, Hope, and Healing

Step into a world of harmony and healing with *Gospel for Peace*, an inspiring collection of songs that transcend boundaries and speak to the heart of humanity. This album weaves together powerful melodies and profound messages, calling listeners to embrace peace, love, and compassion in their daily lives.

From reflective prayers like *"Make Me an Instrument of Your Peace"* to uplifting anthems such as *"Blessed Are the Peacemakers"* and *"Together We Sing"*, each track carries the essence of hope and a deep yearning for a better world. With themes of unity, service, and spiritual connection, *Gospel for Peace* is more than music – it's a movement, a prayer, and a call to action for peacemakers everywhere.

Created by Jay Joyful, an artist devoted to spreading peace, love, and joy through music, this album is a heartfelt expression of his mission to inspire hope and unity. Jay's soulful compositions and heartfelt lyrics invite listeners to walk the path of peace and transform the world, one note at a time.

Let this music guide your soul, inspire your heart, and remind you that true peace begins within.

Available on all well-known streaming platforms.

www.Joyful-Life.org